Programming in
PARLOG

International Series in Logic Programming

Series Editor
Keith Clark, Imperial College of Science and Technology

Associate Editors
Bob Kowalski, Imperial College of Science and Technology
Jean-Louis Lassez, IBM, Yorktown Heights, USA

Editorial Board
K Furukawa (ICOT, Japan)
H Gallaire (ECRC, Munich, FRG)
J W Lloyd (Bristol University, UK)
J Minker (Maryland, USA)
J A Robinson (Syracuse University, NY, USA)
S-A Tärnlund (Uppsala University, Sweden)
M H van Emden (University of Waterloo, Canada)
D H D Warren (Bristol University, UK)

Other Titles in the Series:
Parallel Logic Programming in PARLOG: The Language and its Implementation   Steve Gregory

Programming in
PARLOG

TOM CONLON
Moray House College, Edinburgh

ADDISON-WESLEY PUBLISHING COMPANY

Wokingham, England · Reading, Massachusetts · Menlo Park, California
New York · Don Mills, Ontario · Amsterdam · Bonn · Sydney
Singapore · Tokyo · Madrid · San Juan

Cover designed by Marshall Henrichs and
printed by The Riverside Printing Co. (Reading) Ltd.
Typeset by Quorum Technical Services Ltd, Cheltenham
Printed in Great Britain by T. J. Press (Padstow), Cornwall

First printed 1989

British Library Cataloguing in Publication Data
Conlon, Tom *1954–*
    Programming in PARLOG.—(International
    series in logic programming).
    1. Computer systems. Programming languages.
    Parlog
    I. Title   II. Series
    005.13'3

    ISBN 0–201–17450–2

Library of Congress Cataloging in Publication Data
Conlon, Tom, 1954–
    Programming in PARLOG / Tom Conlon
        p.   cm. — (International series in logic programming)
    Bibliography: p.
    Includes index.
    ISBN 0–201–17450–2
    1. PARLOG (Computer program language)   2. Logic programming.
    3. Parallel programming (Computer science)   I. Title.   II. Series.
    QA76.73.P194C66 1989

                                                                    88–25119
                                                                        CIP

Foreword

Although there are now many introductory books on programming in PROLOG, this is the first such book about its younger sibling, PARLOG. Indeed, to my knowledge, it is the first tutorial book to appear on the subject of parallel logic programming.

What is PARLOG? First, it is a logic programming language: PARLOG programs comprise Horn clauses, which can be read declaratively as sentences of first-order logic. In this respect PARLOG resembles PROLOG, and PROLOG programmers should have little difficulty in recognizing and understanding a PARLOG program. In fact, some application programs can be written equally well in either language, using almost identical code.

The beauty of logic programming is that programs have a declarative semantics and so can be understood independently of their execution. However, the *raison d'être* of any programming language is its behaviour, or operational semantics, and this is where PARLOG and PROLOG differ fundamentally. PROLOG has an operational semantics designed for 'problem solving' applications, with its ability to search for all solutions to a relation. But it is essentially a sequential language: a PROLOG program must, in general, be executed sequentially in a predefined order.

This brings us to the second aspect of PARLOG: as a parallel programming language. Operationally, a PARLOG program describes a system of concurrent processes, rather than a single thread of control. Execution is controlled by programming communication between processes, rather than by sequencing. This means that the PARLOG programmer naturally thinks parallel, formulating his problem in terms of processes sending messages to each other.

When Keith Clark and I began to design PARLOG, we had two objectives. Firstly, declarative languages had long been considered prime candidates for implementation on parallel machines, due to their freedom from side-effects. It seemed likely that a logic language that had a concurrent operational semantics could be mapped onto a parallel architecture much more naturally than PROLOG. This would provide at least one way to realize the promise of parallel implementation of logic programming.

Secondly, many classes of application are naturally expressed in terms of communicating processes. For this concurrent programming, it would be hard to imagine a higher-level language than PARLOG. In recent years PARLOG, and related languages, have been successfully applied in many areas, such as operating systems, process control, simulation, parallel algorithms and artificial intelligence. Parallel logic programming has also been shown to have connections with other high-level programming formalisms, including object-oriented programming and constraint programming as well as functional programming.

For all these reasons, a familiarity with the concepts of parallel logic programming will prove useful, if not essential, to anyone with an interest in Fifth Generation computing, parallel processing, artificial intelligence or language design.

Tom Conlon is a great communicator as well as a PARLOG expert, and this is reflected in his book. Here he presents the language as a succession of clearly defined concepts and discusses each one thoroughly before introducing the next. Each idea is explained meticulously from several angles and illustrated by unusually interesting and well-chosen examples. In particular, the author has been careful to emphasize both the logic and parallel aspects of the language throughout the book.

This outstandingly well-written book is an accessible and enjoyable introduction to parallel logic programming and I recommend anyone wishing to learn the subject to read it, preferably trying out the ideas on a PARLOG language system. In this way, the reader can hardly fail to gain a thorough appreciation of the principles and practice (and fun!) of PARLOG programming.

Steve Gregory
London
May 1988

Preface

This book introduces PARLOG, a revolutionary new programming language. The word **PARLOG** is an abbreviation for 'Parallel Logic', and the name itself proclaims the language's innovative credentials: it projects a new vision of programming rooted in the concepts of concurrency and declarative logic. For PARLOG programmers, the old orthodoxies – based on the ideas that programs could only be understood imperatively, as lists of machine commands, and could only be executed sequentially in step-by-step, drill-sergeant fashion – have been demolished well and truly, and the 'new computing' of the Fifth Generation is already a reality.

But as yet the PARLOG programmers form only a tiny elite. They represent the modern equivalents of those earlier pioneers who heralded past revolutions in computing: those such as the 1950s FORTRAN vanguard who recognized the superiority of a language which was higher-level than the former machine codes, or the 1970s logic programmers who understood the significance of PROLOG. The history of such developments tells how in time, others gained access to the new concepts and the benefits of a more powerful intellectual problem-solving tool were shared. For this book, the main motivation was a belief that a knowledge of PARLOG ought to be far more widely spread – and sooner rather than later.

Two other convictions influenced the book. The first was the belief that new and powerful ideas need not be less accessible than those that are established or commonplace. PARLOG seems to demonstrate this well: its programs are composed of a very modest subset of logic that is executed by computing machines in a uniform, uncomplicated way. What is marvellous – and unexpected in the discovery – is how the combination of these two things brings all the power of general-purpose, communicating concurrent processes. The second, and related, conviction was that it would be in the best interests of teaching and learning PARLOG to fully exploit the language's origins in logic programming. There is no 'rigour' in this book, but there is a determined effort to assist the reader to construct a coherent body of concepts. And the glue that binds them all together is the central theme of logic programming, namely: the relationship between a program's logic and its behaviour – concurrent behaviour, in the case of PARLOG.

Readership

The book is aimed at computer programmers, teachers and students of computing science and artificial intelligence, and anyone with an interest in Fifth Generation computing. It assumes no prior knowledge of its subject matter and hence could be used as an introduction to logic programming and to concurrent programming. In part this orientation is due to an ideal, that the book should be accessible to the widest possible readership; but it is also a pragmatic recognition of the fact that the sheer newness of PARLOG makes unsafe the usual kinds of assumption about relevant prior knowledge. At the same time an important aim for the book has been to provide for a potentially very diverse audience. An understanding of PROLOG for example will certainly do no harm and references to PROLOG are made at several points in the text, but not so as to disadvantage readers unfamiliar with the language.

Structure, content and use of the book

The book's structure should assist in deciding how best to use the contents. All chapters open with a preview and most close with a summary. These features should support an intelligent access to the material by the reader. Early chapters offer tightly-defined exercises to promote and test understanding: in later chapters the exercises become more open-ended and the treatment is generally more free-ranging. Throughout the book encouragement is given to experimenting with the ideas on an actual PARLOG system.

The contents divide naturally into five parts. The first part is represented by Chapters 1 and 2 which offer a general (non-language-specific) introduction to the ideas of logic programming. These chapters are more or less independent from the rest of the book and are mainly included to provide some key background concepts; they could be omitted by readers who have prior logic programming experience (through PROLOG for example). Chapters 3 and 4 describe PARLOG's operational strategy, using a carefully measured approach designed to avoid the 'culture shock' that could result from a first exposure to parallel logic programming. What emerges is a simple model of program behaviour, the so-called 'test-commit-output-spawn' model, that should form the basis of a deep understanding of how PARLOG programs work. The third part comprises Chapters 5 and 6 in which the implications of the operational strategy are gradually exposed. Concurrent algorithms and interacting processes are the subject matter: readers from all backgrounds will want to study this material carefully. Chapter 7 introduces the metalevel constructs that are unusually powerful in PARLOG. The fifth and final part comprises Chapter 8, which takes the form of three case-studies. These represent substantial program developments, each aimed at a distinct application area. This chapter is likely to be of special interest to programmers with an interest in PARLOG as an applications language. A set of appendices complete the book: one summarizes PARLOG syntax, another relates PARLOG to its two close neighbours GHC and Concurrent PROLOG, and a third is a bibliography.

Availability of PARLOG

All the programs in this book have been tested on at least one of the two PARLOG systems in existence at the time of writing. These are Imperial College's SPM and Steve Gregory's own PC-PARLOG, which presently run on Unix machines and PC-DOS micros respectively. PC-PARLOG and a 'sister' implementation known as MacPARLOG (for the Apple Macintosh series) should be commercially available by the time this book goes to press. Contact:

Parallel Logic Programming Ltd
PO Box
Twickenham, London

for details. Hopefully these implementations will spread widely and will rapidly be joined by others. There should be no difficulty in using this book with any future implementation: the text adheres to standard PARLOG syntax with only a small core of assumed primitives (listed in an appendix). Features that might be system-specific are avoided throughout.

Of course, PARLOG systems based on conventional (uniprocessor) hardware cannot convert any of the concurrency specified by a PARLOG program into true parallelism. Both SPM and PC-PARLOG simulate parallelism by a timesharing behaviour. This is not important from a learning point of view. In fact, neither need it matter greatly from a programming point of view, because although the speed-up that should come from parallel execution is obviously not realized on such systems there are at least two other good reasons (apart from speed-up) for programming in a concurrent language. The first is that concurrent programs are higher-level: a degree of abstraction becomes possible in which the order of doing things becomes a detail that programmers can choose to ignore. The second is that many problem specifications – for simulations, for example, or for systems software – are inherently concurrent, and concurrent problems have solutions that are most naturally formulated in concurrent terms.

Yet the future undoubtedly lies with multiprocessor hardware. It seems certain that affordable parallel computers will arrive fairly soon, and when this happens PARLOG programmers will be in an almost unique position: their concepts – and indeed their programs! – should adapt more or less effortlessly to the new systems. A fortunate side-effect is that this book could have a rather longer life than the majority of computing books!

Acknowledgements

Firstly, I acknowledge the debt that I owe to Steve Gregory. Most importantly, as PARLOG's principal architect Steve has made an outstanding contribution to the development of computing. But also, it was Steve who in 1985 suggested that I might undertake this book; since then his encouragement and advice (to say nothing of his ever-prompt supply of the most up-to-date PARLOG system software!) have been unceasing. I am grateful also for support given to me by Steve's colleagues, including Reem Baghat, Keith Clark, Jim Crammond, Ian Foster, David Gilbert, and Graem Ringwood, who form the PARLOG Group at Imperial College. The dynamism and creativity of this Group has generated an output of research papers that has been a continuous source of stimulation for this book. Thanks are due to Ian Crorie, Peter Ross and Rajiv Trehan who smoothed my access to SPM on SUN and VAX machines in Heriot-Watt and Edinburgh Universities. My ideas on teaching logic programming have benefited from many discussions with practising teachers and with members of the former PROLOG Education Group: in particular I would like to thank Jonathan Briggs and Peter Cope. My colleagues at Moray House College, especially Peter Barker, should be thanked for creating an environment in which such work as this is possible. It scarcely needs saying that none of the people acknowledged here have in any way contributed to this book's errors, weaknesses, omissions and ineptitudes. For these I claim exclusive credit.

   Finally, Jean Casey has to endure a partner whose free time is mostly devoted to such matters as the pursuit of parallel logic programming. She bears it well and I am thankful.

Tom Conlon
Edinburgh
May 1988

Contents

Foreword   v

Preface   vii

Chapter 1   Introducing logic and logic programming   1
            Preview   1
      1.1   Logic foundations   1
      1.2   Propositional logic   2
      1.3   The logic programming concept   3
      1.4   A logic program in PL   3
      1.5   An operational strategy for PL   9
      1.6   Limitations of propositional logic   11
      1.7   Predicate logic   12
      1.8   The Horn clause form   15
      1.9   Implications and assertions   16
      1.10 Atoms and terms   17
      1.11 Problem representations in HCF   18
      1.12 The declarative semantics   23
            Summary   25
            Exercises   26

Chapter 2   From logic to control   29
            Preview   29
      2.1   Top-down inference   29
      2.2   Top-down resolution   32
      2.3   Examples of program execution   37
      2.4   Operational semantics   39
      2.5   Relating the two semantics   42
      2.6   Using structured terms   43
      2.7   Input and output substitutions   46
      2.8   Standard list relations   49
            Summary   52
            Exercises   53

Chapter 3   Assertional PARLOG programming   57
            Preview   57
     3.1   Mode declarations: inputs   57
     3.2   Or-parallel search   60
     3.3   Thinking about or-parallelism   61
     3.4   Sequential search   63
     3.5   And-parallel conjunctions   64
     3.6   Thinking about and-parallelism   65
     3.7   Sequential conjunctions   66
     3.8   Mode declarations: outputs   67
     3.9   Test-commit-output   68
     3.10   Committed choice non-determinism   71
     3.11   Shared variable conjunctions   73
     3.12   From processors to processes   76
     3.13   Primitive relations   77
     3.14   Differences from PROLOG   80
            Summary   82
            Exercises   83

Chapter 4   Process = Test-commit-output-spawn   85
            Preview   85
     4.1   Implication clauses   85
     4.2   Spawning concurrent processes   88
     4.3   Multiple clause procedures   90
     4.4   Guarded clauses   94
     4.5   Some concepts refined   97
     4.6   A database example   98
     4.7   Properties associated with guards   100
     4.8   Recursive processes   102
     4.9   Stream communication   118
     4.10   Review of evaluation strategy   122
            Summary   124
            Exercises   125

Chapter 5   Concurrent algorithms   127
            Preview   127
     5.1   I/O for program testing   127
     5.2   List pair relations   130
     5.3   Merging lists   133
     5.4   Partitioning lists   137
     5.5   Sorting lists   141
     5.6   Searching binary trees   144
     5.7   An ordered tree search   148
     5.8   Inserting into a binary tree   150
     5.9   Building trees from lists   154
     5.10   Comparing tree profiles   157

5.11 Finding a path in a graph   161
      Summary   168
      Exercises   169

Chapter 6   Interacting processes   171
      Preview   171
6.1   Producers and consumers   171
6.2   Two-way communication   174
6.3   Client-server interactions   178
6.4   Two-way synchronization   180
6.5   Exploiting incremental feedback   183
6.6   Incomplete messages   187
6.7   Solving the response-routing problem   192
6.8   Lazy producers   195
6.9   Lazy client-server interactions   201
6.10 Biased and fair behaviour   202
      Summary   205
      Exercises   206

Chapter 7   Metalevel programming   209
      Preview   209
7.1   A database interface   209
7.2   Data representation and access   211
7.3   A lazy set constructor   214
7.4   Metacalls and shells   215
7.5   Multitask I/O   217
7.6   Fail-safe shells   220
7.7   Defining meta-predicates   222
7.8   Unification-related primitives   225
      Summary   227
      Exercises   227

Chapter 8   Applications of PARLOG   229
      Preview   229
8.1   A parallel system simulation   229
8.2   A concurrent sentence parser   239
8.3   SLIM: a 'front-end' for PARLOG   252

Appendix A   GHC and Concurrent PROLOG   269

Appendix B   PARLOG syntax and primitives   275

Bibliography   281

Index   283

1

Introducing logic and logic programming

1.1 Logic foundations
1.2 Propositional logic
1.3 The logic programming concept
1.4 A logic program in PL
1.5 An operational strategy for PL
1.6 Limitations of propositional logic
1.7 Predicate logic

1.8 The Horn clause form
1.9 Implications and assertions
1.10 Atoms and terms
1.11 Problem representations in HCF
1.12 The declarative semantics
     Summary
     Exercises

PREVIEW   This chapter informally describes some of the most fundamental concepts of logic programming. Logic itself is introduced through its propositional form, which has a particularly simple syntax and semantics. Using this logic we show how problems can be represented as logic programs and we consider how such programs could be executed on a computer. We then extend the concepts to embrace predicate logic, in particular the Horn clause form that is identified with all current logic programming languages including PARLOG. The focus here is on the declarative, machine-independent interpretation of Horn clause logic programs. Chapter 2 will discuss these programs from an operational (execution) point of view.

If you are already familiar with the underlying ideas of logic programming then both this chapter and the next could be skipped. PROLOG experts, for instance, could proceed directly to Chapter 3 which introduces the distinct operational semantics of PARLOG. On the other hand, the presentation here is fairly novel and it is able to anticipate (and hence hopefully, lessen) some of the difficulties that may be involved in learning PARLOG.

1.1 Logic foundations

In one form or another, logic has served as a language of formal description for at least two thousand years. For philosophers, logic has been a vehicle for expressing beliefs; for mathematicians, it has been a

1

language of axioms, proofs and theorems; and now for computing scientists – easily the most recent customers! – logic has become a means of representing and processing information.

Logic programming is still quite new and unanimity has yet to be reached on some quite basic issues. One of them is: how deep a study of logic itself is necessary for successful logic programming? We take the view that whilst a lengthy study probably isn't essential, a general understanding of the foundations of logic is certainly useful. Such an understanding can help us in reasoning about program correctness, for example, and in the context of parallel computing this will turn out to be even more important than before.

The earliest logic was Aristotle's **syllogistic logic** which specified nineteen different classes of argument. These classes, or **syllogisms**, were supposed to capture all possible ways of expressing beliefs and establishing their consequences. Actually syllogistic logic does no such thing: but the inadequacies were hardly recognized until the nineteenth century, when George Boole attempted to remedy them. His **propositional logic** remains important today. Following Boole the richer form of **predicate logic** was developed. This language is powerful enough, as Bertrand Russell showed, to represent almost the whole of mathematics. It is in predicate logic that most of the logic programming languages, including PARLOG, are based. More precisely, current logic programming languages are based on a subset of predicate logic which is known as the **Horn clause form** (after Alfred Horn, the logician who investigated it originally).

Propositional logic makes a good place to start. Although very simple, this language can nonetheless be used to introduce some of the key ideas. Then we can extend into predicate logic and the Horn clause form that is associated with PARLOG. In this way we shall build secure foundations for the chapters that follow.

1.2   Propositional logic

In the language of propositional logic (PL) we construct sentences or **formulae** according to a very simple syntax. The most basic kind of formulae are the **atomic propositions**, each one denoted by a symbol which is a single upper-case letter. Each atomic proposition is intended to represent some situation or statement which is either true or false. For example:

P: The voltage on port 5 is high.
Q: All registers are empty.
R: The power is off.

More complex formulae are constructed by combining atomic propositions using the **connectives**. There are five main connectives, as shown in the following table.

Connective	Informal Name	Formal Name
∧	and	Conjunction
∨	or	Disjunction
¬	not	Negation
←	if	Implication
↔	if and only if	Equivalence

For example, if P, Q and R represent atomic propositions then among the more complex formulae we can make are the following:

P ∧ Q, Q ∨ R, ¬P, P ← Q, Q ↔ R

Given the earlier meaning for the atomic propositions, it is easy to work out the situations that these more complex formulae represent:

P ∧ Q: The voltage on port 5 is high
and all registers are empty.

Q ∨ R: All registers are empty
or the power is off.

¬P: The voltage on port 5 is *not* high.

P ← Q: The voltage on port 5 is high
if all registers are empty.

Q ↔ R: All registers are empty
if and only if the power is off.

With more complex formulae than these, parentheses could be introduced to make clear what meaning is intended. For example

¬R ∨ (P ∧ Q):   The power is *not* off
or the voltage on port 5 is high
and all registers are empty.

Notice how the English language version here could be misinterpreted, where the formal logic representation is unambiguous. Perhaps we should put parentheses in the English too!

As these examples show, the legal formulae of PL have an easily understood syntax. In fact, we can completely define the syntax using just two rules:

(1)   An atomic proposition such as P, Q and R is a legal formula.

(2)   If S and T are legal formulae, then so are S ∧ T, S ∨ T, ¬S, S ← T, and S ↔ T.

So much for syntax. What about the **semantics** of the language? That is, how do we decide what any particular formula *means*? In the world of natural language, the concept of 'meaning' is made enormously complex by such factors as people's differing understanding of words and the subtle ways in which the context of use affects the interpretation. Logic reduces semantics to the simplest imaginable form: it boils all meaning down to **truthvalues**. That is, any formula – if it has any meaning at all – evaluates to either true or false.

To evaluate any formula, such as

$$(M \wedge N) \vee O$$

logic requires that we first assign a truthvalue to each atomic proposition. How we do this is a matter for us to decide, and usually it will depend on what M, N and O are supposed to represent (for instance, if M represents: 'silicon is cheaper than platinum' then we would probably interpret it as true). Suppose that we agree on:

M	N	O
true	false	true

Once we have selected the assignment of truthvalues to propositions (the **interpretation**, as it is known) logic tells us how to evaluate the whole formula. It does this by providing a set of **semantic rules**, one for each connective, that show how truthvalues should be combined. We shall give the complete set of semantic rules shortly. In our example just two of the rules are involved and the evaluation is quite straightforward:

(1)   Since M is true and N is false,

   $(M \wedge N)$ is false by the rule for and.

(2)   Since $(M \wedge N)$ is false and O is true,

   $(M \wedge N) \vee O$ is true by the rule for or.

Notice that one thing that logic does *not* do is tell us how to interpret the atomic propositions. It is up to us to interpret each one as we choose – as either true or false, according to our beliefs. The role of logic is to show *what follows from* our chosen interpretation. In the example above, logic shows that if we accept the interpretation in that M and O are both true and N is false, then we must also regard $(M \wedge N) \vee O$ as true. Unless we are to be inconsistent, we must accept that which our beliefs imply. This explains why most logicians (perhaps contrary to popular opinion) regard their subject not as the study of truth, but of *consistency*.

But perhaps this digresses too far. Let us return to the semantic rules, of which there are five altogether; one for each connective. They are mainly obvious. For example, the rule for 'and' tells us that the formula S1 ∧ S2 should be interpreted as true if and only if S1 and S2 are both interpreted as true. This rule can be neatly expressed in a **truth table** like this:

	S1 ∧ S2	S1 true	S1 false
S2	*true*	true	false
	false	false	false

In contrast, the rule for 'or' makes clear that S1 ∨ S2 should be interpreted as false if and only if both S1 and S2 are interpreted as false formulae:

	S1 ∨ S2	S1 true	S1 false
S2	*true*	true	true
	false	true	false

The 'not' connective when applied to a formula reverses its truth-value:

S	¬S
true	false
false	true

Less intuitively obvious is the semantic rule for 'if':

	S1 ← S2	S1 true	S1 false
S2	*true*	true	false
	false	true	true

That is, S1 ← S2 is taken as true unless S1 is false and S2 is true. The truth table shown here may not quite square with your intuitive understanding of the English meaning of 'if', but it is the generally accepted formal logic definition nonetheless. In passing, notice that mathematicians more commonly write the arrow in reverse, often putting

$$P \rightarrow Q$$

where we shall write

$$Q \leftarrow P$$

Our convention may seem a little strange at first, but logic programming languages have standardized upon it and so we shall follow suit.

The semantic rule for the 'if and only if' connective is suggested by its formal name of 'equivalence'. The truthvalue of the formula S1 ↔ S2 is true precisely when S1 and S2 have the same truthvalue. That is:

S1 ↔ S2		S1	
		true	*false*
S2	*true*	true	false
	false	false	true

Having established the semantic rules, we can now apply them to discover the meaning (truthvalue) of an arbitrarily complex formula. Essentially, the trick is to substitute into the formula the truthvalue of each atomic proposition, and then to use the semantic rules to 'boil down' the resulting expression to a single truthvalue.

Suppose for example we wish to discover the truthvalue of the formula

$$(\neg A \vee B) \leftrightarrow (C \wedge \neg B)$$

under the interpretation in which A and B are regarded as false and C is regarded as true. Substituting truthvalues we get

	(¬false ∨ false) ↔ (true ∧ ¬false)	{by direct substitution}
=	(true ∨ false) ↔ (true ∧ true)	{by the semantic rule for 'not'}
=	true ↔ true	{by the rules for 'or' and 'and'}
=	true	{by the rule for 'if and only if'}

Notice that in general we must regard as meaningless a formula containing propositions for which we do not have an interpretation. There are exceptions to this, however. The formula

A ∨ ¬A

evaluates to **true** regardless of how we interpret A, and similarly

A ↔ ¬A

is invariably false. Formulae of the first kind are usually called **tautologies** and those of the second kind are known as **contradictions**. Much of the classical study of logic has involved investigating these special classes of formulae. The activity of logic programming, however, has a very different flavour.

1.3   The logic programming concept

Logic programming depends on the idea that human beings and computers can cooperate effectively in problem-solving when logic is used as the language of communication between them. In this concept, to solve any specified problem requires two main stages:

(1)   the *representation stage*: the programmer finds a suitable formal logic representation of the problem (usually called a **logic program**).

(2)   the *execution stage*: the programmer submits the logic program to the computer, perhaps after making some machine-dependent modifications. The computer applies automatically controlled deduction to the logic program order to produce the solution.

An example will make this concrete. We shall specify a problem, write a program that represents the problem in PL, and consider how a computer might manage to execute the program successfully.

1.4   A logic program in PL

As our example, consider the (somewhat hypothetical) problem of whether a certain input buffer is full. Three things are known that should help to solve the problem:

(1)   the input buffer is full if the test byte has an odd parity;

(2)   either the test byte has an odd parity or the LED is illuminated;

(3)   the LED is not illuminated.

In order to represent the problem in logic, let us first assign some proposition symbols to parts of the description. Say:

> I: The input buffer is full.
> P: The test byte has an odd parity.
> L: The LED is illuminated.

Then we can express the three things that are stated as 'known' using the respective formulae:

> I ← P
> P ∨ L
> ¬L

Since these formulae correspond to the given information, they must each be regarded as having the truthvalue true. We can be sure of this even though we are not told directly the truthvalues of the atomic propositions.

The problem is to find the truthvalue for I and this can be boiled down to the symbolic logic form:

> I ← P
> P ∨ L
> ¬L
> ――――
> ? I

We will come across this kind of representation quite frequently, so let us be clear about what it means. Above the line we have the **logic program**. It comprises a set of formulae that specifies the information needed to solve the problem. Since we believe the given information to be accurate, we can safely interpret each formula as having the truthvalue true. Below the line is the **query formula** or **goal**. It identifies the problem requirement as one that asks: 'What truthvalue should be given to this formula?'. Sometimes we shall use the term 'logic program' more loosely, in a way that encompasses the query in addition to the formulae of the program proper.

The computer program that can process a representation in the above form is called a **logic interpreter**. The task of a logic interpreter is to try to infer from the program formulae the truthvalue of the query. With the example given here, a logic interpreter should have no problem: it would output something like

> I is true

perhaps after a very short delay. In the next section we will consider how this is achieved.

Notice that the computer does all its work at the level of abstract symbols. In the example above, the computer manages to reach the solution without having any knowledge of input buffers, test bytes, or whatever, since what it actually processes is the programmer's symbolic representation of the problem. The responsibility for making sound mappings between real-world situations and formal logic is the programmer's, and this includes interpreting the computer's reply as well as initially representing the problem.

1.5   An operational strategy for PL

How might a logic interpreter work? In order to be useful, it will have to respond reliably to any arbitrary logic program that we might choose to submit. Remembering that a logic interpreter is itself a computer program, it seems that this requires that we identify some uniform strategy for executing logic programs in the language of PL.

The requirement that the operational strategy be *uniform* suggests that human-oriented logic processing methods might not be suitable. For example, how would we as humans 'execute' the logic program developed earlier? Recall that the program is

$$I \leftarrow P$$
$$P \vee L$$
$$\underline{\neg L}$$
$$? \, I$$

We might reasonably proceed with the deduction along the following lines:

Since $\neg L$ is true, L must be false
  (by the rule for 'not').
Since $P \vee L$ is true and L is false, P must be true
  (by the rule for 'or').
Since $I \leftarrow P$ is true and P is true, I must be true.
  (by the rule for '$\leftarrow$')
Thus the problem is solved #

To human intelligence, this seems fairly straightforward. At each step a semantic rule is applied to one of the formulae. If all goes well, the truthvalues of the atomic propositions are exposed one by one until eventually the solution to the query becomes revealed. This 'free-proof' approach is the one that a human mathematician would probably find most natural.

Unfortunately, it is rather difficult to transfer the mathematician's skill at 'free-proof' into the kind of watertight, uniform strategy that a logic interpreter would be required to embody. The difficulties are not trivial

even for the elementary language of PL. We shall not inv[e]
further, however, for it turns out that a quite different approac[h]
the **truth-table strategy** offers a very straightforward operatio[n.]
The truth-table strategy requires that a table be constructed t[o]
truthvalues of the program formulae and of the goal for a[ll]
interpretations of the atomic propositions. That done, the p[r]
solved by checking the truthvalues of the query formula for eac[h]
tation which satisfies all the program formulae. If these values a[re]
then the answer to the query itself is true.

An example will make it clearer. To execute the program a[bove]
start (or rather, the PL interpreter starts) by building a table like

Propositions			Program Formulae			Goal
I	P	L	I ← P	P ∨ L	¬L	I
true	true	true				
true	true	false				
true	false	true				
true	false	false				
false	true	true				
false	true	false				
false	false	true				
false	false	false				

These rows specify all possible interpretations for the propositions in
the program. Now we complete each row, using the semantic rules to
determine each entry as shown in the table below.

Propositions			Program Formulae			Goal
I	P	L	I ← P	P ∨ L	¬L	I
true	true	true	true	true	false	true
true	true	false	true	true	true	true (*)
true	false	true	true	true	false	true
true	false	false	true	false	true	true
false	true	true	false	true	false	false
false	true	false	false	true	true	false
false	false	true	true	true	false	false
false	false	false	true	false	true	false

What does all this tell us? Of the eight possible interpretations there is only one (on the row marked ('*')) that gives the truthvalue true to all the program formulae. Unless we disown the program, this is the only interpretation in which we can believe. And since this interpretation also assigns true to the goal, we must accept this too or else we are inconsistent. Hence we conclude as before that the truthvalue of I is true.

The general approach of the truth table strategy will be clear. Firstly, construct the table, with one row for each possible interpretation for the propositions. Secondly, mark with a star those rows in which all of the program formulae are revealed as true. This identifies the interpretations that are consistent with the program. Thirdly, if in each one of these 'starred' rows the goal is also marked as true, then conclude that the program implies that the goal is true; if they each mark the goal as false, then conclude that the program contradicts the goal, that must therefore be false.

At least two other outcomes are also possible. Firstly, there may be no starred rows, because there is no interpretation that satisfies all the program formulae simultaneously. This shows that the program is **internally inconsistent**: by writing it the programmer has described a situation which is impossible. Secondly, it could happen that there are starred rows, but some of them show the goal as true and others show it as false. In this case we can neither conclude that the program implies the goal, nor that it contradicts it. A program that produces this outcome is said to be **under-specified** because, in effect, it does not contain enough information to answer the query one way or the other. Example 3 at the end of this chapter includes instances of internally inconsistent and under-specified programs.

The truth-table strategy has two main features that commend it as the operational basis of a logic interpreter for PL. Firstly, it is a straightforward routine, tedious for humans to execute but simple enough to implement as an effective computer program. Such a program need not be limited to a sequential form of execution: since the rows of the table can be completed independently of one another, a parallel computer could proceed by constructing some or all of the rows simultaneously. Secondly, the same uniform strategy will reliably execute any logic program – even detecting programs that are inconsistent or underspecified. A less welcome characteristic seems to be the rate at which the table expands as problems grow larger: the number of rows doubles with each additional proposition symbol.

1.6   Limitations of propositional logic

Notwithstanding its attractions, the language of PL will not serve for serious logic programming. The crucial weakness of the language is its *coarseness*. By representing a whole 'chunk' of information with a single-letter proposition symbol, too much detail is concealed. The programmer's representation of the problem may be easy to construct, but the benefit is largely illusory because the finished program is typically too crude to make useful deductions possible.

A simple example will illustrate. Consider this:

> The problem is to determine whether Smith must retire. Three things are given: that Smith is a cybernetician, that Smith is 55 years old, and that the retirement age for all cyberneticians is 60.

By common sense, the solution is obviously 'no'. But now consider a representation of the problem in PL. A reasonable assignment of atomic propositions seems to be:

R: Smith must retire.
C: Smith is a cybernetican.
A: Smith is 55 years old.
S: All cyberneticians retire at 60.

This produces the logic program:

```
C
A
S
? R
```

Plainly the correct solution is not computable from this program. The trouble is that the program gives no hint that some of the propositions represent information of a related kind – for example, that R, C and A all relate to Smith and that S and A both relate to to the ages of individuals. By 'wrapping up' the problem description in proposition symbols we have concealed the connecting relationships that would enable the deduction to take place.

Of course, it is possible that with some extra effort we could find a better way to represent this problem as a PL program. But the coarseness of propositional logic is a real obstacle. In predicate logic we will find a language that permits a more useful representation of problems, and hence better logic programs, to be constructed.

1.7 Predicate logic

There is enough in the predicate form of logic (more precisely, First Order Predicate Logic – let us call it FOPL for short) to fill a lifetime of study. Fortunately, our requirements for logic programming are modest. Almost all current logic programming languages – including PROLOG and PARLOG – are based not in the whole language of FOPL but in a restricted sub-language of it. Hence we shall only briefly outline full FOPL before settling on the sub-language.

As a simple example of FOPL, consider the sentence 'The chip is made of silicon'. In FOPL this could be represented by the formula

made_of(chip, silicon)

whereas in PL we might have assigned a single atomic proposition, say

M

to express the same thing. The contrast is obvious. PL lumps the whole 'package' into a single proposition symbol. FOPL constructs a formula from three component terms, which here were: made_of (the **predicate** or **relation** term), chip, and silicon (the **argument** terms). As we shall see, the effort of constructing this more complex formula is more than repaid by its increased expressiveness.

Formulae like the one above, that are constructed simply by associating a predicate with a group of arguments, are the most basic kind of formulae in FOPL. They have the formal name of **atomic formulae**, or just **atoms** for short. The name is a good one because all the more complex formulae of FOPL are built from these atomic components.

Other examples of atoms are:

made_of(cabinet, plastic)
spins(disk)
distance(power_supply, processor, 25)

FOPL does not dictate how predicates and arguments should be composed in order to represent any particular item of information. A rough (very rough!) rule of thumb is that predicates often correspond to verbs and arguments to nouns – but there are usually many possibilities, and we just have to make the choice as to which seems best. For example, the third formula above seems a reasonable way to represent a sentence such as 'The power supply is 25 centimetres from the processor', but there are alternatives such as the atoms

measurement(25, power_supply, processor)
distance_from_power_supply(processor, 25)

that could also be considered. In practice some representations tend to facilitate inferencing whereas others obstruct it, as we shall see later.

More complex formulae can be constructed by combining atoms using the same five connectives as in PL. Here are some examples:

'The disk spins or it is silent':
spins(disk) ∨ silent(disk)

'The cabinet is not made of plastic and is 30 centimetres from the power supply':

¬made_of(cabinet, plastic) ∧ distance(cabinet, power_supply, 30)

'The disk is silent if and only if it is not spinning':

silent(disk) ↔ ¬spins(disk)

FOPL lets us make a statement describing *all* objects having a certain property without us having to write a formula about each one. For example, to say that 'Everything is silent' we need only write

∀X silent(X)

The ∀X should be read as 'for all X'. X is an example of a variable (identified by the capital letter). The symbol ∀ is known as the **universal quantifier**: its appearance in front of a variable tells us that the formula stands for all those formulae such as

silent(disk)
silent(power_supply)
silent(keytop)
. . .

that can be generated by substituting a specific term – any term – for the variable. These generated formulae are known as the **instances** or **instantiations** of the formula that has the universal quantifier. This capability to write a single formula that represents many others is one factor that makes FOPL far more expressive than PL. Here are some examples showing the universal quantifier attached to more complex formulae:

'Everything is silent that is not spinning':

∀X (silent(X) ← ¬spin(X))

'Everything is made of plastic or silicon':

∀X (made_of(X, plastic) ∨ made_of(X, silicon))

'Nothing that is made of silicon is spinning':

∀X (¬spin(X) ← made_of(X, silicon))

The only other symbol of FOPL is ∃, which is a second type of quantifier. This is the **existential** quantifier: it enables us to make a statement describing the existence of some object having a certain property, without us having to specify *which* object it is. For example, to say that 'something is silent' we may write

∃X silent(X)

The ∃X should be read as 'there exists an X'. The presence of ∃X before a formula indicates that there is *at least one* substitution of a non-variable term for the X in the formula which makes the formula true. The identity of the term is not specified: the point is that the existence of at least one such substitution is being guaranteed.

The two different quantifiers can be applied together to the same formula. For example, we can represent the information that 'everything is made of something' by writing

∀X ∃Y made_of(X, Y)

('for all X there exists a Y such that X is made of Y'). Brackets can be inserted to make clear the scope of the quantifiers, as in the example

∀C (∃G guarantee(C, G) ← computer(C))

('Every computer has a guarantee').

These then are the elements of full predicate logic. Having seen it briefly flower we shall now at once prune it rather hard – hard enough in fact to exclude most of the examples of formulae that have been shown here. The sub-language of Horn clauses – which is the language of PARLOG – is very much simpler to describe, for it is limited to a restricted class of FOPL formulae that can be represented in a very simple standard form.

1.8   The Horn clause form

At this point, it is reasonable to ask why it should be necessary to restrict ourselves to a mere subset of FOPL. Why should we not write logic programs that make use of the whole language? The short answer is that nobody has yet demonstrated an effective operational strategy on which a logic interpreter for full FOPL could be based. Writing programs in full FOPL is one thing: finding some way to run them is another.

This is where the Horn clause form (HCF) of logic comes in. HCF is a much-slimmed sub-language of FOPL, but it is still reasonably expressive. (In fact, it has been shown that anything which can be represented in full FOPL can be translated into a logically equivalent HCF representation – although the effort can be substantial and the result may look much more awkward than the original). But the crucial point is that HCF is simple enough for machine processing. Effective operational strategies for it exist that have been incorporated into practical logic programming systems, PROLOG and PARLOG being two examples. The next few sections will ilustrate the combination of representational power with the potential for automatically controlled deduction that makes HCF so attractive from a logic programming standpoint.

1.9   Implications and assertions

The language of Horn clauses is made up of formulae – usually called **clause formulae** or simply **clauses** – of just two kinds. Clauses of the first kind are known as **implications** and these have the syntax

> H ← T1 ∧ T2 ∧ ... ∧ Tn

where the H and each T represents an atom (as described earlier). There can be any number of Ts on the right-hand side of the clause, but one and only one H must appear on the left. Some examples of implications are:

> natural_number(N) ← integer(N) ∧ greater(N, 0)
> left_of(X, Y) ← left_of(X, Z) ∧ left_of(Z, Y)
> parent_of(M, C) ← mother_of(M, C)

(You can probably guess the intended meaning of each of these.) Clauses of the other kind are known as **assertions** and syntactically these are just atoms. Some examples are:

> integer(3)
> left_of(robot1, robot2)
> mother_of(freda, billy)

the intended meanings of which are obvious. The distinction between implications and assertions is in a sense artificial – an assertion can be regarded as an implication that has zero atoms on the right-hand side.

No kinds of formulae other than assertions and implications are permitted. In particular, the connectives ∨, ↔, and ¬, and the existential quantifier ∃ are not available in HCF. Quite simply, we must manage to represent the world without them. Neither does the universal quantifier ∀ ever explicitly appear in a clause; but its absence is apparent rather than real, because all variables appearing in an HCF formula are *implicitly* universally quantified. For example, the three implications above are identical in meaning to the formulae

> ∀N   (natural_number(N) ← integer(N) ∧ greater(N, 0))
> ∀X ∀Y ∀Z (left_of(X, Y) ← left_of(X, Z) ∧ left_of(Z, Y))
> ∀M ∀C   (parent_of(M, C) ← mother_of(M, C))

respectively. Leaving out the quantifiers saves time and effort and it helps a little in simplifying the syntax of HCF, but in reading any clause with variables it is essential to remember them. For instance, the clause

> likes(X, Y) ← likes(Y, X)

should be read formally as: 'For all X and for all Y, the relationship likes(X, Y) holds true if the relationship likes(Y, X) holds true'. A less formal reading is: 'Everyone likes anyone who likes them'. The less formal reading is more natural, but it too recognizes the significance of the invisible universal quantifiers.

1.10   Atoms and terms

Clauses are made up of atoms and so we had better be precise about what legally constitutes an atom. Notice first that atoms represent **relationships** between individuals: the nature of the relationship is identified by the predicate and the individuals are specified by the arguments. (Although an atom with only one argument should really be regarded as representing a **property** rather than a relationship.) Any atom has the form:

predicate(argument1, argument2, ..., argumentk)

The integer k is known as the **arity** and is usually fixed for each particular predicate. (If the arity is zero then the brackets can be omitted). In order to be syntactically legal, the predicate has to be a (non-numeric) **constant**, which is a special type of **term**. The arguments can be terms of any type. There are four types of term, as follows:

(1)   *Constants* are either:

    (a)   *alpha* constants, which begin with a lower-case letter but may include letters, digits and underscore characters; or

    (b)   *numeric* constants, which are just numbers; or

    (c)   *quoted* constants, which may contain any sequence of characters enclosed in quotes.

(2)   *Variables* are like alpha constants but they begin with an upper-case letter.

(3)   *Lists* are sequences of terms separated by commas, with square brackets enclosing the whole.

(4)   *Structures* have the same syntax as atoms.

The table below gives some examples of each type of term.

Constants	made_of, robot1, 25, -3.5, '47b North Street'
Variables	X, N, Name, Salary
Lists	[1, 2, 3, 4], [red, green]
Structures	tree(Left, Root, Right), car(ford, 1910)

Lists and structures are the compound terms of Horn clause logic and these types have a crucial part to play: they act as the data structures of logic programming.

1.11   Problem representations in HCF

At this point, it will help to study some examples of simple logic programs written in the language of HCF. The question of how the programs could be executed will be tackled after the matter of semantics has been properly considered. The important thing here is to gain a feel for the activity of representing problem specifications in this new form of logic.

Example 1   The lucky numbers problem
    Henry wants to know whether 18 is one of his lucky numbers.
    He believes that 4 is lucky and that 7 is lucky. He also believes
    that any number is lucky if it is the sum of two other numbers
    that are lucky.

To represent the problem in logic, let us invent a predicate lucky where the meaning of lucky(N) is intended to be: N is a lucky number. Then Henry's problem could be expressed by the query

    ? lucky(18)

The problem specifies that 4 and 7 are lucky. This can be represented by two assertions:

    lucky(4)
    lucky(7)

Henry's other belief is more general. It is that any arbitrary number N, say, is lucky if it is the sum of two other lucky numbers N1 and N2, say. This can be represented by the implication:

    lucky(N) ← lucky(N1) ∧ lucky(N2) ∧ sum(N1, N2, N)

Note that the three conditions in the body of this rule could appear in any sequence. The ordering is not logically significant. Neither is the ordering of the three different clauses within the definition of the lucky relation.

What about sum? If we had to define this relation, we could do so by writing an infinite set of assertions:

```
sum(0, 0, 0)
sum(0, 1, 1)
sum(1, 0, 1)
sum(1, 1, 2)
sum(1, 2, 3)
sum(2, 0, 2)
sum(2, 1, 3)
sum(2, 2, 4)
sum(3, 0, 3)
. . .
```

This is perfectly reasonable from the theoretical standpoint but it would be very tedious in practice! Instead we shall assume the existence of some suitable implicit definition. (A practical logic programming system always provides a set of built-in or *primitive* predicates that efficiently pre-define the most elementary relations, such as those for basic arithmetic).

The completed program, showing clauses that have been numbered for convenient referencing later, is:

```
lucky(4)                                            [1]
lucky(7)                                            [2]
lucky(N) ←                                          [3]
      lucky(N1) ∧
      lucky(N2) ∧
      sum(N1, N2, N)
? lucky(18)
```

The reason for writing the third clause over several lines is to improve readability, but this is only a matter of taste.

Of course, there are other possible representations. Just as there are usually several ways of expressing the same information in terms of natural language, so it is with logic.

Example 2   The citizenship problem

The problem is to determine whether Jerry is a citizen of Bigland. A person who was born in Bigland is a Bigland citizen, and so is a person who is married to someone who is a Bigland citizen. Jerry was born in Littleland. He is married to Mary. Mary was born in Bigland.

Again, it is helpful to start by inventing a suitable query. In this example we might choose

        ? citizen(jerry, bigland)

where the intended logical reading of citizen(Person, Country) is: Person is a citizen of Country. Notice that the terms jerry and bigland have lower-case initial letters because they are constants – upper-case initials denote variables.

Now we can write the program clauses. On inspection, it appears that for the definition of citizenship it will suffice to define two clauses as follows:

        citizen(Person, bigland) ←
            born(Person, bigland)
        citizen(Person, bigland) ←
            married(Person, Spouse) ∧
            citizen(Spouse, bigland)

Each implication represents 'one half' of the citizenship definition. We have introduced two new predicates born and married because they seemed to be necessary; their intended meanings will be obvious.

The rest of the information contained in the problem becomes the assertions:

        born(jerry, littleland)
        married(jerry, mary)
        born(mary, bigland)

So the logic program is:

        citizen(Person, bigland) ←   [1]
            born(Person, bigland)
        citizen(Person, bigland) ←   [2]
            married(Person, Spouse) ∧
            citizen(Spouse, bigland)

        born(mary, bigland)   [3]
        born(jerry, littleland)   [4]

        married(jerry, mary)   [5]
        ? citizen(jerry, bigland)

Conventionally, distinct clauses that contribute to the definition of the same relation are grouped together. The group is often called the **procedure** for the relation – so we can speak about the citizen procedure, the born procedure, and so on. Notice in passing how blank lines have been inserted between different procedures. Again, this is only a matter of taste.

Example 3 The ancestors problem

Given the family tree shown below, the problem is to name all the ancestors of Bob. A person's ancestors are defined as the person's mother and father, together with the ancestors of the mother and father.

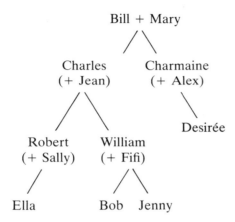

Again, it helps to start by anticipating the query. The question is to find all persons A, say, such that A is an ancestor of Bob. A suitable query might be:

    ? ancestor(A, bob)

where the intended logical reading of ancestor(A, Person) is: A is an ancestor of Person. The definition of ancestors includes the two rules that a person's mother is an ancestor, and so is a person's father. In logic, we can represent these rules as:

    ancestor(A, Person) ← mother(A, Person)
    ancestor(A, Person) ← father(A, Person)

The definition given in the problem specifies two other cases besides these. Firstly, the ancestors of a person's mother are ancestors. That is, if M is the mother of Person and A is an ancestor of M then A is also an ancestor of Person. In logic:

    ancestor(A, Person) ←
        mother(M, Person) ∧
        ancestor(A, M)

There is a corresponding rule for the ancestors of a person's father:

> ancestor(A, Person) ←
>> father(F, Person) ∧
>> ancestor(A, F)

That completes the representation of the ancestor relation. To finish the program we need only add the definitions of father and mother as specified by the family tree diagram. These can be expressed by a set of assertions for two predicates mother and father where, for example, the intended logical reading of mother(X, Y) is: X is the mother of Y. Then the program becomes:

father(bill, charles)	[1]
father(charles, robert)	[2]
father(bill, charmaine)	[3]
father(charles, william)	[4]
father(charmaine, desiree)	[5]
father(robert, ella)	[6]
father(william, bob)	[7]
father(william, jenny)	[8]
mother(mary, charmaine)	[9]
mother(mary, charles)	[10]
mother(jean, robert)	[11]
mother(jean, william)	[12]
mother(alex, desiree)	[13]
mother(sally, ella)	[14]
mother(fifi, bob)	[15]
mother(fifi, jenny)	[16]

> ancestor(A, Person) ←   [17]
>> mother(A, Person)
>
> ancestor(A, Person) ←   [18]
>> father(A, Person)
>
> ancestor(A, Person) ←   [19]
>> mother(M, Person) ∧
>> ancestor(A, M)
>
> ancestor(A, Person) ←   [20]
>> father(F, Person) ∧
>> ancestor(A, F)

> ? ancestor(X, bob)

Notice that we haven't tried to represent all the information that is specified by the family tree, such as the facts about who is married to whom. This is simply because it doesn't seem necessary for solving the problem in hand.

1.12   The declarative semantics

Now that we have established the syntax of HCF, we can turn to the matter of semantics. The key question here is: what is the *meaning* of a set of program clauses? The likelihood is that we already have an informal understanding of the answer. Let us explore this intuitive grasp of semantics and see if we can make it precise.

Consider as an example the lucky numbers problem. We would probably all agree that in any reasonable interpretation of the program, the formulae lucky(4) and lucky(7) will have to be accepted as true formulae since they are directly asserted by the first two clauses. What contribution to the overall meaning is made by the third clause? It enables us to infer the existence of further lucky numbers. For example, we can show that lucky(11) is logically implied, since we have agreed to accept lucky(4) and lucky(7) and since sum(4, 7, 11) is a known fact. This simple proof of lucky(11) comprises a single inference step (that is, one application of the implication clause).

Similar proofs (perhaps longer ones) could be constructed to establish the validity of other formulae such as lucky(8), lucky(12), and so on. In fact, the program could be regarded as a *shorthand* for the complete set that begins

{lucky(4), lucky(7), lucky(8), lucky(11), lucky(12), lucky(14), ..}

and that lists every integer for which the **lucky** property is implied according to the program clauses. This suggests a definition of 'meaning' for logic programming: a program's meaning *comprises the collection of individual things that its clauses logically imply*. The 'things' are variable-free atomic formulae (sometimes called **ground** formulae) each of which represents some particular relationship or property.

This interpretation of meaning, which is based in logical implication, (or logical consequence) is known formally as the **declarative semantics**. The word 'declarative' is intended to have the sense of 'self-evident'. Notice that the declarative semantics gives an interpretation of programs that is entirely machine-independent: the concept of logical implication is fixed and does not depend on any computer's behaviour, so the meaning of a program according to the declarative semantics is the same regardless of how the program might eventually be executed on some physical machine. A second aspect of this view of meaning is that it becomes strictly unnecessary to relate a program's meaning to notions of truth and falsehood – we need only be concerned with whether a particular formula is, or is not, a logical consequence of the program clauses, and not with whether the formula is true or false in some absolute sense. (On the other hand, we usually *do* intend the program clauses to serve as a model of some part of the real world and this makes it intuitive, and useful, to think loosely of meaning in terms of truthvalues.)

As another example, consider the citizenship problem. We developed for this problem a program that defined three predicates: citizen, born and married. According to the declarative semantics, the meaning of this program is the set of all atomic formulae which are implied by the program clauses. This set is small enough to list in its entirety. It is:

{married(jerry, mary), born(mary, bigland), born(jerry, littleland), citizen(mary, bigland), citizen(jerry, bigland)}

The first three of these are given by assertions and the last two can be proved with the help of the implications. Notice that the presence of the last formula in the list shows that the query for the citizenship program should be answered in the affirmative.

Let us now generalize this into an overall logic programming perspective. Any logic program will fit the pattern shown below. Above the line is a set of clauses that (hopefully) describes the information needed to solve the problem. Below we have the query, sometimes called the **goal** or **goal clause**. We regard the query as posing the question: is this clause logically implied by the program clauses? Or equivalently: *is this clause part of the meaning of the program*? In the lucky numbers example, where the goal is lucky(18), the answer must be 'Yes' because we can construct a proof of the goal from the program clauses. The proof requires a small number of inference steps and uses all three clauses.

CLAUSES

?QUERY

Where the goal clause contains one or more variables, we regard it as posing a slightly different question. A query with variables asks: is there some set of substitutions of ground terms for variables that makes this clause one that is logically implied by the program clauses? For example, the goal ancestor(X, bob) in the ancestors example asks: is there a replacement for X that makes this formula a logical consequence of the program? In this example, an inspection of the program shows that the answer is 'Yes' since X = fifi, for instance, leads to a proof by clauses 15 and 17. Notice that the programmer is likely to be interested in the identity of the substitution rather than just the fact of its existence.

A slightly different viewpoint may appeal to the mathematically inclined. We can regard the program clauses as the **axioms** of some hypothetical theory. The query then represents a **prospective theorem** or **hypothesis** that is to be proved. According to the declarative semantics, the query should be answered positively if the goal is provable as a theorem from the axioms (program), and negatively otherwise. Where the query contains variables we shall want to extract from a completed proof any replacement values that were made for such variables, since these may contribute to the solution.

All of this suggests what 'running' an HCF logic program on a computer is actually about. It is an attempt to construct a proof of the goal from the program clauses. Hence, a logic interpreter is really a special kind of automatic theorem prover. In the next chapter we shall discuss this in detail.

SUMMARY

With this chapter we have covered ground fundamental not only to PARLOG, but to logic programming in general. The summary below is a reminder of some of the most important points.

- We introduced logic programming via Propositional logic (PL), which has a very simple syntax. A semantics for PL can be based on the idea of assigning an interpretation true or false to each atomic proposition. We saw how problems could be represented as logic programs written in PL, and how these programs could be executed using an operational strategy based on truth-table construction. However, PL is too coarse to be of much practical use for logic programming.

- Next we looked at the much more expressive language of Predicate logic (FOPL). Instead of proposition symbols FOPL provides atomic formulae with variables. Unfortunately, a suitable logic interpreter for full FOPL has yet to be built.

- We saw that a sub-language of FOPL known as the Horn clause form provides an effective compromise. The formulae or clauses of HCF are of a simple standard form (assertions and implications) and the language is reasonably expressive. We noted that in practice, logic programming languages have standardized on this form of logic.

- We then turned to semantics. A purely logical, machine-independent interpretation of programs is given by the declarative semantics, which specifies that a program means whatever its clauses logically imply. According to this interpretation, a solution to a query for a goal containing variables is any set of replacements for the variables that makes the goal a logical consequence of the program clauses.

EXERCISES _____

1.1 Assuming the interpretation given in the table shown, evaluate (that is, determine the truthvalue of) the following formulae of PL:

   (a) $\neg$P

   (b) $\neg$P $\leftrightarrow$ Q

   (c) P$\vee$(Q $\vee$ R)

   (d) (Q $\vee$ R) $\leftarrow$ P

   (e) $\neg$(Q $\wedge$ R) $\leftrightarrow$ $\neg$R$\vee$$\neg$Q

   (f) (($\neg$P$\vee$Q) $\leftarrow$ P) $\leftarrow$ R

Interpretation:	P	Q	R
	false	false	true

1.2 By making a suitable assignment of proposition symbols, express the problems below as logic programs in PL.

   (a) The problem is to determine whether today is a weekday. Three things are known:

      (i)   Today is either a weekday or it is a weekend-day.

      (ii) It is a weekend-day if and only if I am not working today.

      (iii) I am working today.

   (b) The problem is to determine whether the printer is defective. Four things are known:

      (i)   Either the printer is defective or the computer is.

      (ii) The computer is not defective if the power is on and the LED is glowing.

      (iii) If the LED is glowing then the power is on.

      (iv) The LED is glowing.

1.3 Simulate a PL interpreter by manually constructing truth tables for the PL programs shown below. What should be the output in each case?

   (a) S

      T$\vee$R $\leftarrow$ S

      $\underline{\neg T \leftarrow S}$

      ? R

   (b) $\neg$M

      $\underline{M \leftrightarrow N}$

      ? M $\vee$ N

(c) P ∨ Q
     ¬(P∧Q)
     Q ← P
     ─────────
     ? Q

(d) P ↔ Q
     R
     ¬Q
     P ← R
     ─────────
     ? P

(e) (I ∨ J) ← K
     ¬K
     K ← J
     ─────────
     ? I

1.4 Construct logic programs in the language of HCF to represent the following problem specifications.

   (a) The problem is to determine whether John likes anyone. He likes people who like him. Also, he likes anyone who likes someone whom Mary likes. Ian and Bob like Mary and so does Jane. Mary and Bob like one another. Ian likes John. {Use only the predicate likes, where the meaning of likes(X, Y) is: X likes Y}

   (b) The problem is to determine whether 32768 is a power of two. It is known that two is a power of two, and that any number that is double a power of two is also a power of two. {Use only the predicates power and sum, where sum is as before and power(X, Y) means: X is a power of Y}

   (c) The problem is to find out whether the robot in the diagram can pass from point 1 to point 5. It can pass between any two points that are directly linked by an arrow, but only in the direction indicated. It can also pass from one point to a second point if an arrow connects the first point to a point from which it can pass to the second point. {Use only the predicates pass and arrow, where pass(X, Y) means: the robot can pass from X to Y, and arrow(X, Y) means: an arrow connects X to Y}

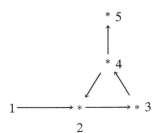

2

From logic to control

2.1 Top-down inference
2.2 Top-down resolution
2.3 Examples of program execution
2.4 Operational semantics
2.5 Relating the two semantics

2.6 Using structured terms
2.7 Input and output substitutions
2.8 Standard list relations
    Summary
    Exercises

PREVIEW   The last chapter introduced logic and the concept of a logic program, with the emphasis on the purely logical interpretation of programs that is given by the declarative semantics. In this chapter we shall focus on the operational interpretation – that is, we study the behaviour by which a computer could execute logic programs. Firstly we describe the general method of proof construction that is known as top-down inference. In the language of HCF this becomes top-down resolution, and we examine the two decision rules – the goal selection rule and the clause choice rule – which must be defined to specify a full operational semantics. We discuss some of the general issues that arise from the need to ensure that the computer's deductions from the programmer's logic are effectively controlled. Finally, we introduce structured terms with examples that aim to bring together all the main ideas that have so far been covered.

    With this chapter we complete our language-independent introduction to the basic concepts of logic programming. This should position us nicely for the advance to PARLOG's operational strategy in Chapter 3.

2.1   Top-down inference

The declarative semantics tells us what the answers to a particular logic program should be. For example, it tells us that Yes, Yes and X = fifi respectively are correct answers for the three logic programs developed in the last chapter (Section 1.11). What the declarative semantics does *not* do is prescribe how a computer should obtain these answers. For that we need an *operational strategy* – that is, a uniform, effective evaluation procedure by which a computer can interpret logic programs in the language of HCF.

You may recall that when we were working in the propositional form of logic, we discovered a suitable operational strategy based on constructing truth tables. In HCF a truth table approach is a non-starter, however. This is because a clause containing a variable effectively represents an infinite number of propositions, thereby giving rise to truth tables that are potentially infinitely large. A more promising idea is the obvious one: we could try to define an operational strategy that seeks to construct proofs directly. On the other hand, the practicality of this approach could be questioned. For as we noted earlier, the mathematician's skill at 'free proof' is generally very difficult to capture within a computer program.

At this point we can reveal a crucial advantage of the language of Horn clauses. It turns out that everything that can be proved from an HCF program can be proved using just one simple proof method known as **top-down inference**. This method is the basis of the operational strategies that are embodied in PROLOG, PARLOG and most other logic programming languages.

Top-down inference tries to prove the goal by working backwards. It starts with the goal and then reasons down through the implication clauses, ultimately, hopefully, reaching the assertions. Hence it is sometimes called 'backwards reasoning' or 'backwards chaining'. This approach contrasts with 'forwards reasoning' which would start with the assertions and then work upwards through implications in the hope of eventually reaching the goal. Notice that forwards reasoning is the style in which mathematicians traditionally present their proofs, but backwards reasoning is recognized nonetheless as an equally valid strategy for solving problems.

We can best demonstrate top-down inference by means of an HCF-like program that uses the simpler propositional logic syntax. (In the next section we shall extend the idea to 'proper' logic programs with formulae in Horn clause form.) Consider the following program:

$$A \leftarrow P \wedge Q \qquad \qquad [1]$$
$$A \leftarrow R \wedge P \qquad \qquad [2]$$
$$Q \leftarrow R \wedge T \qquad \qquad [3]$$
$$R \leftarrow S \qquad \qquad [4]$$
$$S \qquad \qquad [5]$$
$$S \leftarrow R \qquad \qquad [6]$$
$$\underline{P \qquad \qquad \qquad} \qquad [7]$$
$$? \, A$$

Top-down inference always starts by attempting to select a formula that looks like a promising 'candidate' formula to solve the goal. In this example, the goal is

$$? \, A$$

and there are two formulae – namely, the first two program formulae – that might be used (backwards) to solve it. Let us select as our candidate the second of these, which is:

A ← R ∧ P

The formula is interpreted as saying: 'To prove A, try to prove R and P'. So the new goal formula becomes

? R ∧ P

– if we can prove both of these then A will have been proved. Now, we can tackle the two individual goals any way we choose. Suppose we pick R first. For this goal the fourth program formula is the only candidate; interpreting it backwards, this formula says: 'To prove R, try to prove S'. This gives the new goal formula

? S ∧ P

A useful step now is to apply the fifth formula: it states that S is a fact. Facts, of course, need no further proving. So the goal formula is reduced to

? P

and now the seventh formula finishes the job. We have constructed a proof that the original query formula is logically implied by the program clauses.

A neater notation for representing top-down inference proofs is helpful. We can illustrate it as follows, using as an example the proof that we have just discovered:

```
? A
? R ∧ P                                                    [2]
? S ∧ P                                                    [4]
? P                                                        [5]
? #                                                        [7]
```

This simply lists the successive goal formulae in sequence. Each line after the first represents a single step of top-down inference, with an index to show which program formula was applied to produce the new goal formula from its predecessor. A hash character marks the successful completion of the proof.

In case you are still unconvinced about the validity of top-down inference, notice how the proof can be read from bottom-to-top as a conventional forwards reasoning proof. This way it reads: 'We know P by formula seven, and so from formula five we can deduce S ∧ P. Now four proves R ∧ P from this; and hence two gives the proof of A'. Top-down inference just reasons in the opposite direction. At each step we can regard the current goal formula as representing a set of problems that remain to be solved. Each inference step applies a program formula to produce a new set of problems from the existing set. The aim is to end up with an empty set of problems, for then we know that the proof of the original query goal is complete.

Top-down inference provides a basic approach by which a logic interpreter could execute programs. However, it does not in itself determine a fully defined operational strategy. This is shown by our example, in which at several points we had to make decisions of our own. Nor were the decisions inconsequential. You may have noticed that if at the first step we had selected as candidate formula the first program formula rather than the second then the proof would have been obstructed (delayed or even missed altogether). In fact, with consistently bad choices – see formulae 4 and 6 – it would even be possible to enter an endless 'loop' (admittedly no human would fall into this trap, but a machine might be caught by it). In general, top-down inference does not prescribe which program formula to select next when there is more than one possible candidate, and neither does it prescribe which individual goal to try to solve next from a goal formula that contains several goals. A practical, computer-driven logic interpreter will need to incorporate specific strategies for making these decisions.

Finally, let us restate the guarantee that comes with top-down inference. It promises that *if the goal formula really is logically implied by the program, then there will exist a top-down inference proof for it*. As we shall see, this guarantee is a precious gift of logic theory but it cannot work miracles. Knowing that a proof exists is one thing: finding it is another.

2.2   Top-down resolution

We can apply the method of top-down inference directly to programs written in the language of HCF. The principle is the same: the attempted proof starts with the query goal and works backwards through the implication clauses (hopefully) towards the assertions. The main difference is that compared to the propositional logic example above, we now have slightly more work to do at each inference step. The steps are called **resolution inference steps** and hence the proof method is named **top-down resolution**. In this section we shall study the individual resolution steps and in the next section we shall construct some complete proofs.

Each resolution step involves a goal atom and a program clause: the two are 'resolved' together to produce a new goal formula from the old goal atom. But first, the goal atom and the clause head must be made syntactically identical by an operation that is known as **unification**. When the atoms contain variables, the unification typically generates values – variously known as **substitutions**, **instantiations** or **bindings** – for these variables. As we shall see, a substitution that is made for a variable in the goal atom can be regarded as producing **output** whilst those made for a clause variable can be regarded as providing **input**. Output substitutions contribute values to the final solution; input substitutions are passed into the atoms in the right-hand side of the clause and these instantiated atoms become the new goal formula.

Let us make this concrete by describing some examples. Below we consider four, each representing one resolution step in a (hypothetical) top-down resolution proof.

Example 1
Consider the goal

> ? spins(disk)

and suppose the program contains a clause

> spins(disk) ← power(disk, on)

The goal is identical to the head of the clause. Hence unification between the two atoms is a trivial one that succeeds without generating any substitutions. The new goal becomes:

> ? power(disk, on)

as given by the right-hand side of the clause.

That completes one top-down resolution step. We can picture it as follows:

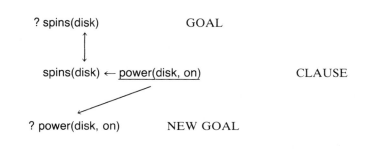

Example 2
Suppose that the goal is

> ? faulty(processor)

and the program clause chosen for resolution is

faulty(Item) ← power(on) ∧ dead(Item)

The goal atom faulty(processor) is not quite identical to the atom faulty(Item) at the head of the clause. However the two atoms can be unified (made identical) by making a substitution for the variable. If we put

Item = processor

in the goal then the unification is complete. Making this substitution in the tail of the clause produces the new goal formula

? power(on) ∧ dead(processor)

The substitution that is generated by the unification here is an example of an **input substitution**. The name comes from an analogy with conventional computing in which goals are likened to procedure calls, clauses to procedure definitions, and unification to parameter passing: in our example, the goal faulty(processor) is acting like a call to a faulty procedure that is defined by the clause, and in effect the goal supplies the input processor for the variable (formal parameter) in the clause.

We can picture this resolution as:

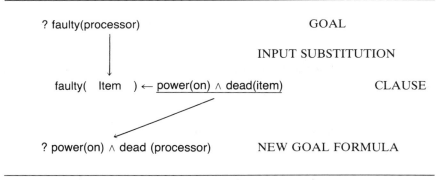

? faulty(processor)	GOAL
	INPUT SUBSTITUTION
faulty(Item) ← power(on) ∧ dead(item)	CLAUSE
? power(on) ∧ dead (processor)	NEW GOAL FORMULA

Notice the logical justification for this step. In effect, it is based on a 'backwards reasoning' interpretation of the rule

faulty(processor) ← power(on) ∧ dead(processor)

that is just a specialized instance of the program clause – it is the version of the clause in which the variable has been replaced by a particular term. We are entitled to make such a specialization because the variable in the clause is (implicitly) universally quantified.

Example 3
Let the goal be

salary(smith, X)

and suppose that the program clause that is chosen for attempted resolution is

salary(smith, 10000) ← grade(smith, clerical)

Unification between the goal salary(smith, X) and the clause head salary(smith, 10000) succeeds, generating the substitution X = 10000 for the variable in the goal. Making this substitution produces the new goal

? grade(smith, clerical)

and if this new goal succeeds then the effect will be to show that X = 10000 is a solution to the original problem about Smith's salary.

A substitution like the one here, which is made for a variable in the goal, is called an **output substitution**. We can think of it as providing the answer, or a part of the answer, to the original problem. Again, the name comes from the analogy with conventional computing: in this example the goal salary(smith, X) is acting like a call to a salary procedure that is defined by the program clause, where the procedure if successful will output the value 10000 for the variable of the call. Because of this analogy, we sometimes refer to a goal as a **procedure call** or alternatively, a **relation call**.

We can picture the resolution step in this example as follows:

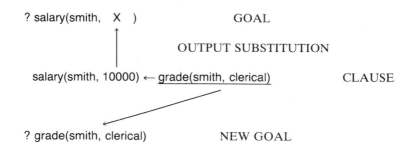

However, we must treat output substitutions with rather more caution than is necessary for input substitutions. This is because in general, an output substitution is logically justified *only* if the new goal formula that results from the resolution step turns out to be solvable. In our example, we will not have proved anything about Smith's salary until we have established that his grade is clerical; if it turns out to be something different, then the substitution X = 10000 may be incorrect. So it is not safe to replace X on a once-for-all basis at the time of the resolution step. Perhaps it is best to regard 10000 as a *potential* binding for X, but as one to which we should not become committed prematurely.

Example 4
Let the goal atom be

> ? statusbits(1, X, 0, Y)

and suppose that the program clause for resolution is

> statusbits(X, X, Y, Z) ← high(X) ∧ high(Y) ∧ low(Z)

The unification requires care. If we try to match the goal with the head of the clause as it is written then the duplication of variable names between the two (they both contain X's and Y's) could cause confusion. The difficulty is easily remedied by renaming the variables in the clause. Variable names are arbitrary after all, and providing it is done consistently throughout the clause the renaming makes no logical difference. So let us rewrite the clause as

> statusbits(V1, V1, V2, V3) ← high(V1) ∧ high(V2) ∧ low(V3)

say. Now unification can proceed. As usual, the aim is to find a set of substitutions that will make the goal atom

> statusbits(1, X, 0, Y)

syntactically identical to the clause head

> statusbits(V1, V1, V2, V3)

A little thought shows that it can be done. The unification requires the input substitutions

> V1 = 1, V2 = 0

for variables in the clause and the output substitution

> X = 1

for a variable in the goal; notice how the latter arises indirectly, from the repeated occurrence of V1 in the clause head. The other substitution required is

> V3 = Y

This last one is interesting: it is an example of what is sometimes called **sharing**. When two free variables (that is, variables without existing bindings) are unified, neither receives a value directly but any future substitution that involves either one of them will automatically apply to the other. For reasons that will become clear later, it will be convenient for us to regard this situation as a special kind of input substitution.

With these substitutions the unification is complete. The resolution step now computes the new goal formula as:

? high(1) ∧ high(0) ∧ low(Y)

which is obtained by applying the input substitutions to the atoms in the right-hand side of the (rewritten) clause. Of course, the same note of caution applies to the output substitution made here as for the last example. If it turns out that the new goal formula can be solved, then X = 1 together with whatever value is found for Y will be a solution to the original goal formula. But should the new goal formula be unsolvable then the output substitution X = 1 may be incorrect. So either we must be prepared somehow to 'undo' bindings that turn out to be unjustified, or else we must defer making them until a permament commitment to these values seems to be safe.

A picture of the resolution step treated by this example is shown below:

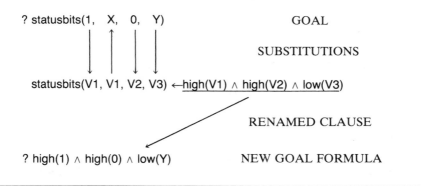

2.3   Examples of program execution

To illustrate program execution by top-down resolution, we shall now simulate the execution of the three programs that we developed earlier in the language of HCF. Each execution constructs a top-down resolution proof of the kind that a logic interpreter would be expected to generate: it comprises a sequence of goal formulae starting with the query and ending with the empty clause, where each successive goal formula is obtained from its predecessor by means of a single resolution step. It is important to realize that the execution sequences shown are not the only ones possible:

they just happen to be 'good' ones in the sense that at each step goal atoms and clauses are chosen that shorten the execution. The issue of decision-making strategy is important and we shall turn to it after the examples.

The notation used below is the concise form that was introduced previously. Each line shows the goal formula produced by one resolution step: an index specifies which program clause has been resolved and any output substitutions generated by the step are also shown. You may find it helpful to follow these executions through whilst referring to the programs given earlier (Section 1.11).

1   The lucky numbers program

```
? lucky(18)
? lucky(N1) ∧ lucky(N2) ∧ sum(N1, N2, 18)                      [3]
? lucky(N2) ∧ sum(7, N2, 18) {N1 = 7}                          [2]
? lucky(11) {N2 = 11, using: sum(7, 11, 18)}
? lucky(M1) ∧ lucky(M2) ∧ sum(M1, M2, 11)                      [3]
? lucky(M2) ∧ sum(7, M2, 11) {M1 = 7}                          [2]
? lucky(4) {M2 = 4, using: sum(7, 4, 11)}
? #                                                            [1]
```

Recall that sum is assumed to be a 'primitive', that is, a predicate for that there is some effective inbuilt definition. Notice also here that for convenience, variables were re-named in the second use of the lucky implication clause so that distinct variables appearing anywhere in the proof have different names.

2   The citizenship program

```
? citizen(jerry, bigland)
? married(jerry, Spouse) ∧ citizen(Spouse, bigland)           [2]
? citizen(mary, bigland) {Spouse = mary}                      [5]
? born(mary, bigland)                                         [1]
? #                                                           [3]
```

3   The ancestors program
There are six solutions, corresponding to Bob's parents, grandparents and great-grandparents. A separate individual top-down resolution proof can be found for each solution. Below we show only two of these, giving the solutions X = fifi and X = charles respectively.

```
? ancestor(X, bob)
? mother(X, bob)                                              [17]
? # {X = fifi}                                                [15]


? ancestor(X, bob)
? father(F, bob) ∧ ancestor(X, F)                             [20]
? ancestor(X, william) {F = william}                         [7]
? father(X, william)                                          [18]
? # {X = charles}                                             [4]
```

2.4 Operational semantics

If you have followed the examples above then it will already be clear that top-down resolution does not by itself comprise a full operational strategy for evaluating logic programs. To be precise, it leaves two important kinds of decisions to be made. These are called the **goal selection** and the **clause choice** decisions respectively.

The need to make the first kind of decision arises whenever a goal formula contains a conjunction of more than one goal. We might for example have a goal formula represented by (in propositional logic notation)

$$? P \land Q \land R$$

The question is: which goal atom – P, Q or R – should be selected for attempted resolution next? In theory, it could be any one of them – or even perhaps any combination of two or more could be evaluated in parallel.

The need for the second kind of decision-making arises when the interpreter has selected a goal and it is looking for a clause with which to attempt the resolution step. There could be several such clauses. For example, if goal Q is selected from the goal formula above then it may be discovered that there exist three clauses

$$Q1 \leftarrow S \land T$$
$$Q2 \leftarrow W$$
$$Q3 \leftarrow L \land M \land R$$

in the defining procedure for Q (that is, three clauses for which the head atom has the same predicate as Q). Any one of these clauses might lead to a solution – or maybe none of them lead anywhere! This forces the question: which clause should be chosen? In theory, they could be tried one at a time (in any order) or they could be investigated together in parallel fashion.

As the earlier examples may have suggested, the issues at stake in these two kinds of decisions are different. Basically, the goal selection strategy affects the *efficiency* of a computation whereas the clause choice strategy affects the *completeness*. We can illustrate these points by considering again the goal clause represented by

$$? P \land Q \land R$$

If this evaluation is to succeed then clearly each of the three individual goals will have to be solved eventually. A good ordering may discover values for variables in a way that reduces the number of necessary inference steps, but it can be shown that if a solution to the query exists at all then it can be computed – sooner or later – by any arbitrary pattern of selection. Hence, the goal selection strategy relates to the efficiency of computation. Suppose now that the goal Q is selected; the clause choice strategy now faces the three clauses

$$Q1 \leftarrow S \wedge T$$
$$Q2 \leftarrow W$$
$$Q3 \leftarrow L \wedge M \wedge R$$

Assuming that one or more solutions to Q exist, the only certain way to find them is to be prepared to search all three clauses. A clause choice strategy that falls short of exhaustive search (by ignoring one or more clauses, say) may miss one or more solutions. For such a strategy, the set of solutions that is produced operationally may be *less than the complete set* that is logically implied. This is what is meant by saying that the clause choice strategy determines the completeness of the evaluation.

The differences between the existing logic programming languages essentially reflect different rules or strategies on which the goal selection and the clause choice decisions can be based. Once we have fixed on a strategy for making both kinds of decision, we will have upgraded top-down resolution into a fully-fledged operational strategy. This defines an **operational semantics**, which simply means a precise specification of how top-down inference will be controlled in the evaluation of any particular goal. Another way of saying this is to say that once we know the interpreter's strategy for selecting goals and choosing clauses, we will be able to predict the machine's behaviour (or at least, predict the range of possible behaviours) in executing any logic program.

The issues involved in appraising the various alternatives are complex questions of logic programming language design. However, it will be worthwhile briefly to summarize the strategies that have been adopted by two contrasting logic languages: PROLOG and PARLOG.

2.4.1 Summary of operational semantics: PROLOG

PROLOG is currently the most widely known logic programming language. Its goal selection strategy is to evaluate any conjunction of goals in left-to-right order. The clause choice strategy is based on a top-to-bottom (that is, textually highest first) search of all clauses in the defining procedure: a 'backtracking' mechanism removes variable bindings made for a goal by one clause when the investigation of that clause is ended and the next clause is chosen for attempted resolution with the goal.

PROLOG's strategy is totally sequential. The language was aimed at, and has proven to be remarkably successful on, traditional single-processor computers. Programmers who understand the PROLOG operational strategy can often improve the efficiency of PROLOG programs by a judicious sequencing of clauses within procedures and of conditions within the bodies of clauses. Furthermore, a 'cut' primitive is available that can be used to limit the extent of the clause search.

Notwithstanding the top-to-bottom clause search behaviour, PRO-LOG's operational strategy is not complete in the sense described above. This is because a non-terminating execution may prevent the sequential search from reaching solutions. For example, if the procedure for Q is re-specified as

Q1 ← S ∧ Q1
Q2 ← W
Q3 ← L ∧ M ∧ R

then PROLOG's search may never get beyond the first clause. If solutions are only computable by the second or third clauses then a 'looping' behaviour could mean that these solutions will never be discovered by the evaluation. It should be noted that even for programs that do not loop, PROLOG's completeness is often affected in practice by programmers' use of the 'cut'. Furthermore, the ordering of clauses and conditions is often such that programs behave with tolerable efficiency only in a single intended pattern of use.

2.4.2 Summary of operational semantics: PARLOG

PARLOG's operational strategy will be described in detail and at length in the chapters to come. Here it is sufficient to indicate some key features of the language. Firstly, PARLOG's basic goal selection strategy is to evaluate any conjunction of goals in parallel. The clause choice strategy is also basically a parallel search, with all clauses in the defining procedure for the goal investigated simultaneously.

This description will be significantly qualified later. We will explain for instance how the goal selection strategy is influenced by the use of programmer-specified **mode declarations** that may force a goal evaluation to suspend until sufficient input data has been made available to it by other goals in the conjunction. We will also show that the parallel search through the clauses of a procedure extends only up to to a certain point, the so-called point of **commitment**, the location of which the programmer can specify: after reaching this point the evaluation becomes irreversibly committed to a single clause. Bindings that would be made by any clause to the goal's variables are held back until (if ever) the clause has been selected for commitment.

An important consideration in the development of PARLOG is that the language should be efficient on parallel computers of various design. The fact that bindings in PARLOG are never retracted (that is, a binding made to a goal variable upon commitment of the evaluation to a clause is permanent) helps to achieve this efficiency, and programmers are free to use mode declarations as well as various operators available in the language to optimize the performance of PARLOG programs. However, the commitment to a single clause means that PARLOG is not complete. An evaluation can only return at most one solution to any goal variable. (Although a program can always be formulated such that the single solution is a *list* that represents a set of individual answers to the intended problem.) Further, the presence of mode declarations means that a PARLOG procedure typically supports only one pattern of call. This will be fully explained, along with the implications for programming style, in the coming sections of this book.

2.5   Relating the two semantics

As will by now be clear, any particular logic program has *two* distinct semantic interpretations. The declarative interpretation is the logically fixed, machine-independent one: it views the logical content of the program only, and judges that the program means whatever it logically implies. The operational interpretation on the other hand is machine-dependent: it views the behaviour of the program under the control of some particular computer-based logic interpreter, such as PROLOG or PARLOG, and judges that the program means whatever is producible from it under a run-time evaluation. A 'PROLOG machine' and a 'PARLOG machine' may produce different results (that is, different subsets of the set of logically valid solutions) to the same query even if the programs being queried have logically equivalent content. The distinction between the logical and the operational semantics could be regarded as the difference between the *what* and the *how*: the declarative interpretation specifies *what* the problem is and the operational interpretation specifies *how* it will be solved by some specific strategy for controlling inference.

Notice that the activity of programming has always involved these two components of 'what' and 'how'. A programmer using an imperative language such as Pascal (say) typically begins with a specification of *what* the problem is and then proceeds to consider *how* it can be solved. The traditional approach to the 'how' part is to try to design an algorithm – a recipe for machine behaviour – the correctness of which for the 'what' part can be very hard to justify. In logic programming, algorithms result from the application of controlled inference to the programmer's logic: the concerns of logical adequacy can be separated from those of operational performance. Robert Kowalski has suggested that the relationship can be represented as

Algorithm = Logic + Control

Many people consider that the main strengths of logic programming stem from this capability to regard the 'what' and the 'how' as separate aspects, that are however related within the single formalism of logic.

In developing logic programs, both of the two semantics are important but the priorities are different at different times. In general, program development passes through two distinct stages: in the first, **specification** stage, where the aim is to find a formal logic representation of the specified problem, the declarative interpretation prevails; in the second, **execution** stage, where the aim is to modify the logic into a program that runs efficiently on the target system, the operational interpretation dominates proceedings. Another way of saying this is to say that in the first stage we aim to ensure that the necessary solutions are logically implied by the program, and in the second stage we aim to ensure that these solutions will be produced in a satisfatory manner when the program is executed on the machine.

Not all problems permit such a clean and simple separation of concerns. Sometimes the algorithmic (or procedural) view is more natural: in such problems the declarative semantics can be ignored if necessary, and 'logic' programs can be written and read that will, under the control of the intended interpreter, give rise to the necessary behaviour. We shall see in the context of PARLOG (the programs of which support a rich procedural interpetation) that such an approach need not be in any way difficult or unnatural. The point is that our programming in general cannot afford to disregard entirely either viewpoint, neither the operational nor the declarative: logic programming gives support to both views, and permits them to be distinguished, and manages to do these things within the single formalism of Horn clauses.

2.6   Using structured terms

All our examples so far have described relationships between very simple objects such as names and numbers. Simple types of term such as alpha and numeric constants have been quite adequate to represent such objects. We now introduce **structures** and **lists**: the so-called **structured** or **compound** types of term that are available to help in representing objects that are more complex.

An example of a **structure** is the term

car(ford, 1986, red)

which is composed of four other terms: car, ford, 1986 and red. The first of these is known as the **functor** and the others are the **components** of the structure. The object that the structure represents is some particular car. A term like this might appear in an assertion such as:

drives(henry, car(ford, 1986, red))

for example, that gives us a convenient way to represent Henry's car ownership. A program built from such assertions could be called a **logic**

database, and it can be queried in a very flexible way, as shown by the example below.

```
drives(henry, car(ford, 1986, red))
drives(george, car(renault, 1984, blue))
drives(sally, car(ford, 1985, white))
drives(jenny, car(leyland, 1986, red))
drives(robert, car(ford, 1981, green))
drives(diane, car(fiat, 1983, red))
drives(pete, car(volvo, 1986, white))
```
? drives(X, car(ford, Year, white))

A single resolution step is enough to produce the solution X = sally, Y = 1985 to the query shown here. Notice in passing that structures have the same syntax as assertions, although they represent different kinds of things – a structure represents an object, whereas an assertion represents a relationship between objects.

Of course, the same information could be represented without using structures. We could just have written

```
drives(henry, ford, 1986, red)
```

for example. Structures offer the same kind of advantages as **records** in conventional programming languages: they make it possible for us to 'package' several mutually associated items into a single term. A single variable can then stand in place of the whole package. For example, we can query

```
? drives(jenny, X)
```

to which a solution is X = car(leyland, 1986, red). Note that a free (unbound) variable will unify with any term, including a term that is a structure as here. But variables excepting, a structure will unify only with another structure that has the same functor, and for which the corresponding pairs of components can unify.

The components of a structure can be terms of any type. They could even be structures themselves. Generally, each functor is associated with a fixed number and type of components. This is true to the record analogy and it ensures that structure terms that share a common functor represent objects of the same kind.

Lists are compound terms each of which contains a sequence of terms. The members of a list are separated by commas and square brackets enclose the whole. Here are some examples:

```
[2, 4, 6, 8]
[N, plus, 2.1, minus, 5.7, plus, 6, 'STOP']
[car(fiat, 1983, red), car(volvo, 1986, white))]
[[X, 7], [Y, 3], [Z, 5]]
[]
```

The last example is the **empty list**, which is distinguished by having no members at all.

We can always convert a representation of information that uses structures into one that uses lists instead. For instance, we could rewrite the database example above as:

```
drives(henry, [ford, 1986, red])
drives(george, [renault, 1984, blue])
drives(sally, [ford, 1985, white])
drives(jenny, [leyland, 1986, red])
drives(robert, [ford, 1981, green])
drives(diane, [fiat, 1983, red])
drives(pete, [volvo, 1986, white])
```
? drives(X, [ford, Year, white])

and the response to the query shown would be exactly the same as before. In practice, if the compound object to be represented has a fixed number of components each of which is of a predictable type (like the cars of the database examples above) we usually prefer the structure representation. If the number of components varies dynamically then we must use a list.

As with structures, a free variable will unify with any list. Thus the query

? drives(jenny, X)

to the rewritten logic database will succeed with the substitution X = [leyland, 1986, red]. Two lists will unify if each pair of corresponding terms unifies: for example,

? drives(diane, [Car, Year, red])

succeeds with Car = fiat, Year = 1983.

Lists also have a flexible alternative notation. The 'bar' notation allows us to specify a template or pattern for a list. An example is the pattern

[X|Y]

(read it as 'X bar Y' or 'the list starting X followed by Y'). This pattern can represent any non-empty list: X represents the first term and Y represents all the remaining terms. Sometimes we call the X the **head** of the list and the Y is called the **tail**. For example, in the list

[1, 2, 3, 4]

the head is 1 and the tail is [2, 3, 4]. It would be perfectly acceptable to rewrite the list as

[1|[2, 3, 4]]

which is different from the above in the manner of notation only.

The 'bar' list notation is available for all non-empty lists. Even a 'singleton' list such as

[henry]

can be expressed in it, namely by

[henry|[]]

The special case is that of the empty list: since it contains no terms at all, it obviously has no first term and hence it is unrepresentable in the bar notation.

The notation allows more than one term to appear before the bar, as with

[X, Y|Z]

which represents a list having at least two terms (X and Y represent the first two and Z represents all the rest). For example, another way to write the list

[1, 2, 3, 4]

is

[1, 2|[3, 4]]

The bar can be regarded as a kind of dividing line that is drawn between the terms at the front of the list and all the others.

2.7   Input and output substitutions

The concept of unification can incorporate the list bar notation straightforwardly. A list written in the bar notation will unify with any other list that can be represented by the same pattern, providing corresponding terms will unify. This is illustrated by the following query to the above database:

> ? drives(robert, [X|Y])

To answer the query requires that the lists

> [X|Y]

and

> [ford, 1981, green]

should be unified. The second list can be re-expressed as

> [ford|[1981, green]]

from which it is clear that the unification succeeds with the output substitutions

> X = ford, Y = [1981, green]

You may recall (from Section 2.2) that an output substitution is one that gives a value to a variable in the goal (call), whereas an input substitution gives a value to a variable in the program clause.

A unification between two structured terms can produce both input and output substitutions. For example, a resolution between the goal

> ? test([2, X, Y])

and the clause with head

> test([A, B, 3]) ← . . .

requires a unification that produces the input substitutions A = 2, B = X, and the output substitution Y = 3. (Remember that we agreed earlier to regard cases of sharing, such as B = X here, as representing input substitutions.) We can picture this unification as:

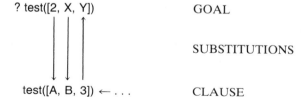

? test([2, X, Y])   GOAL

                             SUBSTITUTIONS

test([A, B, 3]) ← . . .   CLAUSE

Goal	Clause	Substitutions
? test([1, 2, 3])	test([1, 2, 3]) ← . . .	None required
? test([1, 2, 3])	test(A) ← . . .	Input: A = [1, 2, 3]
? test([X])	test([1, 2, 3]) ← . . .	Non-unifiable
? test(X)	test([2, 2, 3]) ← . . .	Output: X = [2, 2, 3]
? test([1, 2, 3])	test([1, 2, H]) ← . . .	Input: H = 3
? test([1, 2, X])	test([1, A, 3]) ← . . .	Input: A = 2; Output: X = 3
? test([1, 2])	test([1, 3]) ← . . .	Non-unifiable
? test([X|Y])	test([3, 4, 5, 6]) ← . . .	Outputs: X = 3, Y = [4, 5, 6]
? test([5, 6, 7])	test([Hd|Tl]) ← . . .	Inputs: Hd = 5, Tl = [6, 7]
? test(X)	test([]) ← . . .	Output: X = []
? test([X|Y])	test([]) ← . . .	Non-unifiable
? test(X)	test(A) ← . . .	Input: A = X
? test(X)	test([A|B]) ← . . .	Output: X = [A|B]
? test([X|Y])	test(A) ← . . .	Input: A = [X|Y]
? test([1|X])	test([A|B]) ← . . .	Inputs: A = 1, B = X
? test(X)	test(pair(1, 2)) ← . . .	Output: X = pair(1, 2)
? test(drives(X))	test(drives(A, B, C)) ← . . .	Non-unifiable

The table shows what happens when unification is attempted between various pairs of goal and clause head arguments. Notice in particular what happens in the case (which will turn out to be a particularly important one for PARLOG programming) where the relation call is

    ? test(X)

and the clause is of the form

    test([A|B]) ← . . .

The terms X and [A|B] can certainly be unified – remember that a free variable like X will unify with any term – and the result is a sharing, just as in the case earlier where two completely free variables were unified. In contrast to the latter situation, however, we regard the unifying substitution here as being an example of an output substitution. Why? It is because the unification with [A|B] imposes a pattern upon the call variable X. Prior to the unification, X could have represented any term – including the empty list: from this time on, X can unify only with non-empty lists. The output to X is one that imposes structure rather than 'real data', but it is an output nevertheless.

2.8   Standard list relations

We shall now discuss a couple of Horn clause programs for processing lists. The programs are for predicates that are in such common use that they have come to be regarded as 'standard' relations. This will also provide a good opportunity to bring together some of the main ideas that we have encountered so far.

The first example is member. The intended logical meaning of member(X, L) is the obvious one: X is a member of the list L. For example,

member(6, [2, 4, 6, 8])

is an instance of the relationship. We seek a definition that is logically both **sound** and **complete**: sound, so that we can never infer from it an incorrect conclusion about membership; and complete, so that we can always infer from it *the entire set* of correct conclusions. (The soundness property is often called **partial correctness** or just **correctness** for short.)

Thinking about the list 'bar' notation helps to write the definition. If we represent an arbitrary non-empty list by [X|Y] instead of just L, we might spot that

the members of the list [X|Y] are the term X together with the members of the list Y

For example,

the members of the list [2, 4, 6, 8] are the term 2 together with the members of the list [4, 6, 8]

In other words, the term at the head of the list is a member; and any term is a member of the list if it is a member of the tail. In logic, then, the general definition can be expressed by two clauses:

member(X, [X|Y])
member(X, [Z|Y]) ← member(X, Y)

The occurence of a member condition in the second clause makes this definition self-referencing or **recursive**.

Notice how the double occurrence of X in the first clause is used to express the fact that a term is a member of a list that has *that same term* at the head. In the second clause the variable is not repeated in the head of the clause: hence the idea is captured that membership is established if the term is a member of the tail. Between them, these two clauses provide a correct (sound) and complete definition of the relation.

As a simple example, we can show that 3 is a member of the list [1, 2, 3, 4] according to the definition. The program corresponding to this problem is

$$member(X, [X|Y]) \qquad\qquad\qquad\qquad\qquad\qquad [1]$$
$$\underline{member(X, [Z|Y]) \leftarrow member(X, Y)} \qquad\qquad\qquad [2]$$
$$? \ member(3, [1, 2, 3, 4])$$

A top-down resolution proof of the goal is:

$$? \ member(3, [1, 2, 3, 4])$$
$$? \ member(3, [2, 3, 4]) \qquad\qquad\qquad\qquad\qquad\qquad [2]$$
$$? \ member(3, [3, 4]) \qquad\qquad\qquad\qquad\qquad\qquad\quad [2]$$
$$? \ \# \qquad\qquad\qquad\qquad\qquad\qquad\qquad\qquad\qquad\qquad [1]$$

Of course, whether some particular logic interpreter could construct this proof would depend on its operational strategy. For PARLOG, the program will need a very slight modification as we shall see later.

In passing, notice that while the member procedure specifies completely what membership *is*, it avoids saying anything about what it is *not*. For example, the fact that the empty list has no members is unstated in the definition, and indeed it cannot be logically deduced. This is quite typical of programs written in the language of Horn clauses, which has the 'if' connective but lacks the 'if and only if' of full predicate logic. The latter would enable us to supply the definition as

> A term is a member of a list *if and only if*
> it is either at the head or else it is a member of the tail.

From this we could construct such proofs as the result that the empty list has no members. On the other hand, this fuller version of the definition allows us to prove nothing more than the Horn clause version about the *positive* occurrences of the relation. Our Horn clause definition is 'complete' in the sense that it logically implies every instance in which membership *does* hold true. Thus, even though it gives only one 'half' of the definition, the half that it does give seems to be the computationally useful half. There is a loose analogy here with conventional databases, in which we strive to include all the facts in which we are interested without concern for the infinity of facts in which we are not.

The second standard list relation is append. The intended logical reading of append(X, Y, Z) is: Z is the list obtained by concatenating (joining) X and Y. For example,

$$append([2, 4], [1, 3, 5], [2, 4, 1, 3, 5])$$

is an instance of the relationship. We seek a general definition, as for member: one that will permit us to derive all the correct inferences (and no incorrect ones) about instances of the relationship.

As with member, there is a special case. If the first list is the empty list then the result of appending is the same as the second list. In logic:

append([], X, X)

In the general case, the first list is not empty. Any such list can be represented by the pattern [X|Y]. Now it is certain that the result of appending [X|Y] to some list Z, say, will be a list beginning with X. The rest of the result might be represented by Rest, say; hence we can at least write the head of a suitable defining clause:

append([X|Y], Z, [X|Rest]) ← . . .

But what is Rest? We may get a clue from the example above, in which

Y = [4], Z = [1, 3, 5], Rest = [4, 1, 3, 5]

The trick is to see that Rest is in fact the result of append-ing Y and Z. This observation enables the clause to be completed:

append([X|Y], Z, [X|Rest]) ← append(Y, Z, Rest)

Then the full definition of append is:

append([], X, X)
append([X|Y], Z, [X|Rest]) ← append(Y, Z, Rest)

As an example, we show how the definition implies the instance of the relation that was given above. That is, we shall 'run' the program:

append([], X, X)   [1]
append([X|Y], Z, [X|Rest]) ← append(Y, Z, Rest)   [2]
? append([2, 4], [1, 3, 5], [2, 4, 1, 3, 5])

A top-down resolution proof is:

? append([2, 4], [1, 3, 5], [2, 4, 1, 3, 5])
? append([4], [1, 3, 5], [4, 1, 3, 5])   [2]
? append([], [1, 3, 5], [1, 3, 5])   [2]
? #   [1]

Notice again that a real logic interpreter (that is, a specific logic programming language) may or may not be able to construct this proof, depending on its particular operational strategy.

We should also be able to use the definition to solve

```
? append([2, 4], [1, 3, 5], X)
```

for X. Since we know that a solution exists – it is the list [2, 4, 1, 3, 5] – there must be a top-down inference proof for it. Here it is:

```
? append([2, 4], [1, 3, 5], X)
? append([4], [1, 3, 5], R)        {X = [2|R]}              [2]
? append([], [1, 3, 5], R1)        {R = [4|R1]}             [2]
? #                                {R1 = [1, 3, 5]}         [1]
```

The solution to X must be extracted from the proof by tracing through the output substitutions. This is straightforward for a computer, but rather tedious by hand:

```
X = [2|R]
  = [2|[4|R1]]
  = [2|[4|[1, 3, 5]]]
  = [2, 4, 1, 3, 5]
```

Again, note that we cannot be certain that any specific logic interpreter will be able to generate this computation without considering its particular operational strategy. As it happens, both PROLOG and PARLOG can solve each of the above problems using the append program more or less exactly as it is written here.

SUMMARY

Here is a review of the main points that have been covered in this chapter.

- We began with the observation that whilst the declarative semantics specifies what the logical answers to a program should be, it does not prescribe how a computer must produce them. For that we need an operational semantics.

- It seemed promising to base an operational strategy on the proof method of top-down inference. This tries to prove the goal from the program formulae by 'backwards reasoning', starting with the goal and working down through the implications towards the assertions. We saw that a top-down inference proof is guaranteed to exist whenever the goal is logically implied by the program.

- When we applied top-down inference to logic programs in Horn clause form, each proof step became a resolution step and the proof method was named top-down resolution. A resolution step combines a goal atom (selected from the goal clause) and a program clause (chosen from the procedure that defines the goal relation) to obtain a new goal atom or atoms. The step first requires a unification between the goal atom and the head of the program clause, that may produce input substitutions (bindings for clause variables) or output substitutions (bindings for goal variables) or both.

- We recognized that top-down resolution does not by itself fully specify an operational strategy. Rules are needed for making the goal selection and the clause choice decisions. Fixing on particular decision rules gives an operational semantics for a logic interpreter. A brief review of PROLOG and PARLOG showed that these interpreters are based on sequential and parallel decision rules respectively.

- Finally we saw that to represent structured objects, clauses can contain structures and lists. We showed how to define two standard relations for processing lists.

EXERCISES

2.1 Find top-down inference proofs for the following logic programs, which are expressed in PL syntax:

(a) $P \leftarrow A \wedge B$ [1]
      $P \leftarrow A \wedge E$ [2]
      $A \leftarrow F$ [3]
      E [4]
      F [5]
      ? P

(b) $P \leftarrow R$ [1]
      $Q \leftarrow S \wedge P \wedge R$ [2]
      R [3]
      $S \leftarrow E \wedge P$ [4]
      E [5]
      ? Q

2.2 Write down any input and output substitutions that result from a resolution step involving the following pairs of goal formulae and program clauses. What new goal clause is obtained in each case?

(a) ? sleeps(henry)
sleeps(henry) ← tired(henry)

(b) ? barks(rover)
barks(D) ← dog(D) ∧ angry(D)

(c) ? made_of(disk, silicon) ∧ spins(disk)
made_of(X, silicon) ← chip(X)

(d) ? supplies(smith, X)
supplies(smith, nuts_and_bolts) ← available(nuts_and_bolts)

(e) ? supplies(smith, X) ∧ cheap(X)
supplies(smith, nuts_and_bolts) ← available(nuts_and_bolts)

(f) ? gives(A, B, bicycle)
gives(santa, mary, X) ← been_good(mary) ∧ wants(mary, X)

(g) ? gives(santa, X, Y)
gives(santa, mary, X) ← been_good(mary) ∧ wants(mary, X)

(h) ? same_files(file1, file2)
same_files(file1, file2) ←
same_name(file1, file2) ∧
same_contents(file1, file2)

(i) ? twinpairs(1, A, 2, B)
twinpairs(X, X, Y, Y) ← onepair(X, Y)

(j) ? even(B) ∧ twinpairs(1, A, 2, B)
twinpairs(X, X, Y, Y) ← onepair(X, Y) ∧ odd(X) ∧ odd(Y)

2.3 Write out a top-down resolution proof (where one exists) for the following logic programs:

(a) Program clauses as in the lucky numbers example, query formula to be ? lucky(15).

(b) Program clauses as in the citizenship example, query formula to be ? citizen(X, bigland).

(c) Program clauses as in the citizenship example, query formula to be ? citizen(bill, L).

(d) Program clauses as in the ancestors example, query formula to be ? ancestor(charles, ella).

(e) Program clauses as in the ancestors example, query formula to be ? ancestor(mary, Person).

2.4 Assuming only the availability of a primitive relation sum as before, write Horn clause programs for the following relations:

(a) even, where even(N) means: N is an even number.

(b)   addup, where addup(N1, N2, S) means: S is the total of all the integers from N1 to N2 inclusively.

(c)   length, where length(List, N) means: N is the number of members of the list List.

(d)   total, where total(Ints, T) means: T is the total of the list Ints of integers.

3

Assertional PARLOG programming

3.1 Mode declarations: inputs
3.2 Or-parallel search
3.3 Thinking about or-parallelism
3.4 Sequential search
3.5 And-parallel conjunctions
3.6 Thinking about and-parallelism
3.7 Sequential conjunctions
3.8 Mode declarations: outputs

3.9 Test-commit-output
3.10 Committed choice non-determinism
3.11 Shared variable conjunctions
3.12 From processors to processes
3.13 Primitive relations
3.14 Differences from PROLOG
Summary
Exercises

PREVIEW This chapter introduces PARLOG's operational strategy. Examples are restricted throughout to assertionally defined programs, which are very simple yet sufficient to illustrate some of the most fundamental concepts of PARLOG, including the use of modes, and-parallelism, or-parallelism, and committed choice non-determinism. All the ideas that are covered here will extend naturally towards a full model of program evaluation in Chapter 4.

It is assumed you have read the previous two chapters of this book, or are otherwise familiar with the basic ideas of logic programming. Readers who are experienced with PROLOG should be able to start here, for example, and they should be helped also by Section 3.14 'Differences from PROLOG' at the end of this chapter.

3.1 Mode declarations: inputs

We shall start with a very simple PARLOG program:

```
mode official_user(?).

official_user('Henry Helpful').
```

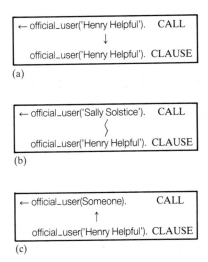

Figure 3.1   (a) Unification requires no substitution: input matching succeeds; (b) Unification impossible: input matching fails; (c) Unification requires an output substitution: input matching suspends.

This program consists of a single procedure. It defines a relation named official_user and although short, with regard to its syntax at least the procedure is quite typical: it comprises a **mode declaration** and some **clauses** (or only one clause, in this example). The clauses form the logical specification of the relation whilst the mode declaration declares the intended pattern of use. For the official_user procedure, the sole clause is an assertion that is intended to represent logically the information that Henry Helpful is an official user of a certain computer system. In the mode declaration the appearance of the question-mark character declares that the single argument of the relation will be used for **input**.

What is meant by an input? Essentially it is a transfer of data from a query (or more generally, from a call) to a clause. An **output** is a transfer in the other direction. By declaring an argument to be an input, we permit the former usage and prohibit the latter. For such an argument it is not enough for the call term to be unifiable with the clause term: the unification must be such that no output substitutions are required. This means that the call must supply *sufficient data to match the clause* before the call can possibly succeed.

To illustrate, consider the three examples that are pictured in Figure 3.1. The first example corresponds to the query that asks whether Henry Helpful is an official user. In PARLOG this query can be represented by

← official_user('Henry Helpful').

As we should expect, this call succeeds. The argument supplied by the call is an identical constant to the argument in the program clause. No substitutions are required to unify the two terms. Since the clause is a simple assertion, the call immediately succeeds and terminates.

The second example is the query

← official_user('Sally Solstice').

The outcome here is also as expected. Unification between the argument of the call and the argument of the clause will fail. In the absence of any other clauses that might solve the call, the evaluation fails.

The third example is slightly more interesting. Here the query is

← official_user(Someone).

The upper-case initial letter means that Someone is a variable. Now the unification of this variable with the term 'Henry Helpful' *could* succeed, but only by making an **output substitution** – the variable in the call would need to become bound to the constant in the clause. This would violate the *input* mode that has been declared for the argument of official_user. Informally, we can think of the call as 'undecidable': its argument does not totally mismatch the clause argument but neither does the call supply 'sufficient data' to satisfy the input mode.

What actually happens in this case is that the unification **suspends**. It is as though the test between the call and the clause is placed on standby whilst waiting for the variable in the call to become bound to some data such as 'Henry Helpful' or 'Sally Solstice', at which point the outcome could be decided one way or the other. As we shall see, in other circumstances – where the query specified a conjunction of parallel calls rather than just one single call – precisely this could happen. But in our example there is no way (short of interruption by the programmer or the system) in which the suspension can be broken. This kind of situation is known as **deadlock**.

These examples suggest the general effect of an input mode declaration. In the evaluation of any relation call, a relation argument that is specified as an input mode argument is subjected to a special, restricted form of unification in which the only permitted substitution is an **input substitution** – one that gives a value to a variable of the clause. A unification that would require that a value be given to a variable of the call – that is, one that would need an output substitution – will suspend. This constrained version of unification is called **input matching** and the requirement that there should be no output substitutions is called the **input constraint**. Of course, if unification is impossible then input matching simply fails. Notice that one consequence of the input constraint is that the official_user program can only be used to *test* for the names of official users; it cannot be used to *generate* a name. This non-invertibility is quite typical of PARLOG programs, as we shall see.

Incidentally, each PARLOG system has its own way of indicating the outcome of a query evaluation. Some may print messages such as 'success', 'failure' and 'deadlock', but others will use different forms of response. A deadlock may cause some systems to 'hang' until the suspension is broken by a keyboard interrupt. The query prompt, which we shall represent by the symbol '←', is also system-dependent.

3.2   Or-parallel search

The program above was not very realistic: it specified only one individual as an official user of the hypothetical computer system. Let us expand the definition of the relation by adding more assertions to specify the names of other individual users. The result is a small database-style PARLOG program as follows:

```
mode official_user(?).

official_user('Henry Helpful').
official_user('Mark Meterman').
official_user('Petra Pathfield').
official_user('Kerry R Kendall').
official_user('Dina Dickson').
official_user('Beatrice Jack').
official_user('Carol Platern').
official_user('Tony Gunball').
official_user('Keith Junket').
official_user('Donald Nugget').
```

The procedure now contains many clauses although of course there is still only one mode declaration. This again specifies that the argument of official_user is to be used for input.

Suppose that we supply to this program the query

```
← official_user('Keith Junket').
```

which asks whether Keith Junket is included among the official users of the system. The behaviour that results from this call is a **parallel search** through the clauses of the procedure. For each clause, input matching is attempted between the argument of the call and the argument of the clause (see Figure 3.2). As soon as the test succeeds with one clause – as it will in this example – the call succeeds and terminates.

Only if input matching between the argument of the call and the argument of the clause fails *for every clause* does the call fail. This happens for example with the query

```
← official_user('Sally Solstice').
```

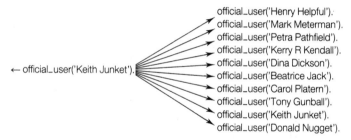

official_user('Henry Helpful').
official_user('Mark Meterman').
official_user('Petra Pathfield').
official_user('Kerry R Kendall').
official_user('Dina Dickson').
official_user('Beatrice Jack').
official_user('Carol Platern').
official_user('Tony Gunball').
official_user('Keith Junket').
official_user('Donald Nugget').

← official_user('Keith Junket').

Figure 3.2   Parallel testing of clauses.

Here none of the input matching tests succeeds. The tests are performed in parallel and all fail, following which the call terminates in failure.

Again, a more interesting (but not very useful) example is when the call argument is a variable. A query such as

← official_user(Someone).

also results in a parallel search through the clauses. But in this case the input matching between the call argument and the clause argument suspends for every clause. The reason is the same as before: the pairs of terms are always unifiable, but to bind the variable in the call would be to violate the *input* mode that has been declared for the relation argument. So the outcome is another deadlock. Hence this procedure also has only a single mode of use: it can be used to *check* for names of official users but it cannot be used to *generate* the names.

The parallel behaviour that we are describing here is an example of **or-parallelism**. The general idea is straightforward: to evaluate a relation call to a procedure that contains more than one clause, PARLOG investigates all clauses in parallel. The name 'or-parallelism' arises from the fact that the call could be solved by the first clause, *or* by the second clause, *or* by the third clause, and so on.

3.3   Thinking about or-parallelism

What exactly do we mean when we say that the clauses of the official_user procedure are searched 'in parallel'? Let us consider briefly the kind of machine behaviour that might be implied.

A possible scenario for the evaluation of one of the above queries on a computer that has an abundance of processors is as follows. One processor is designated as 'supervisor' for the evaluation: this processor will not do all the work itself but will coordinate a number of other, 'worker' processors. Each worker is given a copy of the query along with a single clause with which to attempt input matching. Depending on the result, the worker reports back success, failure or suspension to the supervisor. As soon as the supervisor receives a single success report it can shut down all the workers and terminate the call, announcing a successful outcome to the evaluation. Alternatively, the supervisor might get back only reports of failure in which case the evaluation can be deemed to have failed. If no worker reports success, but one or more report suspension, then deadlock can be reported.

This scenario is completely faithful to the concept of or-parallelism. It guarantees that the number of simultaneous activities is equal to the number of clauses in the procedure. But to run even the small official_user program in this fashion would require a dozen or so processors. If our machine has fewer processors than this then we must slightly adapt the scenario: the supervisor could still share the clauses among the available workers, but now some of the workers must be given more than one clause to test. Such a worker would have to perform **sequentially** the tests with its own allocation of clauses. The overall effect would be to reduce the amount of parallelism but of course the query evaluation should still produce the correct result. In the extreme case of a machine with only a single processor (a **uniprocessor** machine) the one processor would have to complete all the work itself and there would be no parallelism at all. Even so, the evaluation should still produce the correct result.

The PARLOG language has been designed so as to be reasonably efficient on *any* type of computer, whether uniprocessor or multiprocessor. Future computer architectures may well be of diverse type: the number of processors possessed by some particular machine may be as unpredictable (and as configurable) as has been the supply of memory on computers of the traditional sequential design. PARLOG programs do not in themselves carry any assumptions about the number of processors that will be available on the hardware on which the programs will run. *It is the task of the PARLOG compiler, and of the computer's run-time system, to make efficient use of however many processors are available on an individual machine.*

Notice that even if processors are abundant, the 'one clause per worker' scenario may not be the most efficient one. Consider how a team of human workers might cooperate in manually searching a large database of assertions, for example. It may be more efficient to leave some humans idle, whilst others each in parallel undertake a sequential search through several clauses, than to pursue a pure 'one person, one clause' strategy. The latter might impose an administrative overhead that would outweigh the gains arising from the extra parallelism. Correspondingly in the case of PARLOG systems, the details of how an or-parallel search should be implemented are the concerns of those who develop compilers for specific computers.

What this comes down to is that PARLOG programs do not necessarily specify parallelism at all. What they do specify is **concurrency**, which means the *potential* for parallelism. The extent to which the concurrency is converted into actual parallelism (that is, simultaneous execution behaviours) depends on the capabilities of the system on which the program is run. It follows that PARLOG programmers do not, in general, need to worry about processor-level evaluation scenarios at all. We shall return to this shortly.

3.4 Sequential search

Below is a program for official_user that is almost identical to the previous version. The only visible change is that the period at the end of all but the final clause has been replaced by a semi-colon. This makes no difference to the logical reading of the program, but it does affect the operational reading: to evaluate any call the clauses are now searched *one at a time*, in strict sequence, instead of being tried in parallel. The top clause is tested first. If input matching with this clause succeeds then the call succeeds and terminates; if it suspends then the call suspends. Only if input matching with the first clause fails is the second clause tried – and so on. If the searching continues down to the last clause and the input matching with this clause also fails then the call finally fails and terminates.

```
mode official_user(?).

official_user('Henry Helpful');
official_user('Mark Meterman');
official_user('Petra Pathfield');
official_user('Kerry R Kendall');
official_user('Dina Dickson');
official_user('Beatrice Jack');
official_user('Carol Platern');
official_user('Tony Gunball');
official_user('Keith Junket');
official_user('Donald Nugget').
```

In PARLOG syntax the period and the semi-colon are known as the **parallel clause search operator** and the **sequential clause search operator** respectively. The final operator that appears in any procedure is always a period and this should be regarded as **terminating** the procedure.

Later we shall see examples in which the sequential clause search operator is extremely useful. But its usage in the official_user procedure is rather artificial: there is nothing to be gained here by insisting on a sequential search and some worthwhile parallelism might be lost by doing so.

3.5   And-parallel conjunctions

Let us stay with the latest version of the official_user procedure with its sequential clause search operators. Suppose now that the query is a conjunction such as

← official_user('Dina Dickson'), official-user('Keith Junket').

The comma between the calls is the **parallel conjunction** operator. Logically, the query asks whether both the first **and** the second conditions are satisfied by the program. Operationally, the query specifies that the two calls should be *evaluated in parallel*. In this example both calls will succeed, and as soon as this has happened the conjunction will succeed and terminate.

Another conjunction is the query

← official_user('Kevin Arnott'), official-user('Keith Junket').

Here, the first call will fail. As soon as this happens the second call (if it has not already terminated) will be aborted and the conjunction will terminate in failure. Notice that this could mean aborting the second call before its evaluation has been completed, in which case some effort will be saved that would otherwise have been wasted.

One other kind of example needs to be considered. Suppose we enter the query

← official-user(X), official_user('Dina Dickson').

Again PARLOG evaluates the two calls in parallel. The second call succeeds and terminates, but the first suspends (because the variable in the call causes input matching to suspend). The result is that the evaluation of the conjunction suspends. Since there is no way here in which the variable can ever become bound, the outcome is a deadlock.

These examples introduce a different type of parallel behaviour from or-parallelism. It is called **and-parallelism** because it is based upon the parallel evaluation of the individual calls of a conjunction. The concept of and-parallelism extends in the obvious way to a conjunction represented by

← G1, G2, G3, ..., Gk.

containing many calls. PARLOG evaluates all the calls in parallel. If any call fails the evaluation of the entire conjunction fails immediately, possibly aborting some call evaluations that have not yet terminated; if all the calls succeed, the evaluation of the conjunction succeeds; if any call suspends, but none fail, the evaluation of the conjunction suspends.

We could of course submit the same queries to the earlier version of the official_user program that featured parallel clause search operators. If we were to do so then the answers to any query would be the same, although the evaluation behaviour would be different. The individual calls would be evaluated in parallel, as above, but now also for each call the clauses would be searched in parallel. Hence PARLOG's evaluation behaviour would exhibit or-parallelism *in combination with* and-parallelism.

3.6   Thinking about and-parallelism

Let us pause briefly to consider what kind of machine behaviour might be implied by and-parallelism. To illustrate we shall consider again the example of the query

← official_user('Dina Dickson'), official-user('Keith Junket').

submitted to the sequential clause search version of the official_user program (Section 3.4).

Again we can envisage a machine having several processors. To evaluate the query, one processor is appointed to act as 'supervisor': this processor allocates to each of two other 'worker' processors a single call plus a copy of the program clauses. The supervisor then waits while the workers evaluate their allocated calls. For each worker this involves a sequential search of the clauses, with an input match test being performed for each clause, as described in Section 3.4. If either worker eventually reports failure, the supervisor aborts the other worker (if necessary) and terminates the query in failure; if both workers report success then the supervisor terminates the query in success; if one of the workers suspends then the supervisor suspends also.

For a machine with only a single processor this scenario needs to be modified. The single processor must evaluate both calls itself, but it could share its time between them – say, trying the first clause for one call, then the first clause for the other call, then the second clause for the first call, and so on. Of course, a **timesharing** or **interleaving** behaviour like this is sequential but it would *simulate* parallelism. And if the processor ran fast enough then it might be indistinguishable (to an outside observer) from the real thing. Even for a multiprocessor computer an interleaving behaviour will sometimes be necessary. A five-processor machine will be forced into timesharing in order to evaluate a 'parallel' conjunction of six calls, and an n-processor machine will do likewise for an $n+1$ call conjunction, however large n happens to be.

The conclusion then is analogous to that for or-parallelism. The and-parallel operator should be regarded as specifying **concurrency**, which means having the *potential* for parallel execution. The extent to which this potential is realized as genuine parallelism – rather than some form of timesharing – depends upon the nature of the system. It is left to the compiler for each specific machine to transform any PARLOG program into a form of code that exploits whatever capability the machine possesses for a parallel execution. Strictly speaking, whenever we are discussing programs (rather than machines) we should talk about the **concurrent** rather than the **parallel** evaluation of calls and we shall try to be consistent on this point from here on.

3.7 Sequential conjunctions

Later in the book we will encounter situations in which we must insist upon a sequential evaluation for the calls of a conjunction. The query

← official_user('Dina Dickson') & official-user('Keith Junket').

shows how this can be done. The ampersand between the calls here is the **sequential conjunction operator**. Rewriting the query in this way rather than with the parallel operator (comma) does not affect its logical interpretation, but the operational behaviour is different: the calls are now evaluated in strict left-to-right sequence rather than concurrently. In this example (with the program of Section 3.4) the left-hand call will succeed and terminate and then the right-hand call will do the same, enabling the conjunction evaluation to succeed and terminate. But if the first call had failed then the conjunction would have failed and terminated without ever trying the second call. Also, if the first call in the sequence had suspended then the evaluation would have suspended on that call.

It is straightforward to extend this idea to a sequential conjunction containing more than two calls. A query represented by

← G1 & G2 & G3 & ... & Gk.

is evaluated in strict sequential fashion from left to right. If any call fails then the conjunction fails at once (there is no 'backtracking') without trying the remaining calls. If any call suspends, the conjunction suspends on that call. Only if and when the rightmost call succeeds does the conjunction succeed and terminate.

We can freely mix parallel with sequential conjunction operators. In such a mix the parallel operator is regarded as 'binding more tightly' than the sequential operator, so that the query

← G1, G2 & G3.

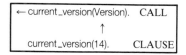

Figure 3.3   Output unification can bind a variable in the call.

has the operational effect of running G1 concurrently with G2 and, when and if these have *both* terminated successfully, *then* running G3. Similarly we may mix the parallel and sequential clause search operators (period and semi-colon) in procedures, and here also the precedence rule is one which regards the parallel operator as binding more tightly.

3.8   Mode declarations: outputs

All the above procedures for the official_user relation are subject to the same operational restriction. They can be used to *check* that named individuals satisfy the relation but they cannot be used for *finding* the names of such individuals. This is because the input mode declaration for the argument of official_user will not allow a variable in the call to become bound; the input constraint causes such a call to suspend. In contrast, a 'finding' version of the procedure would *have to* permit such a binding so as to effect the transfer of the appropriate data from a clause to the call. That is, its argument must be usable for **output**.

A relation argument that is to be used operationally to deliver output must be declared with a mode declaration that shows an up-arrow character (↑). A simple example is:

mode current_version(↑)

current_version(14).

Logically, this program represents the information that the current version number of a certain software system is 14. Operationally it is intended that the program should be usable for *finding* the current version number. The effect of the output mode declaration is to ensure that in the evaluation of any call to the relation, *full unification* will be used with this argument – there is no restriction on the bindings that may be made to variables as there is with input matching. Hence the query

← current_version(Version).

will succeed and will bind the variable Version to the integer 14, as illustrated in Figure 3.3. Notice that this call would have suspended had the mode of the argument been declared as input. To emphasize the distinction from input matching we shall sometimes refer to the unification of output mode argument terms as **output unification**.

In practice, running the above query on a PARLOG system might be rather uninformative. For some systems the query will succeed and terminate but *without* displaying the value that has been given to the variable. As an alternative we can change the query to

    ← current_version(Version) & write(Version).

causing the required value to be displayed. write is a primitive (pre-defined) PARLOG predicate: it has the implicit mode declaration

    mode write(?).

A call to write is used for its display side-effect. The call always succeeds (except in error cases) and hence it has no logical interpretation other than true. Notice the essential use of the sequential conjunction operator in the query. write never suspends, and had the parallel operator been used then this call might have succeeded 'too soon', that is, before its argument had been given a value by the call to current_version. The outcome would be the unhelpful display of the unbound variable Version (or worse, of a term such as _E102 that represents the internal reference to this variable).

3.9 Test-commit-output

The single argument relations that we have discussed so far are not very exciting. More interesting relations usually have at least two arguments, and the PARLOG procedure for such a relation will require a mode declaration that specifies each argument as either an input or an output.

An example of a two-argument relation is owner. The logical reading of owner(file, person) is: the owner of file is person. Its definition is:

    mode owner(?, ↑).

    owner('words.txt', 'Smeaton T.').
    owner('house.pic', 'Fawnes W. R.').
    owner('sort.par', 'Quail S.').
    owner('design.pic', 'Smythe C. T.').
    owner('letter.txt', 'Fawnes W. R.').
    owner('sort2.par', 'Quail S.').
    owner('infer.par', 'McRayne P.').

The mode declaration specifies that the two arguments are to be used for input and output respectively. Hence the expected application of the program is to find (output) the identity of a person who is the owner of a given (input) file. Consider as an example the query

    ← owner('design.pic', Person).

Evaluating this query will cause a concurrent search through the program clauses. For each clause, input matching will be performed between the term 'design.pic' and the first argument of the clause. When the input matching succeeds with the fourth clause, that clause will be selected to solve the call and any other input match tests that are still in progress will be terminated. Output unification between the output arguments of the call and the selected clause will then bind Person to 'Smythe C. T.'. As above, a call to the write primitive could be inserted into the query in order to display this result.

This example is quite typical of PARLOG's evaluation behaviour for calls to assertionally defined relations. Three distinct evaluation stages can be discerned. Firstly, the call **tests** the clauses by input matching for input mode argument terms; secondly, assuming that for some clause the input matching succeeds, the evaluation selects (or **commits to**) this clause; thirdly, **output** unification is performed between the output mode argument terms. For brevity we shall refer to this as the **test-commit-output** strategy. In the next chapter we shall show how the addition of one further stage is enough to extend this strategy to a full model of PARLOG evaluation (that is, to encompass procedures defined using implication clauses).

In passing, PARLOG syntax permits the presence in mode declarations of annotating constants. It would be legal to write

```
mode owner(file?, person↑ ).
```

where the constants file and person have no significance other than to provide comment (for the programmer's benefit) on what information the respective arguments are intended to represent.

As a second example, consider the small_plus relation that is defined below. The intended logical reading of small_plus(N, M, Total) is: Total is the sum of the small integers N and M. The mode declaration shows that the procedure is intended to be used for adding pairs of small integers (of course, the example is artificial in that PARLOG provides inbuilt support for arithmetic as we shall see shortly).

```
mode small_plus(number1?, number2?, sum↑ ).

small_plus(0, 0, 0).
small_plus(0, 1, 1).
small_plus(1, 0, 1).
small_plus(1, 1, 2).
small_plus(2, 0, 2).
small_plus(2, 1, 3).
small_plus(0, 2, 2).
small_plus(1, 2, 3).
small_plus(2, 2, 4).
small_plus(0, 3, 3).
```

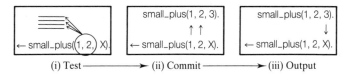

(i) Test ────────▶ (ii) Commit ────────▶ (iii) Output

Figure 3.4   Three stages of evaluation behaviour.

A suitable query might be

← small_plus(1, 2, X).

Figure 3.4 illustrates the evaluation of this query. Firstly, concurrently each clause is tested by input matching between the call and the clause for the two input mode arguments. Secondly, as soon as the test succeeds with the clause small_plus(1, 2, 3) the call commits to this clause. Any input matching that is still being attempted with the other clauses will now be aborted. Thirdly, output unification takes place between the call and this selected clause for the output mode argument, giving the required value 3 to the variable X.

In the test stage of evaluation, input matching must succeed for *all* input mode arguments in order for the test to succeed with a clause. For the query

← small_plus(N, 2, 4).

the test fails for all clauses that do not have 2 in their middle argument positions. This eliminates all but three clauses. However, for these three clauses the test suspends because input matching suspends on the first argument (to succeed would require making a substitution for the variable N of the call, and this is prevented by the input constraint). Hence the call suspends and, since there is no way here to change the situation, deadlock results.

This example shows that the small_plus procedure is not 'invertible' – it cannot be used to perform subtraction. Similarly the owner procedure cannot be used 'backwards' to find the name of a file that is owned by a specified individual. However, both procedures do support a checking pattern of call in which output arguments as well as input arguments are supplied with values, as exemplified by

← small_plus(2, 2, 4).

The fact that PARLOG uses full unification for output means that this query will succeed. This is quite typical of PARLOG procedures: in general each procedure supports only a single pattern of call, as specified by its mode declaration, but a little flexibility exists in that 'finding' procedures can usually be invoked in 'checking' roles.

3.10   Committed choice non-determinism

Both owner and small_plus are *functional* relations. They have the logical property that there is never more than one clause that could be selected for any call, from which follows the operational property that outputs are uniquely determined by inputs. But of course not all **relations** are **functions**. Consider the following procedure:

```
mode characteristic(person?, attribute↑ ).

characteristic(henry, kind).
characteristic(sally, sad).
characteristic(henry, tolerant).
characteristic(donald, angry).
characteristic(sally, kind).
characteristic(henry, ambitious).
characteristic(peter, sad).
```

The logical reading of characteristic(Person, Attribute) is: Attribute is a characteristic of Person. Notice that a person may have more than one attribute – the second argument of the relation is not functionally determined by the first.

This non-functionality has interesting operational consequences. The mode declaration shows that the intended use of the procedure is to find an attribute for a given individual. A suitable query might be

```
← characteristic(henry, X).
```

Evaluation for this query proceeds as usual according to the test-commit-output strategy. Concurrently for each clause, input matching is performed with the first argument. But in this example there are three clauses (three **candidate clauses**) for which an input matching test would succeed. PARLOG resolves this potential conflict by *selecting whichever candidate clause happens to be identified first*. The call commits to this selected candidate clause and output unification is performed for the second argument. This means that the solution found for X could be *any one* of kind, tolerant and ambitious. The evaluation is **non-deterministic** in the sense that the output is not completely determined by the input – part of the decision-making is left to the machine. Notice that the non-determinism disappears if the characteristic procedure is rewritten using the sequential search operator: this would make X = kind the predictable solution.

We should emphasize the distinction between the candidate clauses for a call and the *identified* candidate clauses. An (assertional) clause is a candidate if input matching would succeed between the clause and the call: this is a logical, *static* property that can be determined by inspecting the relevant fragments of text. An identified candidate clause is one for which input matching actually *does* succeed during the evaluation. This is an operational outcome that arises *dynamically* from the run-time behaviour. In general, not all candidate clauses will become identified as such. We can think of the test stage of any evaluation process as a search to discover the identity of at least one candidate clause: the search ends as soon as such a clause is found. In other words

Selected candidate clause = first identified candidate clause

This will form the basis for our discussions from here on, even though it over-simplifies slightly. (On a parallel machine there is the possibility that two or more candidates are identified *simultaneously*, in which case the evaluation simply selects one – by some unspecified method – and disregards the other.) For the query above there are three candidate clauses; one or more of these will be identified by the evaluation process, and exactly one (it is impossible to predict which) will emerge as the selected candidate clause.

For PARLOG, commitments are forever. On selecting a clause to solve a call, output unifications are performed and any binding that this makes to a call variable *is never retracted thereafter*. There will be no return to try any non-selected candidate clauses. This means that a PARLOG query evaluation can only ever compute one solution to the query variables, even if there is more than one solution according to the declarative (logical) semantics. In the above, if the solution X = kind is computed then the solutions X = tolerant and X = ambitious will effectively be overlooked. The computation of only a single solution illustrates the *incompleteness* of PARLOG as a logical inference system. Incompleteness is a direct consequence of the 'committed choice' aspect of the evaluation strategy. The fact that it is impossible to predict which solution will emerge illustrates the non-determinism.

This committed choice non-deterministic operational semantics has a significant effect on the programming style appropriate for PARLOG, as we shall see. An immediate illustration comes from the procedure above: if it really was important to return the complete set of solutions then we would probably choose to re-formulate the procedure using a compound term representation for attributes, as follows:

```
mode characteristics(person?, attributes↑ ).

characteristics(henry, [kind, tolerant, ambitious]).
characteristics(sally, [sad, kind]).
characteristics(donald, [angry]).
characteristics(peter, [sad]).
```

To solve a call to an assertionally defined relation:

(1)   *Test clauses*: attempt input matching between the clauses and the call for the input arguments

(2)   *Commit to one clause*: select the first clause with which input matching succeeds

(3)   *Output results*: perform output unification between output arguments of the call and the selected clause

Figure 3.5   The test-commit-output strategy.

Now the query

    ← characteristics(henry, X).

will produce the solution

    X = [kind, tolerant, ambitious]

which is a list representing the complete set of attributes. The evaluation uses the same test-commit-output strategy, but with the new representation there is only one candidate clause and it is certain that the call will select this clause for commitment.

Figure 3.5 summarizes the evaluation strategy for calls to assertionally defined procedures. When in the next chapter we discuss fully general PARLOG programs (with procedures that include implication clauses rather than only assertions) we shall extend this description to encompass a fourth stage of evaluation. But the basic test-commit-output model, and especially the idea that a call commits (sometimes non-deterministically) to a single candidate clause, will remain valid.

3.11   Shared variable conjunctions

So far the suspension of an evaluation has not been a very productive event: there has been no way out of it when once it occurs. The state in which an evaluation remains permanently suspended is known as **deadlock**. In this section we shall show that suspension need not be the same thing as deadlock. Suspension can and should mean waiting for something that will happen – namely, the arrival of some data – whereas deadlock represents a state of waiting for something that will never happen.

The program below will serve to illustrate. It comprises two procedures that define the relations status and maxfiles. The logical reading of status(Person, Rank) is intended to be: Person is a computer user with status given by Rank. The logical reading of maxfiles(Rank, Max) is: a user of status Rank is permitted up to Max number of files. The mode declarations specify that for both relations the first argument will be used for input and the second for output. Hence the main operational role of the first procedure is to find the rank status of a given individual and the role of the second procedure is to find the maximum number of files that may be owned by people of a given rank.

```
mode status(person?, rank↑ ).

status('Smeaton T.', student).
status('Fawnes W. R.', student).
status('Quail S.', lecturer).
status('Smythe C. T.', student).
status('Fawnes W. R.', programmer).
status('McRayne P.', student).
status('Waddle R. K.', professor).


mode maxfiles(rank?, max↑ ).

maxfiles(student, 50).
maxfiles(lecturer, 150).
maxfiles(programmer, 500).
maxfiles(professor, 300).
```

Now consider the problem of finding the maximum number of files, N, that may be owned by some particular individual. A typical query for this problem might be

```
← status('Smythe C. T.', Rank), maxfiles(Rank, N).
```

The comma indicates that the calls in the conjunction will be evaluated concurrently. However the input mode of the first argument of the maxfiles relation means that the second call will suspend until the variable Rank has been given a value. On this occasion, suspension does not mean deadlock. Eventually the first call will bind this variable to the correct value student. At that point the input matching test between the second call and the first clause of the maxfiles procedure will succeed: the call will commit to this clause and the output binding of N to 50 will be made.

Several points arise from this example. Firstly, notice that the variable Rank is shared by (that is, appears in) both calls of the conjunction. Logically, this means that the two calls do not represent *independent* problems, as has been the situation in previous examples: their respective solutions must agree on the value of this shared variable. Secondly, notice that Rank appears in the output argument position of status and the input argument position of maxfiles. This specifies the dependency between the two problems – the solution of the maxfiles problem depends upon the availability of the solution to the status problem. Thirdly, it should be clear that it is the input constraint acting on the second call that implements this dependency during the evaluation: the input mode of the first argument of maxfiles is what forces this call to suspend until the value of the shared variable is produced by the other call. In fact this kind of synchronization that is imposed by the input constraint (it is usually called **dataflow synchronization**) is the *only* form of synchronization that is provided by PARLOG.

As a second example, consider the problem of finding the value of T where

$$J = 1 + 0$$
$$K = 0 + 2$$
$$T = J + K$$

using the small_plus procedure of the previous section. The problem can be represented as the query

← small_plus(1, 0, J), small_plus(0, 2, K), small_plus(J, K, T).

Here, three calls will be evaluated concurrently. The first two calls each have sufficient data to proceed, but the input constraint will cause the third call to suspend (the mode declaration for small_plus specifies the first two arguments as inputs). However, the suspension will only last for as long as it takes for the first two calls to produce values for the shared variables J and K. When both data become available the third call can commit to a clause and hence the result for T will be produced. Incidentally, notice that the *textual* order in which calls are specified within the query is immaterial. The *same* evaluation behaviour would result from the query

← small_plus(J, K, T), small_plus(1, 0, J), small_plus(0, 2, K).

for example. Textual sequencing never affects the evaluation of a *concurrent* conjunction of calls.

Figure 3.6 represents pictorially the above examples of shared variable conjunctions. These are known as **dataflow diagrams**: each relation call appears as a bubble with connecting arcs to represent inputs and outputs. Data flows in the direction of the arrows down communication channels which are provided by variables that are shared between calls. We think of dataflow synchronization as a mechanism that somehow prevents a bubble or call from 'doing' anything until all of its inputs become available; at that point the bubble sets to work (or 'fires') and produces the appropriate value of output.

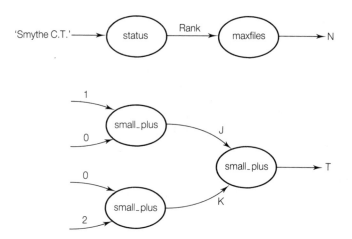

Figure 3.6   Dataflow diagrams.

3.12   From processors to processes

This is a good point at which to review briefly the ground covered so far.
A call represents a problem to be solved. For example, the call

← small_plus(2, 1, N).

represents the problem of finding a replacement for N which satisfies the
requirement that N = 2 + 1. For any assertionally defined relation such as
small_plus, PARLOG solves the call using the test-commit-output strategy.
The test stage can exploit or-parallelism: if there is more than one clause
then the clauses can be tested concurrently. 'Testing' means 'testing a
clause for candidate status', where a candidate clause is one that has the
logical property that input matching between the clause and the call for the
input mode argument terms would succeed. On identifying a candidate
clause the evaluation commits to it and output unification is performed for
the output mode argument terms.

And-parallelism is based on the idea that when a problem can be
represented as a conjunction of sub-problems, the sub-problems can be
solved together. The conjunction represented by five calls

← G1, G2, G3, G4, G5.

specifies five problems that potentially could each be solved by a separate
problem-solving processor (or just problem-solver, for short). If the calls

have no variables in common then the problems are completely independent of one another and there will be no need for communication between
the problem-solvers. More generally, some variables will be shared
between different calls. Mode declarations specify which problem-solvers
are expected to produce (output) the values of these variables, and it is the
programmer's responsibility to ensure that these declarations correctly
distinguish inputs from outputs. The input constraint forces a problem-
solver to suspend until its inputs are available; typically this data is
communicated to it by some other problem-solvers. No special arrangements are needed to implement the communication – the sharing of
variables is all that is required.

Notice that we have talked abstractly in terms of 'problem-solvers'
here. Conceptually it is not crucial that each problem-solver should be
implemented by a separate physical processor. One or more processors
could be used in some interleaving (timesharing) fashion instead: the
details need not concern us. A useful abstraction is the idea of an
evaluation process or simply a **process** for short. A process is the distinct
'chunk' of computation that is required to evaluate an individual relation
call (that is, to solve one problem). For a call to an assertionally-defined
relation it is one application of test-commit-output. To evaluate a query
containing five concurrent calls requires five concurrent processes, each to
evaluate one call, and we can discuss and understand the behaviour of
these processes in test-commit-output terms without referring to the
properties of the physical problem-solvers that will implement (realize)
each process. Given the likely diversity of future computer architectures,
this abstraction is not merely convenient: it is essential.

3.13   Primitive relations

All logic programming languages provide a set of inbuilt or **primitive**
predicate definitions for the most commonly used relations, such as those for
elementary arithmetic. These primitives differ from programmer-defined
relations in having mode declarations that are 'implicit' (see the table that
follows) and calls to them are evaluated by an implicit, system-defined
procedure. Typically also they have a syntax that is infix (that is, the predicate
comes between the arguments) instead of the normal prefix syntax. In this
section we introduce some of the most important primitive predicates of
PARLOG. (A full list of primitives used in this book appears in Appendix B.)

3.13.1   The test unification primitive

The logical reading of the == primitive is as the equality relation.
Operationally it is used for testing that its two arguments are syntactically
identical. A call succeeds only if the arguments can be unified without

Primitive	Implicit Mode Declaration	Purpose
==	mode ==(term1?, term2?).	Test unification
<	mode <(number1?, number2?).	
>	mode >(number1?, number2?).	Inequality
=<	mode =<(number1?, number2?).	testing
>=	mode >=(number1?, number2?).	
is	mode is(result↑, expression?).	Performing arithmetic
read	mode read(term↑).	Accepting input
write	mode write(term?).	Displaying output
not	mode not(?).	Negation-by-failure

binding variables in either argument. If unification would require to bind a variable, the call suspends. Thus the queries

```
← 2 == 2.
← [hit, miss, hit] == [hit, miss, hit].
← car(ford, red) == car(ford, red).
```

all succeed but

```
← X == 5.
← [hit, Z, hit] == [hit, miss, hit].
← [1, 2, 3] == [1|X].
```

all suspend.

3.13.2 Inequality relations

These primitives implement the usual inequality relations and each takes two numeric arguments. Their behaviour is such that a call will suspend if either argument is unbound. Hence the calls

```
← 14 < 165.
← 67 > 66.
```

both succeed and

```
← 5 >= 6.
```

fails, whereas

```
← N =< 6.
```

suspends.

3.13.3   Arithmetic

The is relation is PARLOG's multi-purpose arithmetic expression evaluator. For example, the call

    ← N is 3 + 6.

binds the variable N to the value 9. The second (right-hand) argument of is can be an arbitrary arithmetic expression involving the operators +, −, *, /, and mod, with optional parentheses to indicate evaluation precedence. Examples are

    ← N is 12 − 4.
    ← N is (12 * 4) + 23.
    ← N is 12 / 4.
    ← N is (5 mod 4) + (4 mod 4).

Of course an expression containing free variables is meaningless: the behaviour of is is to suspend until its second argument specifies a **ground** expression – that is, an expression not containing unbound variables. A query such as

    ← N is 3 + A.

will suspend and produce deadlock, for example.

3.13.4   Input and output

write has already been introduced. Its purpose is to display an arbitrary term on the terminal screen. write never suspends but it can be used as the basis of higher-level output procedures that do (as we shall see later). read is the corresponding primitive for input. The query

    ← read(X).

causes a term to be read from the keyboard which then becomes the binding for X. Both read and write may be available in two-argument versions, where the additional argument specifies the channel (window, file or device) for reading and writing: consult your system documentation for details.

    These two primitives are 'non-logical' in the sense that they are used for their input/output side-effects rather than to express logical relationships. Their use often necessitates explicit sequencing control. For example, a query that reads a number N from the keyboard and then prints its square, N2 say, could be specified by

    ← read(N) & N2 is N*N & write(N2).

The second sequential operator is essential here. We could replace the first ampersand with a comma because the is call will suspend until N has been given a value by the read process. But the second sequential operator is necessary to stop the write process from meaninglessly printing the variable N2 (or its internal reference, perhaps something like _E103) before the is call can give this variable its value.

3.13.5   Negation

The not primitive implements the 'negation-by-failure' version of negation that is usual in logic programming. That is, if X is a relation call then not(X) succeeds if and only if X fails as a call. This interpretation is not exactly equivalent to classical negation (we shall discuss this more fully in Chapter 7) but it is close enough for most programming purposes.

In PARLOG, the query

    ← not(1 == 2).

would succeed, as would the query

    ← not(small_plus(2, 2, 3)).

with the previous definition for small_plus. The call

    ← not(3 < 4).

fails (since the call 3 < 4 succeeds). The behaviour of not(X) is to suspend if X suspends, so that

    ← not(N == 3).

suspends (since the call N == 3 does).

3.14   Differences from PROLOG

This section is aimed at readers who, being experienced with PROLOG, will be helped by a brief highlighting of some of the differences between PROLOG and what we have seen so far of PARLOG. Only assertionally defined programs will be considered here. Readers who are unfamiliar with PROLOG can skip this section without any disadvantage.

Firstly, we can note the obvious similarity of syntax. PARLOG syntax is in fact based on that of 'Edinburgh PROLOG' and hence will be very familiar to most PROLOG programmers. There are some differences of course, and the presence of mode declarations in particular distinguishes PARLOG programs from those of PROLOG. But the similarities of syntax easily outweigh the differences.

Since both languages are logic programming languages, the semantics comparison has two parts. The **declarative** semantics of PARLOG is no different from that of PROLOG. In either language the declarative or logical meaning of a program is the collection of things that its clauses imply. Thus, an atomic formula is logically valid if there exists a set of substitutions for variables that makes the formula a logical consequence of the program clauses. This semantics is universal for all logic programs and does not depend on the choice of logic programming language.

It is in the **operational** semantics that we find the significant differences between the two languages. PROLOG's evaluation of any query is sequential whereas PARLOG is of course designed to support a parallel evaluation. We shall indicate the key distinctions in terms of four specific language features: the goal selection strategy, the clause choice strategy, the role of unification and the effect on completeness.

(1) *Goal selection strategies.* PROLOG's goal (call) selection strategy is to evaluate the calls of a conjunction sequentially from left to right. Only one call evaluation (process) is active at any one time. The left to right ('forward tracking') behaviour is complemented by 'backtracking' to re-try earlier calls when a later call fails. As we have seen, PARLOG conjunctions can also specify sequential left to right selection but more typically PARLOG calls are run as concurrent processes. Many processes may be active at any one time and the necessary synchronizations are specified by mode declarations. There is no backtracking: when a call in a PARLOG conjunction fails, the whole conjunction fails immediately.

(2) *Clause choice strategies.* In seeking a clause to solve a relation call, PROLOG sequentially explores the clauses in the defining procedure for the relation. The order in which clauses are tried is the textual order in which they appear. PARLOG uses the test-commit-output strategy described above. Clauses are searched concurrently (although the programmer can specify a sequential testing if necessary) up to the point at which a candidate clause is identified, but only one clause is finally selected to solve the call even if more than one candidate clause exists (committed choice non-determinism). Commitment to a choice of clause in PARLOG is final. There is no prospect as there is in PROLOG of returning to explore the other clauses.

(3) *The role of unification.* When PROLOG seeks to use a clause to solve a call, full unification is attempted between all pairs of corresponding argument terms in the call and the head of the clause. In PARLOG, each relation has an associated mode declaration that

distinguishes between the input and output arguments and the two kinds of argument are treated differently. Following the test-commit-output strategy, PARLOG first attempts input matching beween the input mode arguments. Only if this test succeeds and the clause becomes the selected candidate clause does the output unification take place between the pairs of output mode arguments. Input matching is a restriction of unification that imposes the special constraint (the 'input constraint') that only variables in the clause may become bound. If a call variable would become bound, input matching suspends. The concept of suspension does not exist in PROLOG – there is only full unification that either succeeds or fails.

(4)   *Effect on completeness.* PARLOG is 'incomplete' as a logic language in the sense that some solutions to a call which exist according to the declarative semantics might not be produced by an evaluation. One cause of incompleteness is the use of modes, which means that not all patterns of call are supported – some calls suspend instead of succeeding. Another is the commitment of any call to at most one clause, which means that variable bindings once made are never undone and that at most one solution to any call will be found. PROLOG is 'modeless' and some PROLOG programs do support all possible patterns of call. PROLOG's backtracking strategy can undo variable bindings and can explore multiple clauses, so that for some programs the complete set of solutions to a call can be found. (Nevertheless, PROLOG too is incomplete because the language's depth-first sequential search strategy can cause an evaluation to enter an 'infinite loop' before solutions are discovered.)

As will soon become evident, these differences have a significant effect on the style of programming that is appropriate to PARLOG.

SUMMARY

This chapter has introduced the PARLOG strategy for query evaluation. It has confined attention to assertional programs but the concepts will extend naturally into a full evaluation model for general programs. Here is a brief reminder of the most important points.

- Every PARLOG procedure begins with a mode declaration that specifies which arguments are to be used for input and which for output. Input mode arguments are subjected to a constrained form of unification (known as input matching) that suspends if a call variable would become bound. Full unification is used for output mode arguments.

- To evaluate a call to an assertionally defined relation, PARLOG applies the test-commit-output strategy. Firstly, input matching between input arguments is used to search for a candidate clause; secondly, the evaluation commits to the first identified candidate clause; thirdly, output unification is performed for the output arguments between the call and the selected clause.

- In response to a call, clauses are tested either concurrently (or-parallelism) or sequentially, depending on the programmer's choice of clause search operator. Once the call has committed to a clause, or-parallel activity automatically ceases with the non-selected clauses.

- A conjunction of calls is evaluated either concurrently (and-parallelism) or sequentially, depending on the programmer's choice of conjunction operator. If a variable is shared between two concurrent calls then it acts as a communication channel between them. The input constraint provides the necessary synchronization: typically the variable appears in an input mode argument position of one call and an output mode argument position of the other, and the former call is forced to suspend until the latter call has produced the variable's value.

- PARLOG does not prescribe the manner in which relation calls should map onto physical processors. Instead of talking about processors we speak abstractly about the 'process' of evaluating a relation call. For assertionally defined relations, a process comprises one application of the test-commit-output strategy and results in either the outcome of success, failure or indefinite suspension. A process may or may not be implemented by a single separate physical processor. Evaluating a conjunction of and-parallel calls creates a network of concurrent processes that can be represented pictorially by a dataflow diagram.

EXERCISE

A PARLOG procedure to define a relation file_length is shown below. The logical reading of file_length(File, Length) is: the length of the file File is Length.

```
mode file_length(filename?, byteslong↑ ).

file_length('mydoc.txt', 2305).
file_length('sort.par', 680).
file_length('first.txt', 350).
file_length('data.bin', 3500).
file_length('puzzle.par', 991).
file_length('merge.par', 200).
file_length('merge.asm', 590).
```

Using this procedure, describe PARLOG's evaluation behaviour in response to each of the following queries. For examples (10) to (15) also construct a dataflow diagram.

(1)   ← file_length('first.txt', N).

(2)   ← file_length('stock.pas', X).

(3)   ← file_length(File, Length).

(4)   ← file_length('merge.asm', 590).

(5)   ← file_length('mydoc.txt', L1), file_length('first.txt', L2).

(6)   ← file_length('mydoc.txt', L1), file_length('yourdoc.txt', L2).

(7)   ← file_length('mydoc.txt', L1) & file_length('first.txt', L2).

(8)   ← file_length('data.bin', L) & write(L).

(9)   ← file_length('sort.par', Length), Length < 1000.

(10)   ← Length < 1000, file_length('sort.par', Length).

(11)   ← file_length('sort.par', Length), Length == 680.

(12)   ← file_length('puzzle.par', Size1),
           file_length('sort.par', Size2),
           Size1 > Size2.

(13)   ← read(Fname),
           file_length(Fname, L) &
           write(L).

(14)   ← file_length(F1, L1),
           file_length(F2, L2),
           Total is L1 + L2.

(15)   ← file_length('data.bin', N),
           N >= 128,
           N =< 63535,
           Sectors is N / 512.

4

Process = test-commit-output-spawn

4.1 Implication clauses
4.2 Spawning concurrent processes
4.3 Multiple clause procedures
4.4 Guarded clauses
4.5 Some concepts refined
4.6 A database example

4.7 Properties associated with guards
4.8 Recursive processes
4.9 Stream communication
4.10 Review of evaluation strategy
     Summary
     Exercises

PREVIEW   The previous chapter described the test-commit-output behaviour which characterizes a restricted kind of process, namely the process which is evaluating a call to an assertionally defined relation. This chapter gradually extends that model so as to cover relations defined by fully general procedures. It begins with simple non-recursive unguarded clauses; when such a clause is selected to solve a call there results a spawning of sub-processes, one to evaluate each of the calls given by the clause body. We then describe how a guard may be introduced into a clause in order to specify a more general test for candidate status than is possible by input matching alone. Recursive clauses are shown to give rise to long-lived processes that may produce data incrementally, making possible the stream form of communication between concurrent processes. Our model of process behaviour becomes one of test-commit-output-spawn, where the outcome of the process depends on the outcome of the spawned sub-processes.

4.1 Implication clauses

Suppose that we wanted to define a PARLOG predicate positive that could be used for testing for positive numbers. One way would be to specify an assertionally defined procedure, beginning like this:

```
mode positive(integer?).

positive(1).
positive(2).
positive(3).
positive(4).
positive(5).
positive(6).
    . . .
```
POS1

But this is obviously impractical. Much more convenient is to write the definition as follows:

```
mode positive(integer?).

positive(N) ← N > 0.
```
POS2

This procedure contains only a single **implication clause** which defines the positive predicate in terms of the primitive '>' relation. The arrow in the clause should be read as 'if' and the single atom to its left is known as the **head** or **consequence part** of the clause. To the right of the arrow may come a conjunction of atoms that is known as the **body** or **condition part** of the clause. The variable N is to be understood as representing any arbitrary term (that is, the clause is implicitly universally quantified).

Let us consider how the POS2 version of the procedure works. To answer the query

```
← positive(5).
```

PARLOG will create an evaluation process. The behaviour of this process comprises four stages, that we shall term the **test**, **commit**, **output**, and **spawn** stages, as follows:

Test

The clause is tested for candidate status. A candidate clause is one for which input matching can succeed between the clause head and the call. Here the test succeeds with the substitution N = 5 for the variable in the clause. Notice that this substitution represents a transfer of data from the call to the clause (that is, it is an *input*) which is permitted by input matching – naturally enough! – whereas an attempted transfer in the other direction would not have been allowed.

Commit

Having identified the clause as a candidate for the call, the evaluation commits to it.

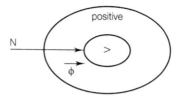

Figure 4.1 Dataflow diagram for positive(N).

Output

The positive relation has no output mode arguments and so there is nothing to do at this stage.

Spawn

A sub-process is created to evaluate the call $5 > 0$ given by the body of the clause (with the input substitution applied). This sub-process will succeed and at that point the parent positive process succeeds and terminates.

How does this compare with the test-commit-output behaviour of the evaluation process for the same call but using the assertional POS1 procedure? With POS1 the test stage would comprise a concurrent test with each assertional clause. But the crucial difference is that with POS1 there is no spawning stage. An assertion can be regarded as an implication with an empty body: when an evaluation process commits to it, there are no sub-processes to spawn and the process just succeeds immediately, as if by default. In contrast, a process that commits to an implication clause does not at that point terminate. Its outcome depends on the evaluation of the goals given by the clause body, which may be affected by inputs (as with N = 5 above) provided by the call. Sub-processes are 'spawned' to evaluate these body calls. The success of the process awaits the successful termination of all the spawned sub-processes.

The dataflow diagram in Figure 4.1 suggests the idea for the POS2 example. It shows the spawned '>' process as a nested sub-process of the positive process: moreover the data that is input to the one is passed through to the other. The positive process can be regarded as the 'parent' of a 'child' or 'offspring' process that (diagrammatically) lives within its own corpus. The parent process is 'committed' to the offspring process in the quite real sense that the parent can terminate only if and when the child terminates, and furthermore the parent's termination state is either success or failure according to the state of termination of the child. Sometimes we might use the term 'reduction' to express the same idea, saying for example that the positive process **reduces to** the '>' process.

In the example above the spawned process succeeds and at that point so too does the positive process. An evaluation with a different outcome is that of the query

    ← positive(−4).

This query creates a positive process that spawns a child sub-process to evaluate the call −4 > 0. Here the child terminates in failure, thereby causing the parent process (the query process) to do likewise.

Notice that if the spawned process suspends, so does its parent. This happens for example with the call

    ← positive(X).

For this example, input matching with the head of the clause succeeds (remember that the only constraint on input matching is that unification should not require output substitutions – it is not necessary for a call to supply 'real data'). The call commits to the clause and a sub-process is created to evaluate the call X > 0. Because of the behaviour of the inequality primitive this spawned process suspends indefinitely. The parent process is left waiting for the result of an evaluation that will never terminate – this is deadlock.

4.2   Spawning concurrent processes

Suppose that the problem is the simple one of adding together four numbers. One way to compute the value of 2 + 3 + 4 + 5 (say) is to make PARLOG evaluate the query

    ← X is 2 + 3, Y is 4 + 5, T is X + Y.   **Q1**

which specifies three concurrent calls to the is primitive. Another way, and one that seems slightly more convenient, might be to present the query

    ← add_four(2, 3, 4, 5, T).   **Q2**

but this assumes the availability of a suitable procedure for the add_four relation. By using an implication clause, it is easy to see how add_four can be defined. A definition is:

    mode add_four(n1?, n2?, n3?, n4?, tot↑).

    add_four(N1, N2, N3, N4, Z) ←
        X is N1 + N2,
        Y is N3 + N4,
        Z is X + Y.

This definition simply generalizes the logic of the query and its logical correctness is obvious. Let us consider the evaluation process that results from the call Q2 above. As before, the process has four stages.

Test

The clause is tested for candidate status. Input matching succeeds for the input mode arguments with the substitutions

N1 = 2, N2 = 3, N3 = 4, N4 = 5

for the variables of the clause, and the clause is identified as a candidate.

Commit

The call commits to the clause.

Output

The output unification is performed for the one output mode argument, producing the binding

T = Z

for the variable of the call.

Spawn

The call reduces to the conjunction of calls

← X is 2 + 3, Y is 4 + 5, Z is X + Y.

which are given by applying the input substitutions to the body of the clause. Three concurrent sub-processes are now spawned, one to evaluate each of these body calls. The situation is now equivalent to that for the query Q1. Eventually all three sub-processes will succeed, producing the required value for Z (and hence for T) and at that point the add_four process succeeds and terminates.

Three points arise from this example of process behaviour. Firstly, it differs from the previous POS2 example in one significant way: the parent process spawns (reduces to) more than one child process. The growth in process numbers is more typical of PARLOG evaluation and in this sense the phrase 'process reduction' is a misnomer. Figure 4.2 gives an abstract picture of an add_four process as a dataflow diagram and Figure 4.3 shows the spawning of sub-processes. The second diagram could be regarded as the 'magnified' version of the first; it 'looks inside' an add_four process and reveals more of the behaviour.

The second point is that it may seem from this example that the output unification stage of PARLOG's test-commit-output-spawn strategy

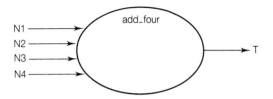

Figure 4.2   Dataflow diagram for add_four(N1, N2, N3, N4, T).

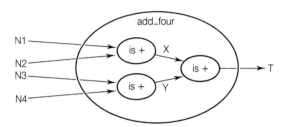

Figure 4.3   The 'magnified' dataflow diagram.

takes place too early. We may ask: why bother to make the binding T = Z before the sub-processes have had a chance to produce useful data for the variable Z? Basically, the answer is that the early binding is necessary to enable effective communication between concurrent processes. This will become clear with the explanation of 'stream communication' later in the chapter.

Thirdly, notice how we could transform the program so that the three spawned sub-processes run sequentially instead of concurrently. It only requires that the parallel conjunction operators in the body of the clause be replaced by sequential operators. After such a transformation, the logical meaning of the relation is unchanged but the behaviour is different: an add_four call now reduces to a sequential conjunction of calls. Only one sub-process is active at a time and their synchronization is imposed explicitly by the programmer's ordering of the calls in the clause body rather than implicitly by the dataflow synchronization behaviour of the is primitive.

4.3   Multiple clause procedures

The examples above referred to relations that were each defined by a single implication clause. More generally a relation is defined by a multiple clause procedure comprising some mixture of implications and assertions.

The add_few procedure shown below is an example. The relation is defined by a (rather contrived) set of five clauses – three implications and two assertions. The logical reading of add_few(Ints, Total) is: Ints is a list of no more than four integers the sum of which is Total.

```
mode add_few(ints?, total↑ ).

add_few([N1, N2, N3, N4], T) ←
      add_four(N1, N2, N3, N4, T).
add_few([N1, N2, N3], T) ←
      X is N1 + N2,
      T is N3 + X.
add_few([N1, N2], T) ←
      T is N1 + N2.
add_few([N1], N1).
add_few([], 0).
```

Each clause of the add_few procedure contributes to the definition a specification of the relation for one particular length of input list. The first clause defines the total for a list of four integers in terms of the add_four relation that was defined previously. The second and third clauses specify the required totals in terms of the primitive is relation. The fourth and fifth clauses are assertions that specify the trivial cases in which the list is a singleton list and an empty list respectively.

Operationally, the mode declarations show that the intended use for the procedure is to produce the total of a given (short) list of integers. Let us follow through the evaluation process of the query

```
← add_few([12, 66, 81], Total).
```

The process has the usual four stages of behaviour:

Test

Concurrently the five clauses are tested for candidate status. Only the second clause is a candidate and for this clause input matching will succeed with the substututions

```
N1 = 12, N2 = 66, N3 = 81
```

for the variables of the clause.

Commit

The second clause is selected to solve the call.

Output

Output unification between output arguments of the call and the second clause produces the binding Total = T for the variable in the call.

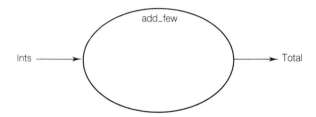

Figure 4.4   Abstract view of the process which evaluates add_few(Ints, Total).

Spawn

The body of the second clause with the input substitutions applied makes the new goal formula

← X is 12 + 66, T is 81 + X.

Two concurrent sub-processes are now spawned to evaluate these calls. Both will succeed, making the bindings

X = 78, T = 159

and this second binding together with the output binding made previously will produce the required value for the variable Total of the query. As soon as the sub-processes terminate in success, so too does the query process.

The important point about the add_few procedure is that not all evaluations will behave like this example. For instance, the evaluation process for a query that specifies a list of four integers will similarly test all clauses for candidate status, but the process will commit to the first clause and the spawning will be of a single add_four sub-process rather than of two is sub-processes. In general the behaviour of an add_few process depends on the pattern of data that is supplied by the call, since this determines which clause (if any) is selected for commitment.

The behaviour of a process can usually be described at more than one level of abstraction. At the most abstract level we can describe all add_few processes as shown in Figure 4.4. They are all just 'black boxes' that accept a list of integers and that somehow manage to output a total. If we want to know more detail then we can look inside the box to see a picture that will be one of those shown in Figure 4.5. The length of input list determines which picture is applicable. In the case of an input list of length four we can describe the process at the 'ultra-magnified' level of detail that is represented by Figure 4.6. This is an example of a process that has two levels of nested sub-processes. The outcome of such an add_few process depends on the outcome of the descendent is sub-sub-processes, and the former terminates only upon termination of the latter.

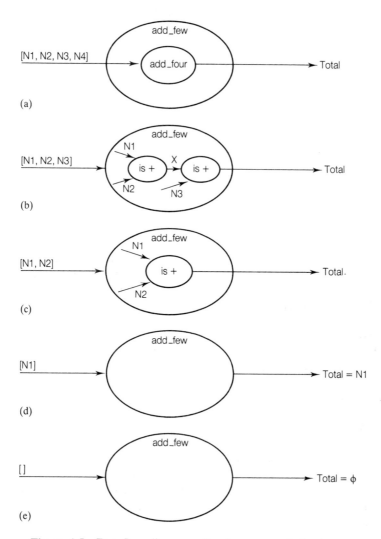

Figure 4.5   Dataflow diagrams showing process behaviour:
(a) add_few([N1, N2, N3, N4], Total)
(b) add_few([N1, N2, N3], Total)
(c) add_few([N1, N2], Total)
(d) add_few([N1], Total)
(e) add_few([], Total).

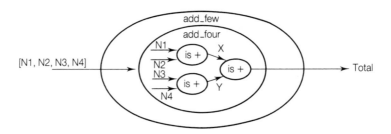

Figure 4.6 'Magnified' version of Figure 4.5(a).

4.4 Guarded clauses

Where a relation is defined by a multiple clause procedure, as with
add_few, the different clauses can be regarded as representing different
problem-solving methods. Each clause 'knows' how to solve the problem
that corresponds to some particular kind of call. Since a PARLOG call can
only ever commit to (at most) one clause, and since commitment is
irreversible (there is no 'backtracking' on the choice of clause) the
importance of selecting the 'right' clause will be obvious. A false commitment would mean that the evaluation process follows a method of
problem-solving that is inappropriate to the call, with the result that the
solution might be missed. It is the programmer's responsibility to make
sure that this does not happen.

We need not worry about the possibility of a false commitment
with the add_few procedure. We can be sure that the appropriate clause
will be selected for any call to this relation because input matching
comprises a sufficient test to discriminate betweeen the clauses (each
clause caters uniquely for one length of input list). However, the pattern-
matching style of test that is provided by input matching is not always
adequate: sometimes we will want to specify a more general test on the
input data.

A simple example is the absolute value relation. The logical
reading of absval(N, AbsN) is: AbsN is the absolute value of N. That is,
AbsN is N if N is at least zero, and is −N otherwise. Operationally we
require a program that can output the absolute value of an integer that is
input. A first, simple-minded attempt to define the relation in PARLOG
is as follows:

```
mode absval(n?, absn↑ ).

absval(N, N) ← N >=0.
absval(N, MinusN) ← N < 0, MinusN is −1 * N.                    ABS1
```

Although this procedure is logically correct and complete, it may fail to produce some answers operationally. The trouble is that both clauses are candidates no matter what the call. For example, if the query is

← absval(5, X).

then a process begins that follows the usual test-commit-output-spawn procedure. In the test stage input matching is performed with both clauses concurrently and potentially it could succeed (with the input substitution N = 5) with either clause. Whichever clause passes the test soonest will be selected for commitment. If this happens to be the second clause then the process will fail as soon as the spawned sub-process 5 < 0 fails. Because of the false commitment the query will have failed where logically it should have succeeded.

The problem arises here because input matching is not a suitable form of test to determine the clause that is appropriate for commitment. The correct test would be a test on the sign of the integer: if the sign is negative then commitment should be to the second clause, otherwise the first clause should be selected. Although the clauses of ABS1 do specify the correct logical conditions N >= 0 and N < 0, these conditions are applied operationally only *after* commitment – which is too late. In remedy we can re-write the procedure so that these conditions become *part of the test for candidate status*, as follows:

mode absval(n?, absn↑).

absval(N, N)   ← N >= 0 : true.
absval(N, MinusN) ← N <   0 : MinusN is −1 * N.   **ABS2**

The condition that now precedes the colon in each clause is known as a **guard**. In the test stage of an evaluation process, a guard specifies a test that must be passed before the clause in which it appears can be selected for commitment. It provides an *additional* test to that of input matching with the clause head and the two tests (which are performed concurrently) must both be passed in order for a clause to be selected for commitment. But whereas input matching can only check the pattern of the data supplied in the call against some fixed 'template' pattern that is given in the clause, a guard can be any condition or conjunction of conditions that specifies an arbitrarily complex form of test. Notice the symbol true that has been inserted into the first clause – this is logically vacuous but it fulfils a PARLOG syntax requirement that a guarded clause must not have an empty body. true is a PARLOG primitive which always succeeds but achieves nothing otherwise.

Let us follow the evaluation of the query

← absval(5, X).

this time using the ABS2 guarded clause version of the procedure.

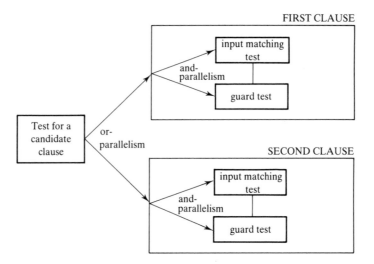

Figure 4.7   Two levels of concurrency in the testing stage of a process.

Test

The two clauses are tested concurrently for candidate status. For each clause, this means performing two concurrent activities: the input matching and the guard evaluation. The input matching can succeed with both clauses, but only for the first clause is the guard valid and as soon as the evaluation of the guard call 5 >= 0 succeeds this clause will be identified as a candidate clause.

Commit

The process is bound to commit to the first clause.

Output

The output unification is performed between the call and the selected clause, producing the binding X = 5 for the call variable.

Spawn

The body of the selected clause contains only the call to the primitive true. This call succeeds immediately and hence the evaluation process just succeeds and terminates.

Notice that there were *two* levels of concurrent activity involved in the test stage of this process (see Figure 4.7). The first is or-parallelism: the two clauses are tested concurrently for candidate status. The second arises from the fact that for each clause, the test actually has two parts – the input matching and the guard test – and the two parts are performed concurrently. This is a kind of and-parallelism: both parts of the test must succeed for the clause to reach candidate status. In the example above the behaviour of the '>' primitive ensures that the guard evaluations suspend until the input matching provides the clause variable N with a value.

4.5 Some concepts refined

We should refine our concepts of PARLOG syntax and semantics in order to take account of guards. The syntax of a general (guarded) clause becomes

    head ← guard : body

where head is an atom and guard and body are both conjunctions of atoms. In the logical interpretation of a guarded clause the commit operator is read simply as 'and' – head is true if guard and body are true. For a clause without a guard the syntax is

    head ← body

that is, the commit operator (colon) is omitted from an unguarded clause. An assertion is an unguarded clause with an empty body and for such a clause the implication operator is ommitted. Appendix B represents PARLOG syntax in diagrammatic form.

Our test-commit-output-spawn model of PARLOG operational semantics easily extends to take account of guards: we simply stretch the definition of a candidate clause. The definition becomes as follows:

For any call, a clause is a candidate clause if

- it is an unguarded clause
  with which input matching would succeed, *or*

- it is a guarded clause
  with which input matching would succeed *and*
  for which the guard with input substitutions applied
  is logically valid.

A 'logically valid' guard is one that specifies a condition that is logically justified by the program clauses. Hence the candidacy (or non-candidacy) of a clause remains a static, declarative property: it can be determined by a purely logical analysis of the call and the program. Operationally, the test stage of process behaviour comprises a search to identify such a candidate clause: for a guarded clause this means testing whether input matching is possible *and* testing whether the guard evaluation succeeds. These two sub-tests proceed concurrently.

As before, a call evaluation (process) can only commit to at most one candidate clause even though more than one candidate clause for the call may exist. The selected clause is the first clause to be identified as a candidate clause.

4.6   A database example

Another illustration of the use of guards is the database-style program below. This program's application is to calculate the annual bonus due to a company employee: the logical readings of the defined relations will be obvious. We shall describe the behaviour of the process that is created to evaluate the query

    ← bonus('D McVean', X).

The process comprises the usual four stages.

Test

Concurrently for each clause of the bonus procedure, the clause is tested for candidate status to solve the call. All tests involve both input matching and guard evaluation. Input matching can succeed for any of the three clauses (with the substitution Person = 'D McVean' for the clause variable) but only for the second clause can the guard call succeed. Notice that for each clause, input matching proceeds *concurrently* with the guard evaluation: however, the guard procedures are such that these calls suspend until input matching produces a value for the variable Person.

Commit

The call now commits to the second clause as the only identified candidate clause. At the point of commitment, any concurrent activity with the non-selected clauses (that is, any input matching or guard evaluation that is still in progress) ceases.

Output

Output unification binds the call variable X to the variable B in the second clause.

Spawn

The body of the second clause now reduces the call to

    ← salary('D McVean', S), B is S/25.

Two concurrent sub-processes are now spawned that evaluate these calls in the usual way. It can be anticipated that they will eventually succeed, binding B to the required value 368 that will thus be given to the query variable X. At that point the bonus process succeeds and terminates.

Notice how the guard evaluations briefly suspended in the test stage of this evaluation process. Even the guard call programmer(Person) for the candidate clause initially suspends until the binding Person = 'D McVean' is made available by the input matching. In general, the possibility arises that a process may suspend *indefinitely* on a guard evaluation and this is another possible source of deadlock. For the database example, the query

← bonus(N, X).

illustrates the point. This call does of course have logical solutions (for example, N = 'D McVean', X = 368 is one of them) but the query only results in deadlock because for each clause of the bonus procedure the guard evaluation suspends indefinitely. Interestingly, all three clauses are candidates for this call – for any one of them input matching would succeed and the guard condition is logically valid (three solutions exist for the guard call programmer(N), for example). But the permanent suspension of the guards prevents any clause from becoming *identified* as a candidate clause and hence the call never commits to a clause.

```
mode bonus(name?, award↑ ).

bonus(Person, B) ←
        programmer(Person) :
        salary(Person, S),
        B is S/20.
bonus(Person, B) ←
        clerical(Person) :
        salary(Person, S),
        B is S/25.
bonus(Person, 100) ←
        technician(Person) :
        true.


mode technician(name?).

technician('A Startwell').
technician('R J Hardy').


mode programmer(name?).

programmer('M McGarty').
```

```
programmer('D Rudell').
programmer('P D Wearie').


mode clerical(name?).

clerical('D McVean').
clerical('S Williams').


mode salary(name?, amount↑ ).

salary('M McGarty', 14500).
salary('D Rudell', 17000).
salary('P D Wearie', 19200).
salary('D McVean', 9200 ).
salary('S Williams', 10500).
salary('A Startwell', 11100).
salary('R J Hardy', 11980).
```

4.7   Properties associated with guards

It is worth stressing that the role of a clause guard is to strengthen the test for candidate status that is made on the clause by a call. Input matching can provide a pattern match on the inputs that are offered by the call, but sometimes this is not sufficient. The option of the guard permits the programmer to specify an extra, more general form of test. The name 'guard' suggests an obvious metaphor: just as a military guard might be posted to prevent wrongful access to a protected area, so a PARLOG guard that is placed before the body of a clause can be regarded as saying to any call something like: 'you must satisfy me before you are allowed to commit to this clause'.

Three important considerations for PARLOG programming are associated with guards. We describe these now, but on a first reading this section need only be skimmed.

4.7.1   The sufficient tests property

Informally, we can think of this as the property of a program for which *every candidate clause for a call is a 'good' candidate*, one that really can solve the call, so that false commitments are impossible. More formally, a program has the sufficient tests property if clause heads and guards are so constructed that, for any call c which is logically valid, and for any clause

c′ ← guard : body

which is such that input matching between c and c' would succeed and guard is valid for the input substitutions – so that the clause is a candidate clause for the call – then body is logically valid also. Notice that the sufficient tests property is purely declarative. We need only inspect the logic of a program to decide whether the program possesses the property – it is not necessary to consider the operational behaviour.

For a program with the sufficient tests property we can make a limited guarantee about the operational behaviour. The guarantee is that if a solution to any call logically exists then a PARLOG evaluation of it will succeed, providing it terminates. The proviso is necessary because the property does not remove the possibility of deadlock. (The database program above – which does have the sufficient tests property – provided a recent example of a logically solvable call that, due to deadlock, does not succeed operationally.) Sometimes this guarantee coming from the sufficient tests property is called the **partial completeness** guarantee: the risk of deadlock is one reason why the 'completeness' on offer is only partial.

It is the responsibility of the programmer to make sure that a program possesses the sufficent tests property. A program not having the property may still run correctly, but the possibility of a false commitment means that some logically valid queries could fail (as with the earlier ABS1 procedure). Typically the remedy is to re-specify the guards so that calls always commit to appropriate clauses.

4.7.2 The minimum guards principle

The database program would still have the sufficient tests property if we re-defined the bonus procedure as follows:

```
mode bonus(name?, award↑ ).

bonus(Person, B) ←
      programmer(Person),
      salary(Person, S) :
      B is S/20.
bonus(Person, B) ←
      clerical(Person),
      salary(Person, S) :
      B is S/25.
bonus(Person, 100) ←
      technician(Person) :
      true.
```

This 'enlarges' the guards of the first two clauses to encompass the salary conditions. But now the tests for candidate status are stronger than is necessary to select the appropriate clause for commitment. Operationally, the effort spent in evaluating one of the salary calls will be wasted: no use will be made of the information that it computes and making the call does not contribute to the correct selection of clause.

This leads to the fairly obvious 'minimum guards' principle, which is really a programming rule of thumb: *always make the guards as small as possible*. Remember that the sole purpose of a guard is to assist the call in committing to the appropriate clause. A guard that is larger than is necessary to fulfil this role is likely to introduce inefficiency. Notice that in general, the smaller the guard the earlier the commitment of a call to a clause, and hence the sooner the output of data: for communicating concurrent processes this is very important, as we shall see later.

4.7.3   The safe guards property

This property is a little less obvious. A program has the safe guards property if the clause guards are so constructed that for any call, *a guard evaluation never attempts to bind a variable that occurs in an input mode argument position of the call*. This is a mandatory property of a PARLOG program and it is essential that the programmer does not breach it. A program having 'unsafe' guards (guards whose evaluations may try to bind input mode call variables) is regarded as illegal and such a program may be rejected by the PARLOG compiler, or alternatively could lead to some form of run-time failure, depending on the system used.

At this stage there is little need to worry about the safe guards property. As long as guards are only used for their intended purpose, which is to *test* the value of the data supplied in the call, their safety is guaranteed. But in Chapter 6 we will describe a powerful programming technique (the 'incomplete messages' technique) that unfortunately makes this class of error more likely.

We should explain why it is that unsafe guards are illegal. The reason why it would not do for a clause guard evaluation to bind an input mode call variable is because *ultimately* the call might not commit to that clause – another clause that is being concurrently tested for candidate status may be selected instead; and on the commitment of the call to that other clause the binding to the variable would remain, even though it is probably not logically justified. (Recall that PARLOG bindings once made are never retracted). Notice that output mode call variables are protected from this danger. The test-commit-output-spawn strategy delays making output bindings until after the commitment stage, so a premature false output binding is an impossibility.

4.8   Recursive processes

Recursive relations – that is, relations that are defined partly in terms of themselves – are very common in logic programming. In this section we study some examples of the processes arising from such relations. Needless to say, our test-commit-output-spawn model of process behaviour applies equally well to these recursion-based processes. We will see that the main difference from the non-recursive processes described hitherto is that the spawned sub-processes of a recursive process can be very deeply nested, so that with recursion we associate processes that are relatively long-lived.

4.8.1 zeroes

Shown below is a definition for the zeroes relation. The logical reading of zeroes(L) is: L is a list containing any number of zeroes.

```
mode zeroes(list?).

zeroes([]).
zeroes([0|Rest]) ← zeroes(Rest).
```

This definition is fairly typical of the simplest sort of recursively defined relation. It requires two clauses. The first clause specifies that an empty list has the zeroes property; this is the special case (sometimes called the 'base case' or 'escape case') for the relation. The second clause specifies the general case: an arbitrary non-empty list satisfies the zeroes relation if the head of the list is a zero and the tail of the list satisfies the zeroes relation. The appearance of a zeroes condition on the right-hand side of the implication clause is what makes the procedure recursive. It is easy to see that the definition is logically correct and complete.

The mode declaration shows that the intended usage is to check that a given list satisfies the relation. Let us consider the process that evaluates the query

```
← zeroes([0, 0, 0, 0]).
```

The behaviour of the process can be described in the usual sequence of four stages.

Test
The two clauses are concurrently tested for candidate status. There are no guards so the test only involves input matching. This can succeed only for the second clause, for which it produces the binding Rest = [0, 0, 0].

Commit
The call commits to the second clause.

Output
The relation has no output arguments so there is nothing to do at this stage.

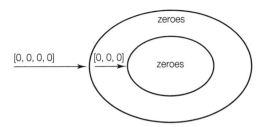

Figure 4.8   A zeroes process with its spawned sub-process.

Spawn

The body of the second clause reduces the query to

    ← zeroes([0, 0, 0]).

and a sub-process is spawned to evaluate this call. If and when this sub-process succeeds our query process will succeed and terminate.

    Figure 4.8 illustrates the evaluation. In fact it is easy to anticipate that in this example the spawned sub-process will indeed succeed. For it will spawn a 'second-generation' sub-process to evaluate the call

    ← zeroes([0, 0]).

which will in turn spawn a third-generation sub-process to evaluate

    ← zeroes([0]).

and finally a fourth-generation sub-process will be created to solve the call

    ← zeroes([]).

At this point the spawning stops. For this process will commit to the (non-recursive) first clause whereby it will succeed directly. In consequence the processes that are its parent, grandparent, great-grandparent and great-great-grandparent will succeed and terminate in turn, this last ancestor being the original query process.

    Figure 4.9 illustrates the complete descendancy of spawned processes and this diagram can be regarded as a 'filling in' of detail left unshown in Figure 4.8. It reveals that the nesting of sub-processes continues with each one consuming a list that is one term shorter than its parent's list, until finally the innermost process for the empty list is spawned that succeeds directly. Only at that point do the earlier generation (outer) processes, including the outermost query process, succeed and terminate.

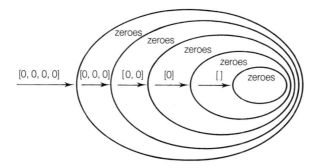

Figure 4.9   The complete descendancy of spawned **zeroes** processes.

In general then, a **zeroes** process could be quite long-lasting. It terminates with the termination of the **zeroes** sub-process that it spawns, but this implies a nesting of processes that could be arbitrarily deep depending on the data supplied by the call. For a query supplying a list of a hundred zeroes an evaluation process needs to complete the nesting of a hundred levels of sub-processes. The process can be imagined as one of drawing one large circle followed by a hundred other progressively smaller concentric inner circles. When the innermost circle is drawn it is immediately erased followed by all the progressively larger circles in turn until finally the first drawn large circle is erased. The drawing of any circle corresponds to the creation (spawning) of a process and erasing the circle corresponds to the termination of that process.

Of course, it is also possible for a **zeroes** process to fail. If some term in the list provided in the call turns out not to be a zero then the input matching stage of the corresponding descendent sub-process will fail and all of the ancestor processes including the originating query process will fail successively.

4.8.2   posints

A second recursive relation, the **posints** relation, is defined below. Logically, posints(P) means: P is a list (possibly empty) of positive integers. Operationally the relation is expected to check that a given list contains only positive integers.

```
mode posints(list?).

posints([]).
posints([I|Ints]) ←
     I > 0,
     posints(Ints).
```

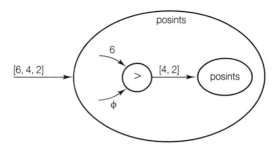

Figure 4.10   A posints process with spawned sub-processes.

Again, let us examine the behaviour of the program by studying a suitable example. The query

← posints([6, 4, 2]).

creates a process that progresses through the usual four stages.

Test

Input matching can succeed only with the second clause, for which the bindings I = 6, Ints = [4, 2] are made.

Commit

The call commits to the second clause.

Output

There are no output arguments to unify.

Spawn

The body of the second clause reduces the call to the conjunction

← 6 > 0, posints([4, 2]).

and two concurrent sub-processes are now spawned to evaluate these calls. The query process will succeed only if and when these two sub-processes succeed.

Figure 4.10 illustrates the posints process and its two spawned sub-processes. It is not hard to predict the outcome: the '>' sub-process will certainly succeed and so too will the posints sub-process, although the latter

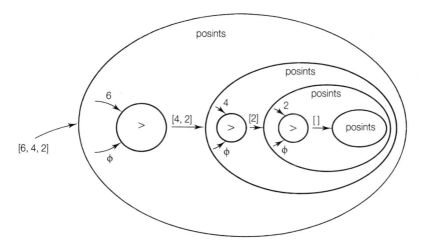

Figure 4.11   Nesting of posints processes.

can be anticipated to take a little longer. For it in turn will spawn two
concurrent sub-processes to evaluate the calls

← 4 > 0, posints([2]).

and the second of these will in its turn spawn two concurrent sub-processes
to evaluate

← 2 > 0, posints([]).

At this point the spawning will stop. By selecting the first clause this final
posints process will succeed directly. This will cause all the ancestor posints
processes to succeed in turn, starting with the most recent and ending with
the query process. Figure 4.11 shows the full nesting of sub-processes that
is produced by the query.

   This posints process exhibits more concurrency than the zeroes
process described above. The latter has only some modest or-parallelism:
in testing for a candidate clause, a zeroes process searches both clauses
concurrently. A posints process also has this or-parallelism but it has
and-parallelism besides, since it generally spawns two sub-processes, an is
process and a further posints process. These two run concurrently,
although the former quickly succeeds and terminates.

4.8.3 member

Chapter 2 described a Horn clause program for the list membership relation. Here is a PARLOG version:

```
mode member(term?, list?).

member(Term, [Term|Rest]).
member(Term, [Head|Rest]) ←
    not(Term == Head) :
    member(Term, Rest).
```

The modes show that the intended use is to check that some given term belongs to a given list. So the query

```
← member(o, [a, e, i, o, u]).
```

will create a typical member process. Its behaviour can be described in the usual sequence of stages.

Test

The clauses of the member procedure are tested concurrently for candidate status. Input matching between the call and the first clause cannot succeed (notice that when a variable occurs in more than one input argument position of a clause, as Term does here, it acts as a check that the corresponding terms in the call are identical). But the second clause is a candidate: input matching will succeed with the substitutions

```
Term = o, Head = a, Rest = [e, i, o, u]
```

for the clause variables, and the guard call not(o == a) will also succeed. Note that the guard evaluation proceeds concurrently with the input matching, but the behaviour of the '==' primitive will cause the former to suspend until the latter has supplied the bindings Term = o and Head = a for the variables of the clause.

Commit

The process commits to the second clause.

Output

This stage requires no action.

Spawn

The body of the second clause (with the substitutions applied) makes the new goal formula

```
← member(o, [e, i, o, u]).
```

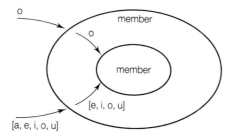

Figure 4.12   A member process.

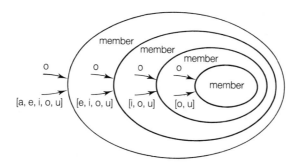

Figure 4.13   The spawned member sub-processes.

The fate of the query process now depends on the sub-process that is spawned to evaluate this call.

The dataflow diagram of Figure 4.12 depicts the member process and its spawned sub-process. (Notice that the diagram does not attempt to show the test stage of the process – dataflow diagrams only show process hierarchy and communications). We do not have to look too far ahead to see that the query process will in fact succeed. Figure 4.13 illustrates this by showing the two further sub-processes that are spawned to complete the evaluation. Because of the (non-recursive) first program clause the inner-most process succeeds directly, thereby causing its parent and its more distant ancestor processes to successively succeed and terminate. But suppose that the query had specified for the first argument a term that was *not* present on the list; then the nesting would have continued until the inevitable failure of the sub-process that was spawned to evaluate the call for the empty list.

Do we need the guard in the member procedure? Logically, the guard is superfluous. Without it the definition still specifies the same relation. But the operational behaviour might become incorrect if the guard is removed. For then both clauses would be candidates for the call (say) member(o, [o, u]), and if the evaluation should select the implication clause then this call will fail where (logically) it should succeed. The presence of the guard makes the assertional clause the sole candidate for such calls. More formally, the guard is necessary to give the program the sufficient tests property.

However, there is a way to make the program behave correctly with the guard removed. This is to introduce the sequential clause search operator as follows:

```
mode member(term?, list?).

member(Term, [Term|Rest]);
member(Term, [Head|Rest]) ←
    member(Term, Rest).                              SEQ-MEM
```

In response to a call, the second clause of SEQ-MEM is only used when the first clause has been found to be a non-candidate. The assertional clause is always tried first. In effect, the sequencing acts here to *implicitly* enforce the test not(Term == Head) for the implication clause, whereas this condition is explicitly expressed in the logic of the previous version. Depending on the system the SEQ-MEM version might be marginally the more efficient of the two procedures, since it economizes on the guard test, but the logical reading suffers: we have to remember that the absence of the sufficient test property is compensated for by the implicit test enforced by the sequencing behaviour.

4.8.4 total

Earlier we defined a relation add_four for adding integers which we later generalized slightly to another relation add_few. More useful than either of these relations is a relation total that can compute the sum of an arbitrary list of integers. A PARLOG procedure for the relation is:

```
mode total(intslist?, sum↑ ).

total([], 0).
total([I|RestInts], Tot) ←
    total(RestInts, PartialTot),
    Tot is PartialTot + I.
```

Let us study the behaviour of the process that evaluates the query

```
← total([2, 3, 5], N).
```

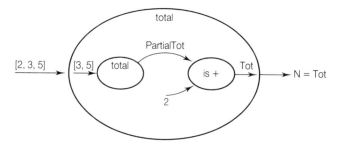

Figure 4.14   The total process spawns a pair of sub-processes.

Test

The clauses are tested concurrently for candidate status. Only the second clause is a candidate and for this clause input matching succeeds with the bindings

$$I = 2, \text{RestInts} = [3, 5]$$

for the variables of the clause.

Commit

The second clause is selected to solve the call.

Output

There is one output argument the corresponding terms for which are now unified. This produces the binding N = Tot for the call variable.

Spawn

The body of the second clause makes the new goal formula

$$\leftarrow \text{total}([3, 5], \text{PartialTot}), \text{Tot is PartialTot} + 2.$$

Two concurrent sub-processes are now spawned to evaluate this conjunction of calls.

Figure 4.14 illustrates this. The pair of spawned sub-processes must terminate before the outcome of the query process can be announced. Notice that the sub-processes are not mutually independent; they share a variable, and hence comprise a very simple network of communicating processes. However, the behaviour is easy to predict. The behaviour of the

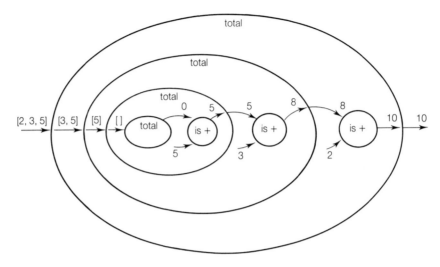

Figure 4.15   The descendancy of spawned total processes.

is primitive will force this process to suspend until the total sub-process produces its result for PartialTot, the shared variable. But the latter will itself reduce to a total process and an is process, and so on: the complete descendency of processes will be as shown in Figure 4.15. Notice that the *first* of the is sub-processes to be spawned will be the *last* to succeed and terminate but when it does so the required value will result for N. In fact, the whole query process will reduce finally to a sequence of three addition operations, with the input constraint acting on the is calls producing the necessary synchronization.

Two final points can be made about the procedure. Firstly, the use of only parallel operators makes the textual order of the two clauses, and of the two conditions within the body of the recursive clause, immaterial. Secondly, the procedure can also solve calls of the form

    ← total([2, 3, 5], 10).

which represents a problem of 'checking' rather than 'finding'. This is a consequence of PARLOG's use of full unification for output.

4.8.5   append

Another relation discussed in Chapter 2 is append. Below is a PARLOG program for the relation. As the modes indicate, the intended usage is to find the concatenation of two given lists.

```
mode append(list1?, list2?, joinedlist↑ ).
```

```
append([], L, L).
append([H|T], L, [H|TL]) ←
    append(T, L, TL).
```

Again, we shall study a sample append process to learn about the program's behaviour. A suitable process is created by the query

```
← append([1, 2], [3, 4, 5], X).
```

for which the logical solution is readily seen to be

$$X = [1, 2, 3, 4, 5] \hspace{4cm} \textbf{SOL}$$

As always, the process has four stages.

Test

Input matching can succeed only with the second clause. The substitutions for clause variables will be:

$$H = 1, T = [2], L = [3, 4, 5]$$

Commit

The process commits to the second clause.

Output

Unification between the output arguments now produces the binding X = [H|TL] for the output argument of the call. Because of the value already given to H, this is equivalent to the binding X = [1|TL].

Spawn

The body of the clause reduces the query to

```
← append([2], [3, 4, 5], TL).
```

A sub-process is now spawned to evaluate this call.

Figure 4.16 depicts the query process and its spawned sub-process. The production of the binding X = [1|TL] in the output stage of this process is very significant. The value [1|TL] can be regarded as a kind of 'first approximation' to SOL, where the rest of the work is left to the spawned sub-process. The latter is expected eventually to produce the binding TL = [2, 3, 4, 5] and thereby to complete the production of the value of X. But even supposing that the sub-process (for some reason) does nothing for a

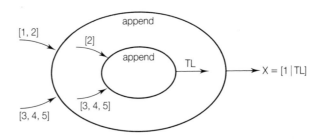

Figure 4.16

long time, the fact is that the first term of the answer list – the integer 1 –
has already been produced by the process. This is the beginning of an
incremental production of the required term.

However, we should satisfy ourselves that the spawned append
sub-process will indeed produce the correct value for TL. To do this, first
notice that the name TL now occurs in both the program and the derived
call. For no other reason than to avoid confusion, we shall rename the
variables in the procedure by (say) postfixing a '1' onto each variable
name, so that the clauses are now taken as

```
append([], L1, L1).
append([H1|T1], L1, [H1|TL1])
    ← append(T1, L1, TL1).
```

The sub-process can now be traced through its own four stages.

Test

Input matching can succeed only with the second clause. The substitutions

$$H1 = 2, \ T1 = [], \ L1 = [3, 4, 5]$$

are made for the clause variables.

Commit

The sub-process commits to the second clause.

Output

The unification of the third argument terms produces the binding TL =
[H1|TL1] for the call variable. The binding on H1 makes this equivalent to
TL = [2|TL1].

Spawn

A sub-sub-process (of the original query process) is now spawned to
evaluate the call

```
← append([], [3, 4, 5], TL1).
```

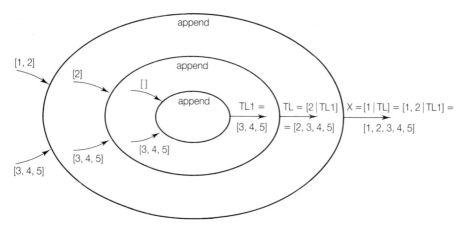

Figure 4.17

Again, the output stage here is very significant. The binding TL = [2|TL1] has produced the integer that is the second term of SOL. Furthermore, it makes X = [1, 2|TL1] the net binding for the query variable and this binding can be regarded as a 'second approximation' to the answer list. The remainder of the work is handed down to the sub-sub-process that is expected to produce the value for TL1.

The story ends here. This last spawned process will succeed directly using the first clause, generating the binding TL1 = [3, 4, 5]. This gives to X the value [1, 2, 3, 4, 5] which can be regarded as the final, *exact* approximation to SOL. At this point the query process succeeds and terminates.

Figure 4.17 extends the previous diagram to show the complete set of spawned sub-processes. We stress that what is important about this example is the *incrementalism*: the value of the solution is a list data structure that is constructed term by term, one term per reduction. The reason for stressing this point will shortly become obvious.

4.8.6 integers

The procedure below defines the integers relation. The logical reading of integers(First, Last, Intlist) is: Intlist is a list containing the sequence of integers in the interval from First to Last inclusively. The first clause asserts that when the endpoints are equal the sequence comprises only the endpoint itself. The second clause specifies the general case in which the first endpoint is less than the second endpoint – here the sequence comprises the first endpoint followed by the sequence that begins at the next integer after that endpoint. Operationally, the mode declaration indicates that the intention is to compute the sequence of integers that lies within a given interval.

```
mode integers(from?, to?, intlist↑ ).

integers(N, N, [N]).
integers(N1, N2, [N1|Rest]) ←
    N1 < N2 :
    Next is N1 + 1,
    integers(Next, N2, Rest).
```

A suitable case for study is the process created by the query

```
← integers(50, 100, Ints).
```

The process behaviour can be traced through the usual four stages.

Test
The clauses are tested concurrently for candidate status. Input matching cannot succeed for the first clause since the duplicate occurence of the variable in the input arguments of the clause comprises a test that could only be satisfied by identical corresponding arguments in the call. But with the second clause input matching succeeds, making the substitutions N1 = 50, N2 = 100. So too does the guard test succeed with this clause; notice that the guard is evaluated concurrently with the input matching, but the behaviour of the '<' primitive makes the guard call suspend until its arguments have become bound.

Commit
The call must commit to the second clause.

Output
The output mode argument terms of the call and the selected clause are now unified, producing the binding Ints = [50|Rest] for the variable of the call. In effect, this is a 'first approximation' to the true value of the answer list.

Spawn
The body of the selected clause reduces the call to

```
← Next is 50 + 1, integers(Next, 100, Rest).
```

Two concurrent sub-processes are now spawned to evaluate these calls.

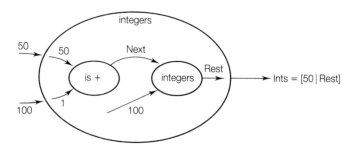

Figure 4.18

Figure 4.18 illustrates the integers query process and its spawned sub-processes. Notice that this process also features incrementalism: the output stage has produced the first integer of the answer list. Even if the spawned integers sub-process does nothing else, the binding Ints = [50|Rest] has given a partial answer to the query.

Of course, the spawned sub-process *will* do 'something else'. Momentarily it will suspend until the is process produces the value of Next (why?) but eventually it will construct the value of Rest, that is it will produce the binding

Rest = [51, 52, 53, ..., 100]

It will do this incrementally, by a succession of further reductions as pictured in Figure 4.19. The nesting will be 50 layers deep and the ultimately spawned sub-process will be to evaluate the call integers(100, 100, RestX). This final process will succeed and terminate directly using the assertional clause, thereby enabling all the ancestor processes to succeed and terminate in turn.

It is straightforward to check that the integers procedure really does produce the required data. The definition can be tested by entering a query such as

← integers(50, 100, Ints) & write(Ints).

Unfortunately this will not demonstrate the *incremental* production of the list. The sequential conjunction operator requires the integers process to terminate before the write process is allowed to begin. In the next chapter we will show how to define a procedure that can display data concurrently as it is produced.

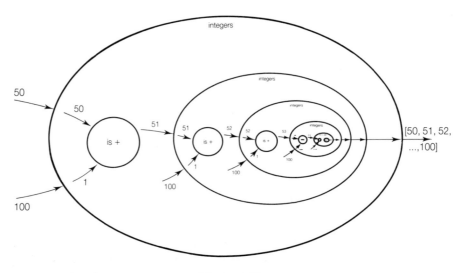

Figure 4.19

4.9   Stream communication

In the previous section we gave procedures for the integers and posints relations. The query

← integers(50, 100, Ilist), posints(Ilist).   **CONJ**

specifies concurrent calls to both relations. The logical reading of CONJ is not very interesting: it asks whether the list of integers from 50 to 100 contains only positive integers and the answer is obviously 'yes'. But the evaluation behaviour here is important for it involves a communication between two long-lived processes.

As we have seen, a parallel conjunction of relation calls creates a network of concurrent processes with shared variables implementing communication channels. For CONJ the network is the simple one shown in Figure 4.20. The shared variable Ilist implements a channel by which data will be transmitted from the integers process to the posints process. The direction of data flow is specified by the declared modes, with the former process acting as producer and the latter as consumer. But the data here is not just an integer or other scalar constant as with previous examples and it will be worthwhile to study this communication closely.

Figure 4.20

As explained above, the integers process will produce the value of its answer list incrementally. The first binding for llist is of the form [50|Rest]. Next the recursively spawned integers sub-process will produce for Rest the binding [51|Rest1], and so on. Over the lifetime of the integers process the variable llist will be affected by the bindings

llist = [50|Rest],
Rest = [51|Rest1],
Rest1 = [52|Rest2],
Rest2 = [53|Rest3],
Rest3 = [54|Rest4],
. . .
Rest48 = [99|Rest49],
Rest49 = [100]

with each successive reduction producing one further binding. These bindings have an incremental effect on the variable llist, as follows:

llist   = [50|Rest],
        = [50, 51|Rest1],
        = [50, 51, 52|Rest2],
        = [50, 51, 52, 53|Rest3],
        = [50, 51, 52, 53, 54|Rest4],
        . . .
        = [50, 51, 52, 53, 54, ..., 99|Rest49],
        = [50, 51, 52, 53, 54, ..., 99, 100]

So we can think of the integers process as producing a 'stream' of integers, with 50 produced first in the stream and 100 last. The stream is shown in Figure 4.21 as a series of blobs each representing an integer dispatched along the communication channel.

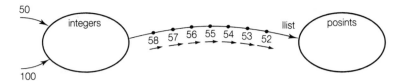

Figure 4.21

Meanwhile, what is the behaviour of the posints process that is running concurrently with the integers process? Recall that the definition of posints is:

```
mode posints(?).

posints([]).
posints([I|Ints]) ←
    I > 0,
    posints(Ints).
```

At first, the shared variable llist in CONJ is unbound and this forces the posints process to suspend. But as soon as the integers process produces the binding llist = [50|Rest], the posints process commits to the implication clause and reduces to two sub-processes to evaluate the calls

    ← 50 > 0, posints(Rest).

The is sub-process quickly succeeds and terminates. The posints sub-process will need to suspend at least until the integers process has produced the binding Rest = [51|Rest1].

Note carefully what has happened with this reduction. In effect, the posints process of CONJ has checked that 50 (the first received term of llist) is a positive integer and it has now reduced to a state of readiness for checking any future terms. The new state is represented by the spawned sub-process that will evaluate posints(Rest). The integer 50 will feature no further in the evaluation – we can think of it as having been 'consumed', that is, removed from the front of the communication channel.

The posints sub-process is unlikely to be held back for long. As soon as the integers process binds Rest to [51|Rest1] the posints process can commit: it will reduce to

    ← 51 > 0, posints(Rest1).

Again, the first of these processes quickly succeeds and terminates. This means that the second member of llist has now been checked and consumed and the posints process is awaiting the arrival of further terms of the list.

Notice how the progress of the posints process in CONJ is constrained by the supply of data produced by the integers process. The input constraint delays each reduction of the posints process until the shared variable llist has become sufficiently bound to permit input matching to succeed. In contrast, there is no such constraint on the integers process which can proceed entirely at its own pace, perhaps even racing far ahead in the generation of integers. It is assumed that the computer's run-time system can cope with any resulting build-up of data: we can think of the channel (variable) as being able to store an arbitrarily lengthy list of terms.

It is easy to anticipate how the communication will terminate. Eventually the integers process will produce, and the posints process will consume, the final integer in the stream. The former will ultimately reduce to the call

    ← integers(100, 100, Rest50).

which will succeed directly with the binding Rest50 = [100]. At this point the integers process will succeed and terminate. Some time thereafter, the posints process will reduce to the call

    ← posints([100]).

in response to which it will spawn two sub-processes to evaluate

    ← 100 > 0, posints([]).

each of which will succeed directly. At that point the query evaluation will succeed and terminate.

This incremental or **stream** form of communication can be likened to a message delivered over a telephone line. The speaker produces a flow of words that is composed and transmitted incrementally. The listener interprets the words as they arrive, building up the meaning in piecemeal fashion. The two participants are active concurrently, but it is the speaker who sets the pace.

For PARLOG, stream communication makes and-parallelism powerful. In the previous chapter, where the shared variable in a parallel conjunction always represented an integer or some other non-structured (scalar) term, a consumer process was typically idle until the producer's work was done. It will now be clear that where the variable represents a list the consumer and the producer can be genuinely active together. Notice that the 'earliness' of the output unification stage in the test-commit-output-spawn evaluation strategy is essential to this capability.

4.10   Review of evaluation strategy

We have now introduced all the key elements of PARLOG's evaluation strategy. This section provides a brief review and offers some reinforcement to the main ideas.

A problem is initially specified as a query, such as

    ← append([1, 2, 3], [4, 5], X).

or more generally, by any goal or call. Logically, a goal asks whether for some substitutions of terms for variables the goal is valid according to the program clauses. Really it is the identity of these substitutions (that is, solutions) in which we are interested. Operationally a process is created to evaluate the goal using the test-commit-output-spawn strategy, as follows:

Test

The process tests the clauses in the relevant procedure looking for a candidate clause. The clauses are tested sequentially or concurrently, depending on the clause search operators specified in the procedure. Candidacy is a *logical* property: those clauses are candidates for which input matching with the call can succeed and for which the guard (if present) is logically valid. But for the process to discover a candidate takes operational effort, in the form of *attempting* the input matching and *evaluating* the guard. For any one clause these two tests proceed concurrently.

Commit

As soon as a candidate clause is identified the evaluation process commits to it. Any concurrent (or-parallel) activity with other clauses automatically ceases at that point. Of course the process may fail at the test stage (if all clauses are found to be non-candidates) or may suspend indefinitely (if the test with some clause suspends indefinitely, but does not succeed with any other clause).

Output

As soon as the process commits to a clause, output unification takes place between the output mode argument terms of the call and those of the selected clause.

Spawn

Here the process spawns sub-processes to evaluate the calls given by the body of the selected clause. A parallel conjunction of body calls will give rise to a concurrent system of sub-processes. The outcome of the process now depends on the ultimate outcome of these sub-processes: the former succeeds only if all the latter succeed. This stage is often termed the **reduction** stage.

Stage of process	Process behaviour	Problem-solving interpretation
Test	Search the defining procedure for a candidate clause	Look for a problem-solving strategy that applies to the problem specification
Commit	Select one candidate clause	Fix on one applicable strategy
Output	Unify output arguments of call and selected clause	Match answer templates of problem specification and selected strategy
Spawn	Create and run sub-processes according to body of selected clause	Solve sub-problems as specified by the selected strategy

Thus far we have always implied that the four stages are strictly sequential. Actually this misrepresents PARLOG very slightly: the design of the language allows that the two latter stages of process behaviour may be concurrent. Conceptually however the output stage is momentary (output unification never suspends) whereas the spawning stage can be long-lasting, so that it does no harm to think of the four steps as strictly sequential.

It may be asked – what is the explanation of process behaviour in terms of logic programming theory? The answer is that a process is an attempt to construct a top-down resolution inference proof of the goal from the program clauses. The test and commit stages represent the choosing of a clause for the first top-down inference step (sometimes called a 'backward chaining' step) and the spawning stage represents the attempt to construct (typically) concurrently a set of proofs of all the goals given by the body of the chosen clause. Commitment of a goal to an assertion means immediate success. For a process that succeeds, the solutions to the goal variables can be extracted from the output substitutions.

Less formally, we can give the stages of process behaviour a generalized problem-solving interpretation as shown in the table above. The test stage involves searching for some suitable problem-solving strategy, that is, a strategy applicable to the type of problem (goal) that has been specified. It may be that only one suitable strategy is available or there could be several: the commit stage selects just one (the first to be found). The output stage links the answer template that is assumed to be supplied in the problem specification with the answer template that comes with the selected strategy. Finally, the selected strategy is executed. Most strategies do not solve problems directly but only show how a problem can be reduced to a set of sub-problems, so that sub-processes must be created to solve these sub-problems. This is the spawning stage: typically it is the spawned sub-processes that are expected to enter details of any solution that is discovered into the answer template.

This interpretation of process behaviour offers a reminder of two key aspects of PARLOG programming style. Firstly, there is the danger of becoming committed to an inapplicable problem-solving strategy: since commitments are irreversible, this is always a disaster. PARLOG programmers are expected to avoid false commitments by constructing programs that have the sufficient tests property. Secondly, in problem-solving it very often happens that where several different problem-solving strategies exist, at least some of them give rise to alternative solutions. PARLOG's behaviour in the presence of more than one candidate clause for a call is to commit non-deterministically to a single candidate. This is an efficient strategy for implementation on parallel machines but it cannot produce more than one solution. If multiple solutions are what is required then the PARLOG programmer must find an alternative representation of the problem – one in which only single candidates exist. This is an issue to which we shall return later.

SUMMARY

This chapter has extended the account of PARLOG evaluation given in the previous chapter to fully general programs. Here is a summary of the most important points.

- To evaluate a relation call PARLOG creates a process that follows the test-commit-output-spawn strategy. Firstly, clauses are tested for candidate status; secondly, the evaluation commits to one candidate clause (the first to be identified); thirdly, the output mode arguments are unified; and fourthly, sub-processes are spawned to evaluate the calls given by the body of the clause. The process terminates when all the sub-processes have terminated.

- The syntax of a guarded clause takes the form
  head ← guard : body. The purpose of guards is to assist each call to commit to the appropriate clause. A guard does this by specifying a more general test on the input data than could be performed by input matching alone. When a process tests a guarded clause for candidate status, the guard is evaluated concurrently with the input matching and both tests must succeed for the clause to be recognized as a candidate for the call.

- A highly desirable property of programs is the sufficient tests property which assures against calls committing to an inappropriate clause. An essential property is the safe guards property which assures against a guard evaluation trying to bind an input mode call variable.

- Recursive relations give rise to processes that can be long-lived, since they may spawn many levels of descendent sub-processes. Such a process can incrementally produce the value of a variable representing a list. If the list variable is shared between two concurrent processes, a stream communication can ensue in which one process operates upon (consumes) the terms of the list concurrently as the other process produces them.

EXERCISES

4.1 The PARLOG program below is intended to be used to compute the larger of two numbers. Is the logic of the program correct? Will the program always behave as it should? Explain your answers and re-write the program if you think this to be necessary.

```
mode larger(n1?, n2?, max↑ ).

larger(N1, N2, N1) ← N1 > N2.
larger(N1, N2, N2) ← N1 =< N2.
```

4.2 Assuming that a suitable program for the larger relation is available, write a PARLOG program for a more general relation largest where the logical reading of largest(Nlist, Max) is: Max is the largest number on the list Nlist. Operationally the program should be able to compute the largest of a supplied list of numbers.

4.3 The program below defines the relation neg_filter. The logical reading of neg_filter(Intlist, PosIntlist) is: PosIntlist is the list obtained by removing negative integers from Intlist.

```
mode neg_filter(list?, poslist↑ ).

neg_filter([], []).
neg_filter([I|Ints], PosInts) ←
    I < 0 :
    neg_filter(Ints, PosInts).
neg_filter([I|Ints], [I|PosInts]) ←
    I >= 0 :
    neg_filter(Ints, PosInts).
```

(a) Is the program logically correct and complete?

(b)   Describe the test-commit-output-spawn stages of the process that evaluates the call

    ← neg_filter([−2, 3, 4, −5], P).

and draw a dataflow diagram to represent the first spawning of sub-processes.

(c)   Anticipate the rest of the behaviour of the process and draw a dataflow diagram to illustrate.

(d)   Does the program have the safe guards property?

4.4   The program below defines the natural_sum relation. The logical reading of natural_sum(Limit, Tot) is: Tot is the total of the natural numbers from 1 to Limit.

    mode natural_sum(limit?, tot↑).

    natural_sum(Limit, Tot) ←
        integers(1, Limit, Ilist),
        total(Ilist, Tot).

The programs for integers and total are assumed to be as given in the chapter.

(a)   Is the program logically correct and complete?

(b)   Describe the test-commit-output-spawn stages of the process that evaluates the call

    ← natural_sum(100, T).

and draw a dataflow diagram to represent the spawning of the two sub-processes.

(c)   Describe the communication of data between the two sub-processes.

(d)   Write a recursive alternative program for natural_sum that only requires the use of the is primitive for its definition. Describe the behaviour of the process that evaluates the above call with this new program for the relation.

5

Concurrent algorithms

5.1 I/O for program testing
5.2 List pair relations
5.3 Merging lists
5.4 Partitioning lists
5.5 Sorting lists
5.6 Searching binary trees

5.7 An ordered tree search
5.8 Inserting into a binary tree
5.9 Building trees from lists
5.10 Comparing tree profiles
5.11 Finding a path in a graph
 Summary
 Exercises

PREVIEW   The PARLOG procedures of the previous chapter specified very simple algorithms. This chapter describes more significant procedures such as those for sorting, searching and constructing common data structures such as lists, trees and graphs. Each procedure is developed from an informal logical specification of the relation that it computes. The operational behaviour of the procedure as a (typically) concurrent algorithm is then indicated, usually by tracing a representative evaluation process through its test-commit-output-spawn stages. Thus the chapter both consolidates an understanding of PARLOG's operational strategy and prepares the reader for the challenge of more realistic programming problems.

5.1 I/O for program testing

Before plunging into concurrent algorithms, let us state the obvious. Complex procedures (or even simple ones) cannot be expected always to work correctly first time through: testing is always essential and debugging is a frequent next stage. Unfortunately, for PARLOG the software tools that can support these activities are still in an early stage of development. The reader should consult his or her own system documentation for details of whatever aids are provided by the PARLOG implementation.

We can however offer some advice on input and output provision for program testing. The simplest approach to interactive testing uses the read

127

and write primitives introduced in Chapter 3. Suppose for example that we have defined a predicate transform (say) that we now want to test. The relation operates over integer arguments and its mode declaration is

    mode transform(?, ↑).

We need not consider the definition: the point is how to test that we have a program that works. A simple, and often useful, type of test is exemplified by the query

    ← transform(12, NewTerm) & write(NewTerm).

which specifies some input directly in the call and which uses the write primitive to display the final value of the variable NewTerm. The sequential operator is essential to hold back the write process because this primitive does not suspend. A slightly more elaborate testing query is

    ← read(Term) & transform(Term, NewTerm) & write(NewTerm).

in which the input to the transform call is obtained from the keyboard by means of the read primitive.

Using the sequencing operators in this way has a drawback. If the transform procedure happens to have a bug that prevents this call from terminating then the call to write will never be made. We shall have no way of knowing (and this could be essential debugging information) whether the required data was produced before the deadlock occurred. A possible remedy is to use a variation upon write that suspends until its argument term has received some kind of binding. Let us suppose that swrite (the 's' is for 'suspendable') is such a variation. Then we could re-specify the first above query as

    ← transform(12, NewTerm), swrite(NewTerm).

using the parallel operator. Now the two processes will run concurrently: initially the swrite process will suspend, but as soon as NewTerm is given some kind of value by the transform process the swrite call will display the value and terminate. Notice that it will do this whether the transform process eventually terminates or not.

The PARLOG data primitive makes it very easy to implement a suitable procedure for swrite. This primitive has the (implicitly declared) mode

    mode data(?).

The behaviour of a call data(X) is to suspend for as long as X remains an unbound variable. When X receives any kind of non-variable binding, the

call succeeds and terminates. (A 'non-variable binding' means exactly that
– it is a binding to any term other than an unbound variable). By combining
data with write, we can define swrite as follows:

```
mode swrite(term?).

swrite(X) ←
     data(X) &
     write(X).
```

Since a data call never fails it can be regarded logically as having the
constant meaning 'true'. Effectively this means that the primitive can be
ignored in the logical reading of a program.

    In the previous chapter we defined an integers relation and noted
that, since an integers process produces the value of its output list
incrementally, a helpful test would be one that displayed the data
concurrently as it is generated. Unfortunately our program for swrite
cannot do this. If we try the query

```
← integers(50, 100, Ints), swrite(Ints).
```

as a test for the relation then the only displayed result will be a term such as
[50|Rest]. The explanation is that this is the first binding made for the
shared variable by the integers process: it is not of course the final value,
but it *is* a non-variable binding and hence enough to make the data call in
the swrite procedure succeed and terminate. In consequence the subsequent incremental binding by the integers process of Rest to the list [51, 52,
..., 100] is not made visible by the test.

    A solution is to define a special suspendable predicate, swrite_list
say, for writing lists. The definition can use swrite, as follows:

```
mode swrite_list(list?).

swrite_list([H|T]) ←
     swrite(H) &
     swrite_list(T).
swrite_list([]).
```

The input mode in this definition will require a swrite_list process to
suspend until the call argument specifies a list pattern. If the list pattern is
non-empty then the process will commit to the first clause, spawning two
sub-processes sequentially. The swrite sub-process will display the term at
the head of the list as soon as this term specifies a non-variable term. The
sequential operator means that the recursive swrite_list sub-process will
display the terms in the tail of the list in their correct order.

    An exercise at the end of this chapter suggests some elaboration. As
written the swrite_list procedure supplies no formatting or punctuation.

Neither does it behave correctly with 'non-flat' lists (lists containing compound terms such as other lists). Furthermore, only one swrite_list process can be usefully active at a time since two such processes running concurrently would probably display their output terms in jumbled-up fashion.

5.2   List pair relations

'List pair' problems make a good place to start. Here are three examples:

- The on_both problem:
  Given a term and a pair of lists, check whether the term belongs to both lists.
- The on_either problem:
  Given a term and a pair of lists, test whether the term belongs to either list.
- The common_term problem:
  Given a pair of lists, try to find a term that is common to them both.

We shall tackle these in turn.

5.2.1   on_both

The first problem suggests defining a relation on_both, where the logical reading of on_both(T, L1, L2) is: T is a term that belongs to both lists L1 and L2. Operationally the relation is to be used only for checking so the mode declaration will specify all the arguments as inputs. A suitable procedure can be defined straightforwardly in terms of the list membership relation defined in Section 4.8:

```
mode on_both(term?, list1?, list2?).

on_both(Term, L1, L2) ←
    member(Term, L1),
    member(Term, L2).
```

Does it work? One way to test the program is with a query such as

```
← on_both(3, [9, 8, 7, 6, 5, 4, 3], [1, 2]).
```

This one should fail. Try a number of test queries to satisfy yourself that the program correctly implements the relation.

The algorithm here is quite simple: to check whether the term belongs to both lists, test each list concurrently. As soon as the test fails for one list the procedure terminates in failure, otherwise it succeeds as soon as membership has been established for both lists. This is an example of the 'restricted' form of and-parallelism: when a problem can be reduced to a collection of *independent* sub-problems, it can be solved by a set of concurrent, non-communicating sub-processes. The normal and-parallel termination mechanism assures an efficient earliest-termination behaviour.

5.2.2   on_either

The second problem suggests that we might define a relation on_either. The logical reading of on_either(T, L1, L2) should be: T is a term that is a member of (at least) one of the lists L1 and L2. The definition is another application for member. For the PARLOG procedure the mode declaration will again specify all arguments as inputs:

```
mode on_either(term?, list1?, list2?).

on_either(T, L1, L2) ← member(T, L1) : true.
on_either(T, L1, L2) ← member(T, L2) : true.
```

(The vacuous true conditions here serve to 'plug' what would otherwise be empty clause bodies, which PARLOG syntax prohibits for guarded clauses). To test the program we could try the query:

```
← on_either(3, [9, 8, 7, 6, 5, 4, 3], [1, 2]).
```

which should succeed. Again, you should check that the program behaves consistently with its logical reading.

The evaluation process for such a query is interesting. The process first tests the two clauses concurrently for candidate status. Because the clause head atoms contain only variables, input matching is certain to succeed for both clauses and so the test for candidacy depends on the concurrent guard evaluations. As soon as one guard evaluation succeeds that clause is selected for commitment and the other guard evaluation is halted. Since the clauses bodies contain only calls to the primitive true, commitment marks the successful termination of the process. In effect the evaluation becomes a 'race' between the guards.

The algorithm here is a neat illustration of or-parallelism. In general, when a problem can be solved by using two or more alternative methods the search for the solution can investigate all methods concurrently. A **guards race** implements this concurrency in PARLOG. Because of the committed choice strategy, or-parallelism cannot continue beyond the guard; but effectively this can cover the entire evaluation, as the on_either problem demonstrates.

5.2.3   common_term

The final list-pair problem is evidently the 'finding' or 'constructive' version of the first problem. We require to define a relation common_term, such that common_term(T, L1, L2) has a logical reading that is identical to that for the earlier on_both relation. The difference is that the procedure for common_term is expected to be capable of *discovering* a suitable value for T instead of merely checking the suitability of some value supplied by the call.

It is natural to ask whether a program similar to that for on_both, but with revised mode declarations, might serve. So as a first attempt let us try the following:

```
mode common_term(term↑, list1?, list2?).

common_term(Term, L1, L2) ←
    member(Term, L1),
    member(Term, L2).
```

Unfortunately this does not represent a usable algorithm. If you test the procedure with the call (say)

```
← common_term(T, [7, 6, 5, 4, 3], [5, 4, 3]), swrite(T).
```

then it will not happen that one of the terms which is common to both lists will be displayed. Instead the result will be a deadlock. The explanation is that the two member sub-processes both suspend (look back at the definition of member to see why this happens). What this example shows is quite typical of PARLOG: changing the mode declarations is not enough – a 'constructive' program usually requires a different logical formulation from a 'checking' program for the same relation.

An alternative definition of common_term that does have a correct behaviour is as follows:

```
mode common_term(term↑, list1?, list2?).

common_term(T, [T|L1], L2) ←
    member(T, L2) :
    true.
common_term(S, [T|L1], L2) ←
    not(member(T, L2)) :
    common_term(S, L1, L2).
```

This procedure specifies a form of **generate-and-test** algorithm. A common_term process *generates* a term from the head of the first list and *tests* it for membership of the second list. Depending on the result the process either commits to the first clause and outputs the term as the solution before terminating, or commits to the second clause and spawns a recursive common_term process to try to generate a solution from somewhere in the tail of the first list.

Notice that the test member(T, L2) occurs in the guard of both clauses. This is necessary to give the procedure the sufficient tests property; if we simply remove the guard from the recursive clause then the behaviour might be incorrect. But the duplication is a potential source of inefficiency. However, the SEQ_MEM version of the list membership procedure (Section 4.8.3) showed how a guard can sometimes be excised by re-specifying a procedure using the sequential clause search operator. We can use the same device here:

```
mode common_term(term↑, list1?, list2?).

common_term(T, [T|L1], L2) ←
    member(T, L2) :
    true ;
common_term(S, [T|L1], L2) ←
    common_term(S, L1, L2).
```

With this version, a process first implements the member test for the term at the head of the first list and *only if this fails* is the recursive clause used to generate alternatives from the list tail. As with SEQ_MEM, the behaviour is completely sequential: the performance may be better than the parallel version (especially on sequential machines) but the logical reading is poorer – the sufficient tests property is lost and we have to reason about the behaviour in order to persuade ourselves that a valid call will not fail.

Can these successful versions of common_term replace on_both? That is, can they operate (unchanged) in 'checking' mode? The answer is a qualified yes: you may like to investigate why the qualification is necessary. Again this is typical of PARLOG – the use of full unification for output means that a 'finding' program can generally double for 'checking' to some extent, even though the converse does not hold.

5.3 Merging lists

A common experience on a two-lane highway is to discover at some point that road-working has caused one lane to close down: the two lanes of traffic must then merge into a single lane. List merging is very similar. Formally, two lists are said to be **merged** into a single list if the single list is some interleaving of all the members of the other two. For example

```
merge([4, 2], [1, 8], [1, 8, 4, 2])
merge([4, 2], [1, 8], [4, 1, 2, 8])
merge([4, 2], [1, 8], [4, 2, 1, 8])
```

are all valid instances of the relation. Notice that the relative ordering of terms on each of the original lists is preserved within the merged list, but

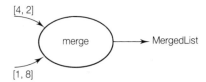

Figure 5.1   A merge process.

given that constraint it otherwise does not matter how the terms are combined. Evidently this relation is not **functional** (in the mathematical sense) – the third argument is not uniquely determined by the first two.

A PARLOG program for merge is shown below. Logically, the first clause specifies that the merge relation holds if the term at the head of the first list occurs at the head of the merged list, providing the remainder of the merged list represents a merge between the terms in the second list and the rest of the first list. You should satisfy yourself that this clause and the other clauses do give to merge(La, Lb, Lm) the logical meaning: Lm is a merge of the lists La and Lb.

```
mode merge(list1?, list2?, merge↑ ).

merge([T|L1], L2, [T|L12]) ← merge(L1, L2, L12).
merge(L1, [T|L2], [T|L12]) ← merge(L1, L2, L12).
merge([], L, L).
merge(L, [], L).
```

Operationally, the program is expected to output the merge of two lists supplied as inputs. A suitable query for test purposes is

← merge([4, 2], [1, 8], MergedList), swrite_list(MergedList).

Figure 5.1 illustrates the merge process that this query creates. To evaluate the call the process will follow the usual test-commit-output-spawn procedure. Both implication clauses are candidates for the call: with the first clause input matching could succeed with the substitutions

T = 4, L1 = [2], L2 = [1, 8]

and with the second clause the substitutions are

L1 = [4, 2], T = 1, L2 = [8]

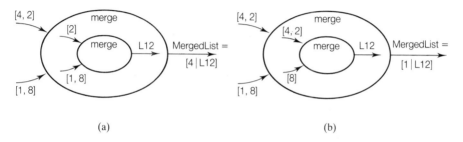

Figure 5.2 Two alternative behaviours: (a) The process commits to the first clause; (b) The process commits to the second clause.

So the process could commit to either clause. Depending on the choice, the subsequent behaviour of the process will be either

> Output: MergedList = [4|L12]
> Spawned sub-process evaluates: ← merge([2], [1, 8], L12)

if the first clause is selected, or else the behaviour will be

> Output: MergedList = [1|L12]
> Spawned sub-process evaluates: ← merge([4, 2], [8], L12)

if the selected clause is the second clause. Figure 5.2 illustrates these two alternative behaviours. Of course, in either case the spawned sub-process has a *similar* pair of alternative possible behaviours. Overall this means that the final value produced for MergedList could be *any one* of those values that are valid according to the logical reading of the relation. Notice that termination is assured: each sub-process has one fewer term to merge than its parent process, so that ultimate commitment to an assertional clause is certain.

The fact that we cannot completely predict the behaviour of the merge evaluation process shows that this procedure is an example of a **non-deterministic** procedure. It specifies an algorithm that does not fully determine or prescribe the progress of the computation but instead leaves part of the decision-making to the evaluation process. The 'non-determined' part is the choice of candidate clause: effectively, when both inputs have terms to offer the machine is allowed to decide from which list to select a term for placing onto the output stream.

The non-determinism of merge has a second possible source. In the query above the inputs to merge were completely specified at the time of the call, but more typical examples are those in which merging acts as a

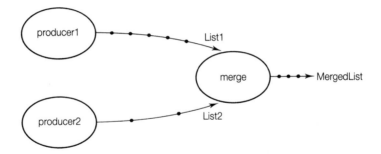

Figure 5.3   Merging of two lists with incremental producers.

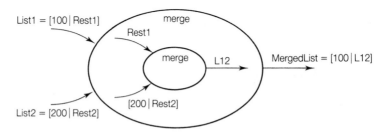

Figure 5.4   A merge process that selects the first clause.

'utility' process with inputs that are produced incrementally by other concurrent processes, as shown in Figure 5.3. A simple example of such a situation is created by the query

← integers(100, 500, List1),
      integers(200, 900, List2),
      merge(List1, List2, MergedList).

in which the producers are integers processes. The behaviour of merge in such a situation is influenced by the rates at which the producers supply data. Suppose for example that the bindings List1 = [100|Rest1] and List2 = [200|Rest2] are immediately made available to the merge process by the integers processes. Then the merge call becomes

← merge([100|Rest1], [200|Rest2], MergedList)

As above, the merge evaluation process can commit non-deterministically to either of the first two clauses. Figure 5.4 illustrates the case where the

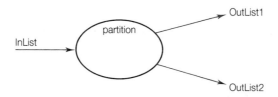

Figure 5.5 A partition process divides a list into two.

process selects the first clause, effectively choosing the integer 100 for the first term of the merged output stream. The next step depends partly on how fast the producer of List1 can generate the second term of this list (which will be the first term of Rest1). The availability of this term will determine whether the spawned merge sub-process is bound to commit to the second clause or whether it could commit non-deterministically to either clause. Thus we see that to compound the *intrinsic* non-determinism of the merge procedure, this computation is also affected by an *extrinsic* time dependency – the outcome partly depends not only on the values of the input lists, but also on the times at which these values are incrementally supplied.

Non-determinism will arise in PARLOG whenever there is more than one candidate clause for a call. It is often called 'don't-care' non-determinism because the uncertainty is acceptable whenever the programmer 'doesn't care' which of the alternative behaviours will result. In the case of merge for example the programmer's attitude might be that one merged list is as good as any other. But note that there is no guarantee that a merge process will not consistently select the *same* clause whenever a choice arises, and hence 'unfairly' favour one input list over the other. The concept of the 'fairness' of an evaluation is important and we shall return to it – and to the general theme of list merging – in the next chapter.

5.4 Partitioning lists

Merging is a process of combining two lists into one. Partitioning is an inverse process to merging in the loose sense that it divides one list into two (see Figure 5.5). If we left unspecified the basis of the division then the algorithm would be non-deterministic, like that of merge: the process itself would choose the output list on which to place each input term. But more commonly the relation is defined with some specified test that determines the partition. We shall confine ourselves to the important special case of

partitioning numeric lists where the test is based on ordering, so that
OutList1 receives all the numbers less than some fixed value and OutList2
receives all those greater than or equal to it. This suggests a four argument
partition relation rather than the three arguments suggested by the diagram.
The extra argument specifies the fixed value or 'pivot' that will be used in
the test.

A program for partition is shown below. The logical reading of
partition(Pivot, InList, LessList, MoreList) is: LessList and MoreList are the
sublists of InList whose terms are less than Pivot and not less than Pivot
respectively. The first clause specifies the partitioning of an InList in which
the head term is less than Pivot; the second clause describes the case where
the head term is greater than or equal to Pivot; and the third clause treats
the final possibility, of an InList that has no head term because it is empty.
Thus we have a complete definition the logical correctness of which should
be clear by inspection.

```
mode partition(pivot?, inlist?, lesslist↑, morelist↑ ).

partition(Pivot, [T|InList], [T|LessList], MoreList) ←
    T < Pivot :
    partition(Pivot, InList, LessList, MoreList).
partition(Pivot, [T|InList], LessList, [T|MoreList]) ←
    T >= Pivot :
    partition(Pivot, InList, LessList, MoreList).
partition(Pivot, [], [], []).
```

Instead of studying a single specific example of a partition process, let us try
this time to be more general. We shall analyse the set of test-commit-
output-spawn behaviours that partition processes could exhibit. The call
being evaluated can be represented by partition(P, In, Less, More), say.

Test

What happens at this stage depends on the bindings of P and In, the
variables occurring in the input mode arguments of the call. The following table sets out the possibilities. This table economizes by disregarding
error cases such as those where In becomes bound to a number or P
becomes bound to a list. It may be tempting also to ignore the possibility
that P is unbound in the call since at first sight perhaps this situation
seems an improbable one. But in fact this is not so: a partition process will
find both P and In initially unbound in any typical conjunction of calls
such as

```
← produce(In, P), partition(P, In, Less, More).
```

	P *unbound*	P *bound*
In is unbound	test suspends with all clauses	test suspends with all clauses
In bound to []	test succeeds with clause 3	test succeeds with clause 3
In bound to [N|Rest]	test suspends with clause 1 and clause 2	test succeeds with clause 1 if N < P or with clause 2 if N >= P

in which a concurrent producer process is expected to generate their values. The table shows that the program behaves satisfactorily in this situation. When P is unbound the process suspends (unless In becomes bound to the empty list in which case the test justifiably succeeds using the third clause).

The input substitutions that result in successful tests are:

- For a test succeeding with clause 1: Pivot = P, T = N, InList = Rest
- For a test succeeding with clause 2: Pivot = P, T = N, InList = Rest
- For a test succeeding with clause 3: Pivot = P

Commit

If the test stage has succeeded with at least one clause, the process now commits to that clause. The table shows that for this process there never is more than one candidate clause, so the behaviour is deterministic – it can be wholly predicted whenever the arguments of the call are known.

Output

The output arguments of the call are now unified with those of the selected clause. Depending on the clause, this produces the bindings:

- For a process committing to clause 1:
  Less = [N\|LessList], More = MoreList
- For a process committing to clause 2:
  Less = LessList, More = [N\|MoreList]
- For a process committing to clause 3:
  Less = [], More = []

The first two cases represent the depositing of a term from the input list onto one of the output lists.

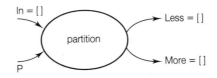

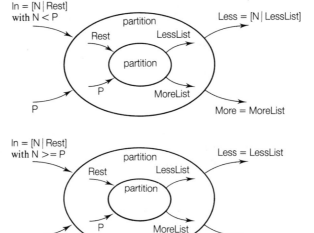

Figure 5.6   Three possible behaviours.

Spawn

The process that commits to the third clause simply succeeds and terminates. When the other two clauses are selected one sub-process is spawned to evaluate the call

    ← partition(P, Rest, LessList, MoreList).

and the rest of the lifetime of the process comprises the running of this sub-process to carry out the partitioning of the remainder of the input list.

    Figure 5.6 gives a pictorial view of this analysis. It shows the three possible behaviours of a non-suspending partition process (that is, of a process that does commit to a clause). We stress that these are *deterministic* behaviours – unlike the case of merge, an individual partition process has no choice. Its fate is decided solely by the data supplied in the call.

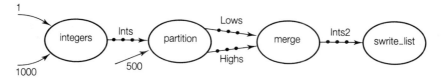

Figure 5.7 Network of processes.

Notice how early it happens in the life of the partition process that the head term N of the input list is placed on the appropriate output list. Even if the spawned sub-process immediately suspends – which will happen unless further data is communicated via In to Rest – this head term is available to any concurrent process that might be waiting for it. For a partition process this means that the output lists are produced incrementally as two streams of terms, where each term results from one successive reduction. Assuming that P has a suitable value the only constraint on the progress of the process is the availability of data for the input list, which in general may itself be being produced as a stream of terms by some other concurrently active process.

By combining merge with partition and some of the relations described earlier we can now construct queries that specify some quite interesting process networks. An example is

```
← integers(1, 1000, Ints),
    partition(500, Ints, Lows, Highs),
    merge(Lows, Highs, Ints2),
    swrite_list(Ints2).
```

This query creates a network of four concurrent processes as shown.in Figure 5.7. The processes are all (relatively) long-lived and the variables that appear in the conjunction are all bound incrementally by their respective producers so that each one implements a stream communication channel; the diagram shows blobs to suggest the flow of a stream of terms. We could think of the processes as the components of a plumbing system (or of an electrical circuit) with the variables acting as water pipes (or wires). What output might this query display?

5.5 Sorting lists

There exist many algorithms for sorting data and an account of their implementation in PARLOG could easily fill a book in itself. Here we shall discuss only one, Hoare's **quicksort**, which is among the best and most elegant. Quicksort is based on a straighforward divide and conquer strategy: first the data set to be sorted is partitioned (in the sense described above) into two parts, then each part is sorted, and finally the sorted parts are re-combined. This implies a recursion the termination of which will ultimately depend on partitioning the data set into such small parts that sorting is trivial (an empty set of data needs no work to make it sorted). The algorithm has an obvious potential for parallel execution in that having partitioned the data into two parts the sorting of the parts can proceed concurrently.

Assuming that the data is represented as a list of numbers, which number should we use as the pivot for partitioning? The most convenient choice is whichever number happens to occur at the head of the list. A disadvantage of this choice is that if the head integer happens to be untypically large or small then the partitioning may not create roughly equal-sized parts, as would be ideal. But this is a price that we will pay. The re-combining of the parts can be accomplished by a simple append, as defined prevously, with the pivot term suitably placed by inserting it into the head of the second sorted list.

Here is an example showing what will be involved in a quicksort process. Notice that steps 2 and 3 are mutually independent: they could be executed in parallel.

To sort the list [6 2 8 9 0 2 1 4 7 5]:

(1)   Partition the tail with 6 as pivot: [2 0 2 1 4 5] and [8 9 7]

(2)   Sort the first list: [0 1 2 2 4 5]

(3)   Sort the second list: [7 8 9]

(4)   Append (with 6 at head of second list): [0 1 2 2 4 5 6 7 8 9]

A PARLOG procedure for quicksort is shown below. The logical reading of qsort(L, SortedL) is: SortedL is a list containing the terms of the list L in ascending order. The recursive clause reads logically as a specification of what it means for a list to be sorted, by stating a set of conditions that can be used to check that one list is a sorted version of another. The operational reading of the program shows how a qsort evaluation process constructs the sorted list by spawning a network of four sub-processes, as pictured by the dataflow diagram of Figure 5.8. Notice the effect of the conjunction operators in the recursive clause, bearing in mind that the sequential operator has higher precedence than the parallel operator. Firstly the partition sub-process runs to completion; then the two concurrent qsort sub-processes are spawned; and finally, when these have both terminated the append sub-process can start. Thus we can imagine a qsort process as having a life of three discrete phases, corresponding to a left-to-right traversal of the dataflow diagram.

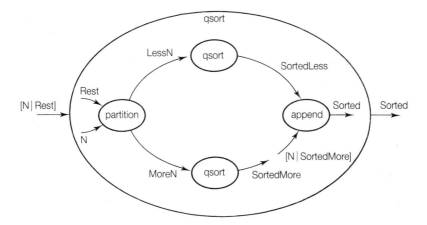

Figure 5.8   A qsort process spawns four sub-processes.

```
mode qsort(list?, sortedlist↑ ).

qsort([N|Rest], Sorted) ←
    partition(N, Rest, LessN, MoreN) &
    qsort(LessN, SortedLess),
    qsort(MoreN, SortedMore) &
    append(SortedLess, [N|SortedMore], Sorted).
qsort([], []).
```

Although this algorithm does give correct results (as you should check for
yourself) it does not specify maximum concurrency. A natural question is:
how would the behaviour be affected if we were to re-write the program
with only parallel operators? Instead of synchronizing the spawned processes explicitly by the use of sequencing operators, this would leave the
modes (that is, the input constraint) to take care of the synchronization.
Let us refer to this all-parallel version as pqsort, defined as follows:

```
mode pqsort(list?, sortedlist↑ ).

pqsort([N|Rest], Sorted) ←
    partition(N, Rest, LessN, MoreN),
    pqsort(LessN, SortedLess),
    pqsort(MoreN, SortedMore),
    append(SortedLess, [N|SortedMore], Sorted).
pqsort([], []).
```

With this version the same sub-processes as in Figure 5.8 are spawned to evaluate a call but now the spawning is wholly concurrent. At first, before the partition sub-process has produced any data, the other spawned sub-processes will all suspend (look at the definitions of pqsort and append to understand why). But the pqsort sub-processes do not stay suspended for long. As soon as they obtain *any* terms from the partition process they begin useful activity.

To illustrate, let us consider as an example the process that evaluates the call

← pqsort([6, 2, 8, 9, 0, 2, 1, 6, 7, 5], S).

This process commits to the recursive clause and immediately spawns four concurrent sub-processes. As soon as the partition sub-process produces some data for LessN and MoreN the two pqsort sub-processes will commit. For example, if partition generates the binding

LessN = [2|LessN1]

then the corresponding pqsort sub-process commits to the first clause and hence spawns four concurrent sub-processes of its own, as shown in Figure 5.9. These sub-sub-processes will suspend for as long as LessN1 remains unbound. But when partition subsequently generates the binding

LessN1 = [0|LessN2]

the first sub-sub-process, which itself is a partition process, will commit and will pass the term 0 onto one of its output channels, enabling one of the pqsort sub-sub-processes to commit and to spawn a further four processes; and so on.

The descendency of spawned sub-processes that is created by a pqsort call is no different from that which would be created by a call with the same input data to qsort. The completely 'filled-in' diagrams of Figures 5.8 and 5.9 would look the same. The difference lies in the relative times at which the sub-processes are spawned. For pqsort, the recursive sub-processes are spawned as soon as this is justified by the production of *any* data by the partition sub-process; whereas the recursive sub-processes of qsort are held back until the partition process has entirely completed its work. On a parallel machine the pqsort version is potentially much faster – although there is likely to be a (system-dependent) penalty associated with the rapid growth in the numbers of processes.

5.6   Searching binary trees

Tree data structures arise frequently in computing: examples are parse trees, directory trees, proof trees, expression trees, and so on. In fact, lists

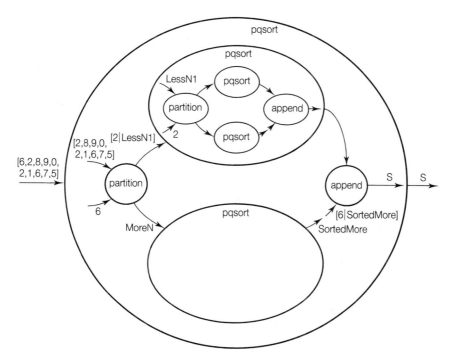

Figure 5.9 A pqsort sub-process reduces as soon as the partition sub-process produces some data.

can be represented as trees also. In this section we introduce some simple tree processing in PARLOG.

Examples of trees are shown in Figure 5.10. These are all **binary trees**, each node of which has at most two 'child' nodes: hence a binary tree comprises a root node and two descendent subtrees, one or both of which might be empty. Data may be stored by terms at each node. In typical applications these will be structured terms but we shall simplify here by dealing with binary trees that contain only constants such as integers. We shall also assume that the data stored on the tree is unique, so that the same term does not occur at two different nodes.

There are several ways to represent a binary tree as a PARLOG term. We shall use a structure with tree as the functor and with three components representing respectively the left subtree, the data at the root node, and the right subtree, as in

tree(LeftSubtree, Root, RightSubtree)

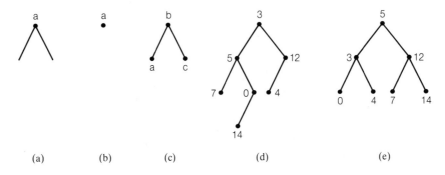

Figure 5.10   Binary trees.

This representation will suffice for every binary tree except the empty tree (the tree equivalent of the empty list) which has no subtrees and no root node. To denote the empty tree we shall use the constant empty. Then the tree shown in Figure 5.10 (a) is represented as

    tree(empty, a, empty)

This tree has only a single node: usually we would illustrate it just as Figure 5.10 (b) that does not bother to show the empty arcs. The tree in Figure 5.10 (c) is represented as

    tree(tree(empty, a, empty), b, tree(empty, c, empty))

and so on. This is an awkward notation to manipulate by hand but of course it presents no problems to a machine.

Given a binary tree an obvious question is to ask whether some particular term is present on the tree. Let us define a predicate on_tree, where the logical meaning of on_tree(Element, Tree) is: Element is a term occurring at some node of Tree. A PARLOG definition of the relation is shown below.

```
mode on_tree(term?, binarytree?).

on_tree(E, tree(Ltree, X, Rtree)) ←
    on_tree(E, Ltree) :
    true .
on_tree(E, tree(Ltree, X, Rtree)) ←
    on_tree(E, Rtree) :
    true .
on_tree(E, tree(Ltree, E, Rtree)).
```

Logically, the two implication clauses specify that an element is on the tree if it is on the left or right subtree. The assertional clause specifies that the element at the root of a tree is on the tree. Operationally, as the mode declaration indicates, the program is intended to check whether a given term belongs to a given tree. Let us consider the query

← on_tree(c, tree(tree(empty, a, empty), b, tree(empty, c, empty))).

which asks whether c belongs to the tree shown in Figure 5.10 (c). The process that evaluates this call begins by testing the three clauses concurrently for candidate status. Because of the duplicate occurrence of the variable E in the assertional clause this clause is a non-candidate. Input matching can succeed with the two recursive clauses and the test for candidacy with these clauses becomes a concurrent test of the guards. The guard call for the first clause becomes

← on_tree(c, tree(empty, a, empty)).

whilst for the second clause it is

← on_tree(c, tree(empty, c, empty)).

These calls are evaluated concurrently. The process evaluating the second guard call will succeed using the assertional clause and at that point the other guard process will be terminated (assuming it has not already failed) and the second clause will be identified as a candidate. The query process will thus commit to the second clause and hence will succeed and terminate.

This example represents an untypically short evaluation but it suggests the general picture. Effectively the on_tree procedure specifies an algorithm in which the search for the term proceeds by examining the root whilst concurrently searching the left and right subtrees. The concurrent searches are implemented by a 'guards race', similar to the racing guards behaviour of the on_either example discussed earlier. But for an on_tree process this can imply guard evaluations that are deeply nested: the process cannot afford to commit to a clause until the very last possible moment, when the term has been found somewhere down the tree. Such 'deep guards' reflect the fact that although there is no more than one candidate clause (the term cannot lie on both subtrees) a significant amount of computation (search effort) is needed to determine its identity.

Another feature of on_tree is the rapid growth in the amount of concurrency. An evaluation process effectively forks into two at each node (see Figure 5.11). This behaviour could lead to a very fast search but the processing costs grow exponentially with the height of the tree. Imagine an idealized parallel machine that converts all the concurrency into true parallelism by allocating one additional processor per node: such a machine would need to have at its disposal roughly half a million

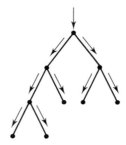

Figure 5.11   An on_tree process forks into two at each node.

processors in order to exhaustively search a fully-laden binary tree with a height of twenty nodes. (Admittedly this is a rather large tree – it would contain over a million terms of data). Analogously, consider a mountain-rescue team whose strategy it is to search a network of paths leading down from a mountain summit by starting at the top and dividing at each fork into two groups. Then to guarantee that after the twentieth fork each path would be searched by at least a single individual, the starting team would need to be more than half a million strong. This approach to solving the problem potentially offers the fastest result possible, but the resource requirements are rather formidable!

5.7 An ordered tree search

If a binary tree is **ordered** then an expensive exhaustive search such as is specified by the on_tree procedure can be avoided. An example of an ordered tree is Figure 5.10 (e). The property of such a tree is that the data on the left subtree for any node is less than the term at the node, and the data on the right subtree is greater than the term at the node. Figure 5.10 (d) is an example of a tree that is *not* ordered – the left subtree of the root node contains terms that are greater than the term at the root, for example.

An ordered binary tree could just be searched blindly by on_tree but this would be wasteful. A much better algorithm is based on the idea of repeatedly comparing the term at each node with the term being searched for; in this way the search can be confined to just one branch of the tree. Let us define a procedure for on_ord_tree to implement this algorithm. The logical reading of on_ord_tree(Element, Tree) is: Element is a term that occurs at some node of the ordered binary tree Tree. A PARLOG definition of the relation is shown below.

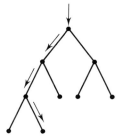

Figure 5.12   An on_ord_tree process commits to one subtree at each node.

```
mode on_ord_tree(term?, orderedbinarytree?).

on_ord_tree(E, tree(Ltree, X, Rtree)) ←
    E < X :
    on_ord_tree(E, Ltree).
on_ord_tree(E, tree(Ltree, X, Rtree)) ←
    E > X :
    on_ord_tree(E, Rtree).
on_ord_tree(E, tree(Ltree, E, Rtree)).
```

Logically, the first clause specifies that an element is on an ordered tree if it is less than the number at the root and it occurs on the left subtree. The second clause expresses the corresponding implication for the right subtree. The assertional clause specifies that the term at the root node is on the tree.

Operationally the behaviour of on_ord_tree is very different from that of on_tree. An on_ord_tree process now quickly commits to a clause on the basis of three simple comparisons between the search term and the term at the current node. The comparisons are concurrent and are effected by guard calls within the implication clauses and by input matching in the case of the assertional clause. If the successful test is the latter then the evaluation succeeds and terminates; otherwise a sub-process is spawned that searches the appropriate subtree. The fact that the tree is ordered justifies the immediate commitment of any call to a single clause or subtree (see Figure 5.12).

For an on_ord_tree process there is no forking and no concurrency other than the limited or-parallelism arising from the tests for candidate status. In terms of our mountain rescue-team analogy, it is as though the search party can unerringly track the correct path by (say) reading the spoor at each branch. There is never any need to divide and there is no advantange in having more rescuers than can be effectively deployed in reading spoor. Even so this algorithm is capable of an impressive

impressive performance. The binary tree mentioned previously that is twenty nodes high will be completely searched within a mere twenty recursive calls, each implementing one set of comparisons between a node term and the search term.

5.8 Inserting into a binary tree

Many operations other than searching can be performed upon trees. We only have to imagine a dictionary represented as a tree (as part of a spell-checking system, say) to suggest some likely requirements: we may need to add new words to the dictionary, delete existing words, re-construct the tree about a different root node, count the total number of words, and so on. Here we shall describe only the common operation of inserting a term into a tree.

Let us postpone dictionary-style trees, which are necessarily ordered trees, and start with trees that are *unordered*. Then in principle, the new term could be inserted anywhere. However it is easier to add a new 'leaf' node to the end of an existing branch than to attempt insertion somewhere into the middle of the tree, so we shall define a relation insert where the logical reading of insert(Element, Tree, NewTree) is to be: NewTree is the tree formed by adding the term Element on to the end of some branch of Tree. The program for insert will have modes declared by

mode insert(element?, unordtree?, newtree↑).

There seem to be three cases to consider and these are shown in Figure 5.13. A special case is where the tree is empty: here there is no choice but to 'insert' the term as the root of a fresh tree that has two empty subtrees. Logically this can be represented as the assertion

insert(H, empty, tree(empty, H, empty)).

In all other cases we are inserting a term into a non-empty subtree, represented by some term of the form tree(L, X, R) where L and R represent the left and right subtrees. Evidently the possibilities are to insert into L and to insert into R. If it is decided to insert H into L then the result will be a tree having a new left subtree. The implication

insert(H, tree(L, X, R), tree(NewL, X, R)) ←
    insert(H, L, NewL).

represents this case, and a similar clause can represent the right subtree insertion. The procedure then becomes:

Term for insertion	Input tree	Output tree

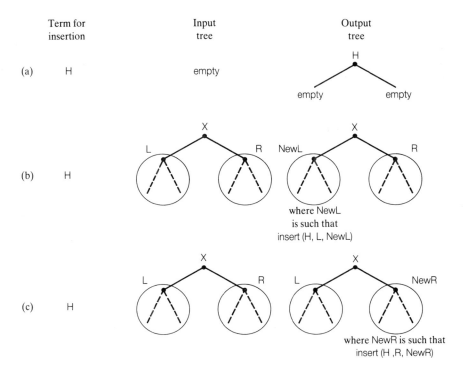

Figure 5.13 Inserting into a binary tree.

```
mode insert(element?, unordtree?, newtree↑ ).

insert(H, empty, tree(empty, H, empty)).
insert(H, tree(L, X, R), tree(NewL, X, R)) ←
        insert(H, L, NewL).
insert(H, tree(L, X, R), tree(L, X, NewR)) ←
        insert(H, R, NewR).
```

To understand the operational reading of this program, let us consider the problem of inserting the term d into the tree shown in Figure 5.10 (c). This corresponds to the query

```
← insert(d,
         tree(tree(empty, a, empty), b, tree(empty, c, empty)),
         T).
```

(printed over several lines here for readability). The evaluation process follows the usual four stages.

Test

Input matching fails with the assertional clause because the middle argument of the call specifies a non-empty tree. However input matching with the recursive clauses can succeed: for the second clause the input substitutions are

$$H = d, \quad L = tree(empty, a, empty), \quad X = b, \quad R = tree(empty, c, empty)$$

and similar substitutions are available for the third clause.

Commit

Both the second and the third clauses are candidates and the process could commit to either one. For the sake of our example let us suppose that the second clause is the selected candidate.

Output

The output argument terms are now unified, producing the substitution

$$T = tree(NewL, b, tree(empty, c, empty))$$

for the call variable.

Spawn

The body of the selected clause now creates a single sub-process

$$\leftarrow insert(d, tree(empty, a, empty), NewL).$$

The behaviour of this sub-process is not hard to anticipate. It too could commit to either the second or the third clause: supposing that the third clause is selected, the output binding will be

$$NewL = tree(empty, a, NewR)$$

and a sub-sub-process will be spawned to evaluate the call

$$\leftarrow insert(d, empty, NewR).$$

This will succeed directly. Using the first clause it will produce the binding

$$NewR = tree(empty, d, empty)$$

and terminate, causing the original insert process to do likewise. Tracing back through the three steps that comprise the 'binding history' of the

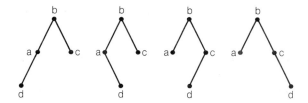

Figure 5.14   Trees producible by the insertion process.

query variable T, we see that the final value is

T = tree(NewL, b, tree(empty, c, empty))
  = tree(tree(empty, a, NewR), b, tree(empty, c, empty))
  = tree(tree(empty, a, tree(empty, d, empty)), b, tree(empty, c, empty))

which is the structure represented by the second diagram of Figure 5.14. Notice that this tree *does* comprise a valid insertion of the term into the tree specified by the query.

Obviously the insert procedure specifies a highly non-deterministic algorithm. In effect, by selecting between the two recursive clauses the process itself decides at each non-leaf node whether the insertion should be made into the left or the right subtree. The ultimate reduction of the evaluation to a sub-process that commits to the assertional clause corresponds to the actual insertion of the term when the end of a branch has been reached. The different choices could have produced *any* of the trees shown in Figure 5.14 and these are all valid solutions according to the logical reading of the relation.

In passing, notice that this example demonstrates that structures as well as lists can be produced *incrementally* by a PARLOG process. The three-stage binding of T in the example above demonstrates the point. The values at each step can be regarded as successive approximations to the final tree value. Is there a structure or tree analogue of the 'stream' metaphor for the incremental production of the terms of a list? We might think of an upturned tree being gradually painted by some artist's brush, where the tree's size, shape and node contents only gradually (and asymmetrically) become visible. This is less intuitive than the concept of incremental binding for lists. However, the chief benefit of incrementalism remains the same: it is that a concurrent consumer process can begin operating upon the structure before its final value has been completely constructed.

A small variation upon the insert procedure obtains a version for ordered tree insertion. We shall assume that the ordered tree contains unique numeric data and that the term for insertion does not already occur on the tree. The definition shown below makes the logical reading of ord_insert(Element, Tree, NewTree) to be: NewTree is the tree formed by adding the term Element on to the end of the appropriate branch of the ordered binary tree Tree.

```
mode ord_insert(element?, ordtree?, newtree↑ ).

ord_insert(H, empty, tree(empty, H, empty)).
ord_insert(H, tree(L, X, R), tree(NewL, X, R)) ←
    H < X :
    ord_insert(H, L, NewL).
ord_insert(H, tree(L, X, R), tree(L, X, NewR)) ←
    H > X :
    ord_insert(H, R, NewR).
```

The logical correctness of the definition should be clear. Operationally, the algorithm here is very similar to that for on_ord_tree except that this procedure *constructs* a term representing the required tree as the search progresses down the appropriate branch. Compared to insert, the main difference is that we now have a procedure that is deterministic: there is never more than one candidate clause for any call. If the tree is empty then the non-recursive clause is the only candidate. For a non-empty tree the guards ensure that an evaluation process selects either the second or the third clause, depending on whether the term for insertion is less than or greater than the element at the root. It is still the case that the term representing the output tree is constructed incrementally, but in contrast to the previous procedure the value that will be computed is entirely predictable when once the arguments of the call are known.

5.9   Building trees from lists

Data stored in a tree can often be accessed much faster than data held in a list. Consider the performance of a list membership test with the earlier procedure for member, for example: regardless of whether the data is ordered, the list can only be searched sequentially. In contrast our on_tree program for searching unordered trees can apply a highly parallel search whilst for an ordered tree the on_ord_tree program can achieve an efficient performance by means of its halving of the search space with every term inspected. The advantages are such that it can be worthwhile to transform list data into a tree structure prior to further processing.

A PARLOG program that builds an unordered tree from a list is shown below. The logical reading of make_tree(L, T) is: T is a tree the nodes

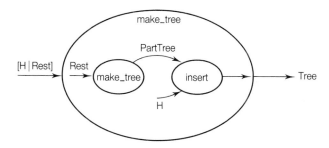

Figure 5.15 A make_tree process.

of which contain the terms of the list L.

```
mode make_tree(list?, tree↑).

make_tree([], empty).
make_tree([H|Rest], Tree) ←
    make_tree(Rest, PartTree),
    insert(H, PartTree, Tree).
```

The logical correctness of the procedure should be clear. The assertional clause specifies that the empty tree corresponds to the empty list. The recursive clause specifies that Tree arises from a list with head term H if PartTree corresponds to the remainder of the list and Tree is obtained by inserting the element H into PartTree. For insert we shall assume the same definition as was given previously: this means that there will be no (intentional) ordering in the tree that results.

  This program does work but its performance may be disappointing. To understand why, consider the behaviour of a typical make_tree process. The process will spawn the pair of sub-processes shown in Figure 5.15. The sub-processes run concurrently but the input constraint on the insert sub-process forces the latter to suspend until the make_tree sub-process produces a term representing a tree structure for PartTree. But of course, the recursive make_tree sub-process exhibits a behaviour similar to its parent; it too spawns a pair of concurrent sub-processes, including an insert process that initially suspends. Ultimately this implies that a make_tree process reduces to a sequence of insertions. The first descendent insert process to terminate will be the very last to be spawned: it will enter the final term of the list into the empty tree. The last to complete will be the first-spawned insert sub-process. This is the one shown in the diagram and it is responsible for inserting the list head term H.

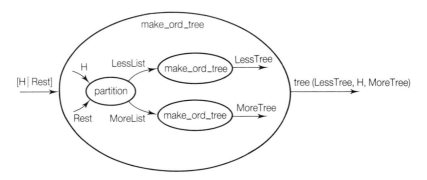

Figure 5.16   A make_ord_tree process.

In passing, notice how make_tree exhibits an 'inherited' non-determinism. Although the make_tree procedure itself is deterministic (there is never more than one candidate clause for a call) the non-determinism of insert means that a make_tree process could construct *any* binary tree that is logically producible from the input list. Obviously this is acceptable only if we really don't care what the finished tree will look like.

Suppose now that the requirement is the much stronger one that the tree constructed from an (unordered) list should be an ordered tree. An easy way to obtain a corresponding program would be to transform the above make_tree program by substituting a call to ord_insert (as defined previously) for that to insert in the body of the recursive clause. However, the resulting program would share with make_tree the sequential algorithmic behaviour. Let us try a different approach instead.

The list-to-tree program shown below is a radically different formulation. The logical reading of make_ord_tree(L, T) is: T is an ordered tree the nodes of which contain the terms of the list L. Observe the conditions specified by the recursive clause: for an ordered tree to be built from a list, the root should be the head term and the left and right subtrees should be built from the lesser and greater sublists arising from a partition of the list using the head term as pivot. The partition relation is as defined previously. You should satisfy yourself that these clauses do form a good logical specification of the make_ord_tree relation.

```
mode make_ord_tree(unordlist?, ordtree↑ ).

make_ord_tree([H|Rest], tree(LessTree, H, MoreTree)) ←
    partition(H, Rest, LessList, MoreList),
    make_ord_tree(LessList, LessTree),
    make_ord_tree(MoreList, MoreTree).
make_ord_tree([], empty).
```

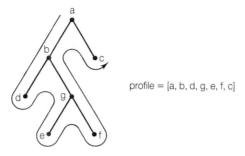

profile = [a, b, d, g, e, f, c]

Figure 5.17   Obtaining a tree profile.

Operationally this program is very different from make_tree. A make_ord_tree process creates a network of three concurrent sub-processes as shown in Figure 5.16. As soon as the process is supplied with some list data as input, it produces a tree as output: the tree has the list head term H as root and it has two subtrees the values of which are constructed by the recursive make_ord_tree sub-processes. The only constraint on the latter is the rate at which the partition sub-process is able to divide the input list into two distinct streams. This algorithm is potentially highly parallel; it specifies a divide-and-conquer behaviour reminiscent of the earlier quick-sort example.

5.10   Comparing tree profiles

A classic tree problem is to determine whether two trees have the same profile. By a **profile** we mean the sequence of node terms that is determined by a left-to-right walk (preorder traversal) around the base of the tree, starting at the root and visiting each node exactly once: Figure 5.17 shows an example. A list provides a suitable representation of the profile. Figure 5.18 demonstrates that trees do not have to be equal to share a common profile, for each tree shown has the profile

[6, 5, 2, 3, 1]

even though the trees are clearly different.

To solve the problem for arbitrary trees let us define a relation same_profile, where the logical reading of same_profile(T1, T2) is: T1 and T2

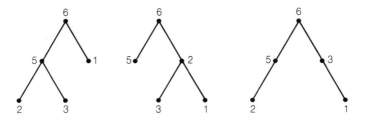

Figure 5.18   Trees with the same profile.

are binary trees having identical profiles. A procedure for the relation is:

mode same_profile(tree1?, tree2?).

same_profile(T1, T2) ←
    profile(T1, L1),
    profile(T2, L2),
    L1 == L2.

(Recall that == is the test unification primitive – it cannot bind variables in either argument). Given the expected meaning for profile, the logical correctness of this program is obvious. The modes of profile will be

mode profile(tree?, list↑).

and a suitable definition will be given below. Operationally, the same_profile program is expected to check that the relation holds for two given trees. A call such as

← same_profile(T1, T2).

where T1 and T2 are bound to terms representing trees, will reduce to the conjunction

← profile(T1, L1), profile(T2, L2), L1 == L2.

This creates the network of concurrent processes shown in Figure 5.19. Providing that the generation and comparison of profiles is incremental, the behaviour should be highly efficient. For the == process will try to match the pairs of corresponding node terms concurrently as these are made available by the profile processes. The key point is that as soon as a pair is received that do not agree, the matching and hence also the

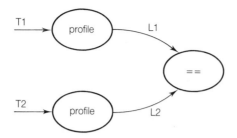

Figure 5.19   The network created by a call to same_profile

same_profile parent process, will fail. For example, if the profiles of the two trees T1 and T2 are actually

L1 = [1, 2, 3, 4, 5, 6, 7]
L2 = [1, 2, 3, 5, 8, 13, 21]

then after a sufficient period of time, the profile process working on the first tree will have produced for L1 the binding

L1 = [1, 2, 3, 4|RestL1]

Potentially, as soon as the second profile process has generated a binding for L2 that is complete at least as far as

L2 = [1, 2, 3, 5|RestL2]

then the == process can detect the mismatch between the two partial profiles. At that point the evaluation will immediately terminate: no work will be wasted on generating and comparing the remainders of the profiles. Of course, where two trees *do* have identical profiles then each profile will have to be produced in its entirety.

Let us now turn to the profile relation. What is required is to find the profile list corresponding to a given tree. Using the same representation for trees as before, the tree is either empty or it is a term of the form tree(Left, Root, Right). In the former case the relationship is trivial: it is

profile(empty, []).

For a general non-empty tree, the rule giving the profile can be induced from examples like the ones shown in the diagrams. The profile is a list that

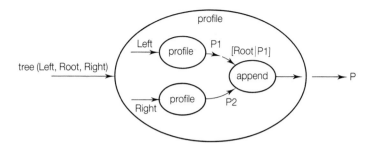

Figure 5.20   A profile process.

always starts with the term at the root. Next come the terms that make up the profile of the left subtree. Finally, the list is completed by the terms from the right subtree profile. We could write this as

profile = [root] + [left subtree profile] + [right subtree profile]

and a straightforward rendering of this in PARLOG, using append to implement the '+', gives the recursive clause. The definition is:

```
mode profile(tree?, list↑ ).

profile(empty, []).
profile(tree(Left, Root, Right), P) ←
    profile(Left, P1),
    profile(Right, P2),
    append([Root|P1], P2, P).
```

Operationally this behaves satisfactorily. A profile evaluation process spawns three concurrent sub-processes (see Figure 5.20). The recursive sub-processes construct the profiles of the left and right subtrees and the append combines the results. The behaviour of append is such that the required output list will be generated incrementally, with the root term produced immediately at the list head. This is exactly what is required for the same_profile program.

We can now test the same_profile program. Its performance should be quite impressive but there is still some scope for improvement. Firstly, the == condition in the procedure is actually unnecessary and it can be removed. If we re-write the clause as

```
same_profile(T1, T2) ←
    profile(T1, L),
    profile(T2, L).
```

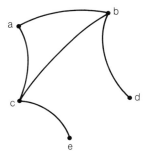

Figure 5.21   A graph.

then the logic obviously remains unchanged but also, less obviously perhaps, the behaviour is still correct. With this version the two concurrent profile sub-processes will compete to make the bindings for L. Whichever process runs more slowly will in effect only be *checking* that its tree's profile agrees with the bindings that have already been made for L by the faster process. If at some point the slower process generates a term that mismatches the corresponding term that has already been supplied then the evaluation fails, exactly as before. This somewhat unusual behaviour is an exploitation of PARLOG's use of full unification for output: usually a call variable in an output argument position is unbound prior to the call, but this need not always be so as the above demonstrates to good purpose.

A second gain in performance would arise from the use of a 'difference list' representation for tree profiles. A difference list specifies a normal list L, say, by means of a list pair [L1, L2], where the pair is such that L2 is a 'tail-end' sublist of L1 and the difference between the pair gives L. In PARLOG procedures the list argument L is usually replaced by a pair of arguments L1 and L2, one input and the other output, in the difference list representation. The main advantage is that list concatenation becomes very efficient – the need for an explicit call to append, such as the one in the profile procedure, can be avoided. The disadvantage is that procedures using difference lists are harder to understand. Difference lists have been quite widely covered in the logic programming literature and the interested reader may like to treat this topic as an investigation.

5.11   Finding a path in a graph

A graph is a data structure consisting of a set of nodes connected by arcs: Figure 5.21 shows a simple example. Graphs can be regarded as a generalization of trees and they find many applications in representing electrical circuits, games, maps, semantic relationships, and so on. Depending on the application the arcs could be annotated with arrows or labels.

Many problems are associated with graphs and much has been written about them. Here we shall treat only one of the more common problems, which is to find a path between a given pair of nodes. For example, given the pair of nodes a and d in Figure 5.21 a valid path would be

a → c → b → d

This is not the only path and neither is it the shortest (in terms of the number of arcs). However we shall not insist on the shortest path. For our purposes, it will be enough to develop a program that returns some valid path (of whatever length) whenever one or more such paths between the specified endpoints exists.

We could represent a graph in PARLOG in several ways. Here we shall use a set of assertions that specify the 'neighbours' of each node, as follows:

```
neighbours(a, [b, c]).
neighbours(b, [a, c, d]).
neighbours(c, [b, a, e]).
neighbours(d, [b]).
neighbours(e, [c].
```

The first of these clauses represents the fact that in Figure 5.21 the node a is attached via arcs to the nodes b and c. This kind of representation contains redundancies in the sense that each arc is specified twice, but on the plus side it means that all the arcs attached to any one node are specified by the same single clause. So by declaring the relation with modes

```
mode neighbours(node?, nextnodes↑ ).
```

we will be able to obtain via a call of the type

```
← neighbours(Node, NextNodes).
```

a list NextNodes of all the nodes attached by an arc to Node. Obviously, one of these nodes must form the next step in any path from Node.

We must now define a relation path, where the logical reading of path(Start, End, P) should be: P is a path connecting node Start to node End. Operationally we want the program to construct paths between given endpoints and so the modes will be

```
mode path(from?, to?, path↑ ).
```

To represent a path we shall use a list containing the relevant sequence of nodes. A trivial case of the relation is where the endpoints are identical so that the 'path' contains just this one node. We can represent this case by the assertion

```
path(Node, Node, [Node]).
```

In the general case the endpoints are not identical, as with the call

```
← path(a, d, Path).
```

Clearly here, Path must start with the node a. Furthermore, the remaining nodes must comprise one way to connect some neighbour of a (the neighbour that is to give the 'next step') to d. Generalizing, this suggests the clause:

```
path(Start, End, [Start|Rest]) ←
    neighbours(Start, Nodes),
    one_way(Nodes, End, Rest).
```

The one_way relation does not have the same meaning as path. Each relation specifies a path between endpoints, but where path insists on a single starting point the corresponding argument of one_way provides a list of equally acceptable alternatives. Logically the reading of one_way(StartNodes, Target, Path) should be: Path is a path from one of the points on the list StartNodes to Target.

The path clauses above seem to provide a good logical specification of what it means to be a path. But to make a procedure with correct behaviour we must guard the recursive clause so that this clause cannot be selected when the assertional clause is a candidate for a call (the sufficient tests property again). The program becomes:

```
mode path(from?, to?, path↑ ).

path(Node, Node, [Node]).
path(Start, End, [Start|Rest]) ←
    not(Start == End) :
    neighbours(Start, Nodes),
    one_way(Nodes, End, Rest).
```

The next requirement is a suitable program for one_way that behaves according to the modes

```
mode one_way(startnodes?, endnode?, path↑ ).
```

We can define this relation mainly in terms of path. Consider for example the call

```
← one_way([b, a, e], d, Path).
```

It may be possible to solve this call by solving

    ← path(b, d, Path).

in which Path uses the first node on the list as starting point. Alternatively it might be solved by the call

    ← one_way([a, e], d, Path).

in which Path starts from one of the nodes on the tail of the list. As to which of these (if either) will succeed there is no prior way of knowing – the evaluation process must be prepared to try them both. It is essential not to commit to either method until it has actually produced a path. This suggests the following PARLOG program:

```
mode one_way(startnodes?, target?, path↑ ).

one_way([Node|Nodes], Target, Path) ←
    path(Node, Target, Path) :
    true.
one_way([Node|Nodes], Target, Path) ←
    one_way(Nodes, Target, Path) :
    true.
```

Logically the correctness of this definition is plain. For it states that given a list of possible starting points and a target, a path could begin at the first starting point or it could begin at one of the others. Interestingly, with this procedure we have managed to define the path and one_way relations each partly in terms of the other: this is a **mutual recursion**.

    The behaviour is also interesting. Figure 5.22 illustrates the evaluation of the query

    ← path(c, d, Path).

The evaluation process for this call quickly commits to the second path clause and supplies the output binding

    Path = [c|RestPath]

Two sub-processes are spawned of which one, the one-way sub-process, suspends until the other neighbours sub-process produces the list [b, a, e] as the neighbours of c, at which point the one_way call becomes

    ← one_way([b, a, e], d, RestPath).

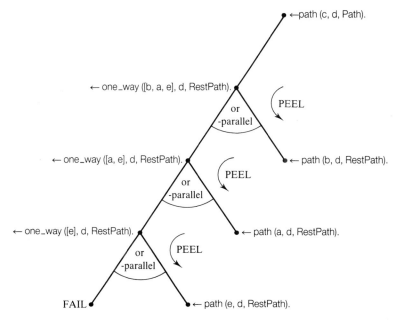

Figure 5.22 Behaviour of a path process.

Because of the definition of the one_way procedure, the query process now reduces to a guards race. The race is between the process that evaluates the call

    ← path(b, d, RestPath).

representing the guard test for the first one_way clause, and the process that evaluates

    ← one_way([a, e], d, RestPath).

representing the second guard test. These two run in or-parallel fashion and the success of either process will cause the termination of the other, and will also cause the query process to succeed and terminate.

Let us ignore the spawned path process and follow the fate of one_way. We can anticipate that this process will create another guards race. One process will evaluate the guard call

    ← path(a, d, RestPath).

and the other is an or-parallel process process to evaluate

    ← one_way([e], d, RestPath).

Again, let us ignore the path process. The lattermost one_way process again reduces to a guards race between processes that test the guard calls

    ← path(e, d, RestPath).

and

    ← one_way([], d, RestPath).

This final process will fail. Hence the outcome of the parent process depends solely on the outcome of the path guards test.

What is happening here? The original path query to find a path starting from the node c has produced three other path processes to evaluate respectively

    ← path(b, d, RestPath).
    ← path(a, d, RestPath).
    ← path(e, d, RestPath).

each of which represents an attempt to construct a path starting from one of the neighbours of c. In effect, the one_way procedure has 'peeled' down the list of neighbours and for each neighbour it has created an individual path process. Although the peeling is sequential (it follows the order in which nodes occur in the relevant neighbours clause) we may reasonably assume that relative to the lifetime of the path processes it does not take long. In effect the path processes run concurrently, with each one being peeled into existence momentarily after its predecessor. Because of the racing guards semantics, as soon as any one of the peeled path processes manages to succeed the others will be halted and the original query process will succeed and terminate.

Effectively the program represents a very simple algorithm for finding a path between two given nodes. It first finds all the immediate neighbours of the start node and for each neighbour it creates a separate individual path-finding process. We could think of the evaluation as a search for the target node that propagates symmetrically outwards from the starting node, as if spreading from the hub of a wheel along the spokes (see Figure 5.23). Unfortunately, this implies an exponential growth in the number of processes that is likely to be even more prohibitive than that for the earlier on_tree program. An interesting exercise is to run the program on your computer with graphs of increasing complexity: you may be surprised to see how quickly your machine's performance degrades.

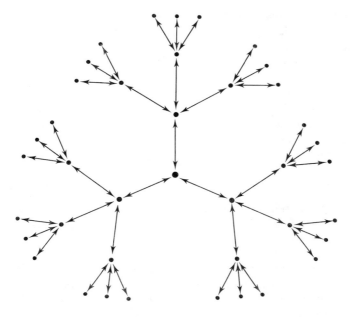

Figure 5.23 Exponential growth.

The costs need not be quite so severe. Notice that any evaluation is likely to produce many duplicated processes: for example, in Figure 5.22 each of the peeled processes will include among its spawned child processes an offspring to evaluate the call

← path(c, d, RestPath2).

(since c is a neighbour of b, a, and e, and vice-versa). Each of these is a replica of the original query process! Some form of **loop prevention** could be implemented to eliminate this redundancy, and loop prevention could also ensure a terminating behaviour for calls seeking non-existent paths (our program does not terminate with such calls because there is always an ever-increasing number of replica processes to work on and to further replicate).

Note that our program is non-incremental in its output of finished paths. Although the query

← path(c, d, Path).

immediately produces the binding Path = [c|RestPath], the variable RestPath thereafter remains unbound until the path is completely constructed, at which point it receives the correct value in a single binding. From a problem-solving viewpoint, it could not be otherwise because the evaluation cannot commit itself to any nodes after c (a certain first step!) until it is known that the nodes actually do contribute to a path: that is, until the path is completed. Operationally, late commitment is an inevitable consequence of the fact that the search for a path becomes a guards race (and hence no output can be delivered until one of the guard evaluations succeeds). Unfortunately this means that any concurrent process that is the consumer of a path may remain suspended until the path process has finished its activity.

SUMMARY

This chapter has described a variety of concurrent algorithms implemented as PARLOG procedures. Some of the main points are summarized below.

- The data primitive enabled us to define swrite_list, a useful program for displaying lists. Unlike the write primitive, swrite_list is 'suspendable' and can run concurrently with a process that may incrementally produce the list's value.

- The on_both program that specifies a term belonging to each of two lists provided a simple example of and-parallelism. The on_either program demonstrated or-parallelism and the concept of a guards race. find_on_both illustrated the point that a 'finding' program for a relation typically requires a different logical formulation from a 'checking' program.

- Combining two lists into one was made possible by the merge program, that featured non-deterministic behaviour. When data is available on both input lists the choice of next term is left to the evaluation process that must select between two candidate clauses. Our version of partition on the other hand was deterministic, with no more than one candidate clause for any call. Both programs demonstrated incremental production of output terms.

- Hoare's quicksort is a sorting algorithm based on a divide-and-conquer strategy. Our implementation used partition to divide an input list of data into two parts that were sorted by concurrent recursive sub-processes and then re-combined by means of append.

- The on_tree program performed an or-parallel search of a binary tree, with the evaluation process forking into two at each node. If the tree is ordered then a search using the on_ord_tree program can avoid the exponential growth of processes.

- Two versions of the list-to-tree program were formulated giving rise to contrasting behaviours. make_tree specified an algorithm that was non-deterministic and sequential. The algorithm specified by make_ord_tree was deterministic and concurrent.

● The same_profile program compared profiles for two trees. An efficient performance was achieved by an algorithm that incrementally constructed and compared the tree profiles.

● In the path-finding program the search for a path from a given node investigated all paths from the node concurrently. The search was implemented by a form of guards race that gave rise to a 'peeling' or-parallel behaviour.

EXERCISES

5.1 Write some programs for typical list-processing operations such as reversing lists, inserting terms into and deleting terms from lists, computing the length of a list, finding a list permutation, etc. Implement your programs and study their behaviour.

5.2 Improve and extend upon the output facilities provided by the swrite_list program. Some suggestions are as follows.

(a) If your computer system supports windowing, implement a variation of the procedure to support windows. Your variation could be declared by

mode winwrite_list(windowid?, list?).

where windowid identifies a screen window. (You will need to consult reference manuals for details of window management for your system). This will enable your programs to produce multiple concurrent output streams that are directed into separate screen windows.

(b) Extend swrite_list so that it (a) produces proper punctuation (brackets, spaces and commas) for lists and (b) can cope with nested lists.

(c) Write a program for swrite_term that can operate upon a PARLOG term of any arbitrary type (including a list containing structures or a structure containing lists).

5.3 Investigate PARLOG implementations of some other common sorting algorithms (for example insertion sort, exchange sort and tree sort). Experiment with different formulations of the logic and alternative control operators and study the effects.

5.4 The following declarations relate to binary tree-processing programs, where the intended logical reading of each relation should be obvious. Write a logic definition for each relation that behaves satisfactorily given the specified modes and describe the algorithms that result when these definitions are executed as PARLOG procedures.

```
mode nodecount(tree?, totalnodes↑ ).
mode balanced(tree?).
mode delete_node(intree?, termtodelete?, outtree↑ ).
mode maxnode(numerictree?, maxnodeterm↑ ).
```

5.5 Try to transform the path-finding program into one that *checks* that a given sequence of nodes represents a path between two given endpoints. Explain any difficulties that you encounter.

6

Interacting processes

6.1 Producers and consumers
6.2 Two-way communication
6.3 Client-server interactions
6.4 Two-way synchronization
6.5 Exploiting incremental feedback
6.6 Incomplete messages

6.7 Solving the response-routing
    problem
6.8 Lazy producers
6.9 Lazy client-server interactions
6.10 Biased and fair behaviour
     Summary
     Exercises

PREVIEW   The previous chapters have shown how the evaluation of a conjunction of relation calls can give rise to a network of concurrent processes. We now focus on the range and types of interaction between processes that can be obtained by different logical formulations. The theme of 'guessers and tellers' is maintained throughout the chapter to demonstrate a variety of interacting process scenarios: for each scenario the underlying ideas are identified and generalized. Recurring topics include those of inter-process communication and synchronization, client-server interactions, avoidance of deadlock and the power of 'incomplete messages' techniques. Thus although the treatment is informal, the chapter describes concepts central to many applications of concurrent programming.

6.1 Producers and consumers

A sometime popular children's game is that of 'guessers and tellers'. There are many variations on the theme but the basic idea is for the children who are playing 'guessers' to hit upon a number or object that has been thought up by another child who acts as 'teller'. This game provides a useful example of communicating concurrent processes. We shall see how each of several variations can be modelled by the evaluation of a suitably formulated PARLOG program: in doing so we shall be learning techniques that are applicable to concurrent programming in general.

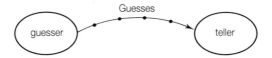

Figure 6.1   Simplest form of game.

The simplest possible version of the game is illustrated in Figure 6.1. Here we suppose that there is a single guessing child and that communication takes place in one direction only, from the guesser to the teller. The guesser advances a stream of proposals while the teller merely listens in silence. When and if the secret object – which is mutually agreed to be a small positive integer, say – is guessed the teller simply ceases to pay attention to any guesses that may follow. This version would be very dull to play but it is a good starting point for PARLOG modelling.

There is an obvious PARLOG representation for this version. A pair of processes like those of of Figure 6.1 could be created by a query containing a conjunction of and-parallel calls such as:

    ← guesser(Guesses), teller(Guesses).   **M1**

where the modes are

    mode guesser(↑), mode teller(?).

The evaluation of the query will give rise to two concurrent processes, one to model each player. Notice how the communication between the players is represented by the shared variable, the value of which can be a list produced incrementally by the guesser process.

A straightforward definition for the guesser relation is as follows.

    mode guesser(guesses↑).

    guesser(Guesses) ← integers(0, 1000, Guesses).

With this rendering the logical reading of guesser(G) is: G is the list [0, 1, 2, 3, .., 1000]. Operationally the guesser process just reduces to an integers sub-process that does the real work. It generates the value of the list incrementally with a succession of bindings of the form

    Guesses = [0|Guesses1]
            = [0, 1|Guesses2]
            = [0, 1, 2|Guesses3]

            . . .

            = [0, 1, 2, ..., 1000]

that can be viewed as the production of a stream of terms, as explained in Section 4.8.6. The behaviour of this process is always the same: it laboriously generates guesses exhaustively through the entire range. In the absence of feedback from the teller process this seems as good a playing strategy as any.

The teller process knows nothing about the guesser's strategy. It simply inspects the guesses as they arrive. A suitable definition is as follows:

```
mode teller(guesses?).

teller([Guess|Guesses]) ←
    correct(Guess) :
    true.
teller([Guess|Guesses]) ←
    not(correct(Guess)) :
    teller(Guesses).
```

where the procedure for correct can be

```
mode correct(guess?).

correct(107).
```

or something similar. Logically, this definition gives to teller(G) the meaning: G is a list containing a term Guess that satisfies correct(Guess). Operationally, a teller process tests the head term of the list and if this term is not the correct answer, it commits to the second clause and spawns a teller sub-process to test the remainder of the list. For example, on receiving the first binding for Guesses the teller call is

```
← teller([0|Guesses1]).
```

and assuming that the guard test correct(0) fails, it spawns a sub-process to evaluate

```
← teller(Guesses1).
```

which awaits another guess for checking. When the binding Guesses1 = [1|Guesses2] becomes available, the sub-process similarly compares 1 to the correct answer and so on. Thus the stream of terms produced by the guesser is consumed one term at a time by the teller. As soon as a term Guess is supplied that satisfies correct(Guess) the corresponding teller sub-process commits to the first clause and terminates, causing the query teller process to do likewise.

Notice that with these definitions the two processes specified in M1 above could run at quite different speeds. The only synchronization between the processes is that arising from the input mode of the argument of the teller relation, which means that this process cannot run ahead of the guesser process. But there is no constraint on how fast the guesser process may progress and there is nothing to prevent this process from producing guesses at a rate that greatly exceeds that at which they can be tested by the teller process. Of course whether this happens is system dependent: if it does happen then no harm need be done (a PARLOG variable can be regarded as implementing a store of infinite size). Perhaps we could think of the guessing player specified by M1 as one who scribbles guesses as fast as possible onto a piece of paper while the teller struggles to keep pace with the checking.

If possible you should check that this program does work. It is a good idea to try it with a query such as

← guesser(Guesses), teller(Guesses), swrite_list(Guesses).

where swrite_list is as defined previously. The solution to the query will be a list value for the variable that represents the entire history of guesses, with the guesser's first effort at the head of the list. The correct answer will be on the list but not (necessarily) as the final term.

Generalization

The interaction between processes specified by M1 (along with our definitions) is typical of the simplest kind of stream interaction. One process is the producer of the value of a list for which another process is the consumer. A shared variable acts as the communication channel: the incremental binding of the variable to the value of the list can be regarded as the sending of a stream of terms down the channel from the producer to the consumer. The input constraint forces the consumer process to wait for data to arrive on the channel, but there is no such constraint on the producer which can run at an arbitrary rate.

The concept of a 'store of infinite size' is fine in theory, but no real system will be able to achieve it. In some situations the racing-ahead of a producer process could be harmful: its data may flood the (finite) available store. This is an issue to which we shall return later.

6.2   Two-way communication

The communication described above is one-directional. In consequence the game continues longer than it should for the guessing player, who would continue generating integers forever were it not for a fortunate restriction of guesses to a finite range. Let us try to model a more realistic version of the game in which the telling player agrees to return a one-off item of feedback to the guesser's efforts: the moment of success will be 'flagged' by a single communication in the other direction, hopefully enabling both players rather than just the telling player to cease play at the appropriate moment (see Figure 6.2).

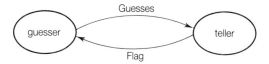

Figure 6.2 A two-way communication.

One way to implement the feedback is to introduce a second variable that is shared between the calls. Hence the query now becomes

← guesser(Guesses, Flag), teller(Guesses, Flag). **M2**

The producer of Flag is the teller process, so the modes are

mode guesser(guesses↑, flag?), mode teller(guesses?, flag↑).

We shall modify the definition of teller given previously so that the Flag variable remains unbound until the correct guess appears, at which point it shall become bound to some suitable token. Any arbitrary constant such as got_it, say, could be used as a token providing it is understood by the guesser process as the signal of a correct guess. A definition for teller that meets this specification is:

```
mode teller(guesses?, flag↑ ).

teller([Guess|Guesses], got_it) ←
    correct(Guess) :
    true.
teller([Guess|Guesses], Flag) ←
    not (correct(Guess)) :
    teller(Guesses, Flag).
```

The test-commit-output-spawn behaviour of a PARLOG process will ensure that the got_it term is output only on receipt of the correct guess.

The guesser procedure must also be modified. Instead of spawning a sub-process producing guesses in a fixed range it should now spawn a process producing integers only while Flag remains unbound. This suggests the definition:

```
mode guesser(guesses↑, flag?).

guesser(Guesses, Flag) ←
    while_guess(0, Guesses, Flag).
```

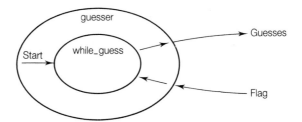

Figure 6.3   Dataflow with while_guess.

where while_guess will have modes declared by

mode while_guess(start?, guesses↑, flag?).

To define while_guess it will help to think about the behaviour required of a process that evaluates a call of the form

← while_guess(Start, Guesses, Flag).

(see Figure 6.3). In the case where the value of Flag is got_it, a correct guess has been signalled by the teller process. No further play is necessary and so the empty list can be output as the value for Guesses. (We may disregard the value supplied for Start – we might expect it to be the correct answer that has just been flagged, but see below). This gives the assertion

while_guess(Start, [], got_it).

In the other case Flag is tested and found to be still unbound. This suggests that more guesses are necessary. Here the value produced for Guesses should be [Start|RestInts], where RestInts represents future guesses that are to begin at Start+1. These future guesses will be produced by a sub-process that inherits the same Flag variable. We can specify this case as follows:

```
while_guess(Start, [Start|RestInts], Flag) ←
    var(Flag) :
    Next is Start + 1,
    while_guess(Next, RestInts, Flag).
```

The guard call features PARLOG's var primitive. This primitive is related to data in that it is used to test the binding of a variable. The behaviour of a call var(X) is to succeed if X is an unbound variable and fail otherwise. This implements the necessary test on the Flag variable in the above procedure.

Bringing this together, the definition for while_guess becomes

```
mode while_guess(start?, guesses↑, flag?).
```

```
while_guess(Start, [], got_it).
while_guess(Start, [Start|RestInts], Flag) ←
    var(Flag) :
    Next is Start + 1,
    while_guess(Next, RestInts, Flag).
```

You should now test this program if possible. A suitable query for testing is

```
← guesser(Guesses, Flag), teller(Guesses, Flag), swrite_list(Guesses).
```

where swrite_list has the usual definition.

The test may reveal a slight flaw: the value produced for Guesses could be a longer list than is strictly necessary. That is, it might not end abruptly with the correct guess as it should do if the guesser process terminates promptly. Depending on your system, the list could contain one or more additional integers.

The explanation is fairly simple. In M2 as with M1 there is no constraint on the rate of progress of the guesser process. It could produce integers much faster than the teller process can check them. If so then by the time the teller gets around to inspecting the term representing the correct guess, the guesser may already have produced others. The got_it response arrives too late to prevent this process from doing the extra work; and notice that there is no way in which the guesser process can identify which of its guesses achieved the success.

Generalization

This interaction exemplifies a two-directional communication between processes with a separate channel to implement each direction of communication. Each process acts as producer for data on one channel and consumer for data on the other. But the channels here implement contrasting types of communication: the Guesses channel implements stream (incremental) communication whilst the Flag channel implements single-binding (non-incremental) communication.

The latter type of communication is very simple but the example shows its main limitation. A single-binding feedback communication provides no 'tight' synchronization: it cannot be used to control the progress of a process in the precise way that can be achieved by the input constraint acting upon the consumer of a stream communication. In passing, the example suggests how dangerous it could be to make (unwarranted) assumptions about the relative speeds of concurrent processes. Unless the processes are tightly synchronized, the result could easily be a 'psychopathic' program that behaves incorrectly on some systems but correctly on others.

Actually, the var primitive is potentially dangerous in itself. A call var(X) may succeed at one instant where it would have failed an instant later, when the variable X had become bound by some other concurrent call. The primitive is 'non-logical' and programs in which it appears may have no convincing logical reading. (The related data primitive is logically less troublesome – since a call to it can never fail, data(X) can always be read simply as true.)

6.3   Client-server interactions

Before improving upon the method of feedback communication it is worth considering briefly how the model above could be extended so as to represent multiple concurrent guessing players. We now envisage a rather disorderly version of the game in which several guessing players generate guesses, each operating as though the others did not exist. Somehow the teller must cope with them all. We shall suppose that the teller is again willing to communicate only a single item of feedback in the form of a got_it message to be sent on receipt of a correct guess. The message should be 'broadcast' to all guessers so that the game may stop for everyone at that point.

Representing this version in PARLOG should require no change to the definition of the guesser procedure. This is because each guesser process is to behave exactly like the single example in the previous model. However, it may appear that the teller procedure needs a radical alteration. For does not a teller process require multiple pairs of input and output channels – one pair to implement the communication with each guesser? If so then the teller relation will become multi-argument, and will presumably require a complex definition. Worse, the definition will need to be updated whenever there is a change in the number of players.

Fortunately a multi-argument relation is not required, as Figure 6.4 shows. This represents a network that accommodates two guesser processes and that will be created by the PARLOG query

```
← guesser1(Guesses1, Flag),
  guesser2(Guesses2, Flag),
  merge(Guesses1, Guesses2, MergedGuesses),
  teller(MergedGuesses, Flag).                          M3
```

The two guess streams are combined into a single stream by a merge process, so that the teller process still operates upon only a single input stream of guesses. Only one output channel is needed because the feedback is the same for both guesser processes: the commonality is implemented in the query by the appearance of the same variable Flag in both calls.

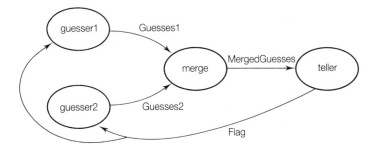

Figure 6.4 Merging two guess streams.

With this model there is no need to change any of the previous definitions. Even from the point of view of the teller process, nothing has changed: the process just consumes a stream of guesses received on one channel and implements a single-binding feedback communication on the other, as before. Of course, the program for merge will need to be updated if there is to be a change in the number of guessers. For two guessers the program can be the one given in the previous chapter: an n-way merge relation can be defined by a clause containing n−1 calls to the standard merge. However it seems preferable to be prepared to modify the definition of the utility merge procedure rather than those of the problem-specific guesser and teller relations.

You may like to try out this version. As programs for guesser1 and guesser2 you could cosmetically modify the earlier program for guesser so that these processes generate guesses over different integer intervals. But notice that this program inherits the defect of single-binding feedback communication as noted above – the guessers are liable to run ahead of the teller, so that by the time the got_it response is communicated each guesser may have produced more integers than is strictly necessary.

Generalization

This interaction can be regarded as a simple kind of **client-server** interaction. In general this is an interaction between a server or resource process (one that controls access to some data or to some external device such as a printer) and one or more client processes that require periodic access to the resource. Here the teller process controls access to the value of the correct answer and this process acts as server to the client guesser processes. By using a merge to combine the input streams the same resource process can service several clients. Because the merge specifies a sequential access to the resource a **mutual exclusion** behaviour, whereby one client's period of access to the resource must not overlap with that of any other, can be

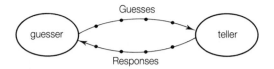

Figure 6.5   Stream feedback communication.

implemented where necessary. Also, providing the merge process is 'fair' in its treatment of the client streams an equitable usage of the resource is certain even if the clients behave differently (by supplying data at varying rates, for example). However, the standard merge is not guaranteed to behave fairly and this is the subject of a later section.

Another important feature of M3 is the **broadcasting** of feedback. Broadcasting refers to the fact that a PARLOG producer process does not select the intended consumer for its data – the data is available to any process or processes that happens to be connected to the right channel (that is, evaluates a call that shares the appropriate variable). But usually a resource process is expected to give different feedback to different clients, making the broadcasting technique inappropriate.

6.4   Two-way synchronization

Let us return to the single-guesser version of the game and imagine that we have a less taciturn telling player who is prepared to provide a limited kind of feedback to each individual guess. The guessing player naturally exploits this by waiting for the response to one guess before venturing another. A typical interaction might be something like this:

```
Guesses   – 0   1   ....   103   104   105   106   107
Responses –   no  no .... no    no    no    no    no   got_it

           ———— Time ————▶
```

This strict interleaving of communication corresponds to a more reasonable and 'conversational' behaviour on the part of the two players.

Figure 6.5 pictures the interaction. The only difference from M2 is the intention to make the shared variable Responses representative of a stream of terms that will be produced incrementally, rather than representing a solitary constant the value of which is produced in a single binding. For Responses the final value will be a list of the form [no, no, no, ..., got_it]. The teller must generate the list synchronously with the receipt of the guesser's integers. The PARLOG model of the interaction can be created by the query

```
← guesser(Guesses, Responses), teller(Guesses, Responses).        M4
```

It is often easier to define the procedure first for the more 'passive' process in an interaction, so let us start with the teller. This process must output a message no for each input term that does not specify the correct answer. For an input that is correct, it should output got_it and terminate. A suitable definition is:

```
mode teller(guesses?, responses↑).

teller([Guess|Guesses], [no|Responses]) ←
        not(correct(Guess)) :
        teller(Guesses, Responses).
teller([Guess|Guesses], [got_it]) ←
        correct(Guess) :
        true.
```

The operational view often seems more natural when we are constructing what is essentially a model of behaviour. But the program does nonetheless give the relation a clear logical reading. You should satisfy yourself that the meaning of teller(Guesses, Responses) is: Responses is a list ending in got_it and containing one term no for each term in the list Guesses up to the first term G that satisfies correct(G). By analysing the logical reading we obtain a cross-check on the understanding of the program that we have gained from studying its operational interpretation.

In a conversation one participant must be prepared to speak first or the result will be deadlock. Here, the responsibility to open communication clearly lies with the guesser. Suitable behaviour will be assured if the process that evaluates the call

```
← guesser(Guesses, Responses).
```

in M4 could immediately supply the binding Guesses = [0|Guesses1] and spawn a sub-process to generate suitable bindings to Guesses1 in syncronization with the receipt of Responses. This suggests the definition

```
mode guesser(guesses↑, responses?).

guesser([0|Guesses1], Responses) ←
        synch_guess(0, Guesses1, Responses).
```

Notice that the spawned synch_guess sub-process must immediately suspend. This is because 0 has been sent as a first message on the Guesses channel and the response to this guess coming from the teller will determine whether the guesser process should terminate or produce further guesses. If the response no is indicated by the receipt of the binding Responses = [no|Responses1] then synch_guess should send the integer 1 as a next guess, and so on. Subsequently it should continue to produce guesses in synchronization with the teller's feedback until the response got_it is obtained, at which point the process should terminate. A suitable definition is:

> mode synch_guess(lastguess?, nextguesses↑, responses?).

> synch_guess(N, [], [got_it]).
> synch_guess(N, [NextGuess|FutureGuesses], [no|Responses]) ←
>   NextGuess is N + 1,
>   synch_guess(NextGuess, FutureGuesses, Responses).

These procedures give to guesser(Guesses, Responses) the logical reading: for some K, Guesses is a list [0, 1, 2, ..., K] and Responses is a list containing K terms no followed by the term got_it. Notice that when conjoined with the logical reading of teller, this makes the logical solution for Guesses in M4 to be: Guesses is the list [0, 1, 2, ..., K] where K is the smallest non-negative integer such that correct(K) is true. This is exactly what is required.

If possible you should implement this version and run M4 to satisfy yourself that the behaviour is as described, and in particular that the teller process does terminate on reaching the correct guess. On a system that supports windowing you should be able to arrange that the bindings made to Guesses and Responses are written concurrently into different screen windows; otherwise a query such as

> ← guesser(Guesses, Responses),
>   teller(Guesses, Responses),
>   swrite_list(Responses) &
>   swrite_list(Guesses).

will be useful. This query will display the teller's responses concurrently as they are produced and when the game ends it will display the 'history list' of the guesses that gave rise to them.

Generalization

This interaction features two communication channels with one-way stream communication on each channel. Such an arrangement can synchronize two processes tightly to one another, as demonstrated by the strict alternation between guesses and responses in the interaction above. Notice that the guesser producer process can no longer run uncontrollably ahead of the teller since the former is constrained by the supply of feedback just as the latter is contrained by the supply of guesses.

Non-termination, and deadlock in particular, is probably the main pitfall to avoid in programming such interactions. Given that a solution to the query logically exists, and given that the program has the sufficient tests property so that a call will not commit to an inappropriate clause, then only the non-termination of some process can prevent a successful operational computation.

Unfortunately deadlock can have subtle causes. Consider this example: a plausible change to the non-recursive clause of the teller procedure is to re-specify it as

```
teller([Guess], [got_it]) ←
    correct(Guess) :
    true.                                            BAD
```

It is a *plausible* change since intuitively, the final response should 'correspond to' the final guess. But with this definition the teller process will deadlock. The deadlock will arise when the teller process eventually reduces to the call

```
← teller([107|GuessesN], ResponsesN).
```

For this call, input matching will suspend with the BAD clause (since the output substitution GuessesN = [] would violate the input constraint) and the recursive clause is a non-candidate (because correct(107) succeeds and hence the guard test fails). To make matters worse, when the teller process deadlocks so too will the guesser since this process will be left waiting for a response that will never materialize.

The kind of error that is represented by BAD could result from a confusion on the programmer's part about the communication sequence that terminates the interaction. It is *not* the case that the answer integer is sent to the teller as the 'final' guess – from the guesser's viewpoint, this integer merely happens to be one further term in a list the tail of which is expected to specify successors. It only *becomes* final when the teller identifies it as correct, sends out the message got_it and hence enables the guesser process to bind the tail variable to the empty list.

6.5 Exploiting incremental feedback

If the telling player can be persuaded to give a little more information in responding to each guess then the guesser should be able to do better than merely generate successive integers. Suppose that the teller is prepared to answer any guess with one of the messages high, low or got_it. Then an intelligent game could result in an interaction such as:

```
Guesses   – 500     250     125     62      93      ... 107
Responses –      high    high    high    low     low     ...     got_it
```

——————— Time ——————→

By using a **binary search** strategy the guesser is now able to locate the correct answer much more efficiently. Each feedback can be used to halve the interval in which the answer is known to lie.

To model this variation of the game does not require much new effort. The interaction between players is still as illustrated by Figure 6.5 and the query M4 can create the corresponding PARLOG processes. We need only modify the definitions for guesser and teller to allow for the different types of message that are to flow along the communication channels.

In the procedure for teller two clauses supplying high and low responses replace the previous single clause that merely supplied no to any incorrect guess. The new definition is:

```
mode teller(guesses?, responses↑ ).

teller([Guess|Guesses], [got_it]) ←
    correct(Guess) :
    true.
teller([Guess|Guesses], [high|Responses]) ←
    high(Guess) :
    teller(Guesses, Responses).
teller([Guess|Guesses], [low|Responses]) ←
    low(Guess) :
    teller(Guesses, Responses).
```

The definition of correct can be as before. A simple way to define high is:

```
mode high(guess?).

high(Guess) ← Guess > 107.
```

and a similar procedure can be specified for low.

The guesser process begins with the knowledge that the correct answer is an integer in the interval from 0 to 1000. It should produce the first guess of 500 immediately and should spawn a sub-process that will produce future guesses synchronously with the teller's replies. A suitable procedure is:

```
mode guesser(guesses↑, responses?).

guesser([500|Guesses], Responses) ←
    synch_guess(interval(0, 500, 1000), Guesses, Responses).
```

Thus the first argument of synch_guess now specifies more than just the value of the most recently generated guess. It is a term of the form

interval(Min, G, Max)

where G is the most recently made guess and Min and Max are the endpoints of the interval into which the search has become narrowed. If the response high is returned from the teller then the guesser knows to restrict the search to the left half of this interval, the midpoint of which should give the new guess. The response low can be handled similarly. This suggests the following definition for synch_guess:

```
mode synch_guess(lastinterval?, nextguesses↑, responses?).

synch_guess(interval(Min, G, Max), [], [got_it]).
synch_guess(interval(Min, G, Max), [NextGuess|Guesses], [high|Responses]) ←
    NewMax is G − 1,
    midpoint(Min, NewMax, NextGuess),
    synch_guess(interval(Min, NextGuess, NewMax), Guesses, Responses).
synch_guess(interval(Min, G, Max), [NextGuess|Guesses], [low|Responses]) ←
    NewMin is G + 1,
    midpoint(NewMin, Max, NextGuess),
    synch_guess(interval(NewMin, NextGuess, Max), Guesses, Responses).
```

This requires a definition for midpoint, where midpoint(N1, N2, M) reads logically as: M is the integer midpoint of N1 and N2. Operationally the program should output the midpoint for two integers that are input. The definition is left to the reader.

Generalization

This is a second example of a two-way synchronized interaction. It shows how stream feedback to a process can *progressively* influence the behaviour of the process (as the guesser's behaviour was determined by the sequence of high, low and got_it messages).

Unfortunately there remains a problem. Suppose that the consumer process is a client-server (resource) process that is expected to service several clients; then the difficulty again arises of routing back the replies. If we try to use merge to combine the inputs from different clients then the client-server process will have no way of knowing where to send each response. For example, consider a re-implementation of the two-guesser game with the latest definitions: as Figure 6.6 shows, we cannot simply connect the feedback stream to all guessers as we did in M3 because then each guesser will receive the responses intended for the others as well as its own (the 'broadcasting' technique is indiscriminate).

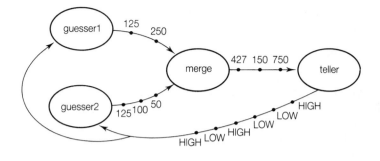

Figure 6.6   Sharing the response stream gives incorrect behaviour.

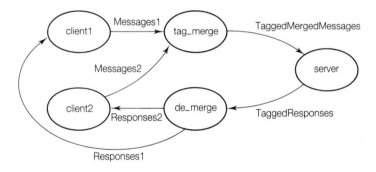

Figure 6.7   A 'message-tagging' solution to the response routing problem.

As before, we are reluctant to resort to a solution that requires that the client-server procedure should be re-defined whenever there is a change in the number of clients.

A possible solution is illustrated in Figure 6.7. This is based on the idea that each message sent by a client process might be 'stamped' or 'tagged' by a special tag_merge process with a label identifying the sender. A de_merge process then uses the tags to address the replies back to the appropriate clients. Although feasible, the price of a 'message tagging' solution to the response-routing problem seems likely to be high both in terms of logical complexity and operational overhead. Fortunately, the next section suggests that it is a price that we do not have to pay.

6.6   Incomplete messages

So far we have assumed a face-to-face interaction between guessers and tellers. However, the game could be played by mail. We can imagine a two-player version in which the guessing player sends the teller a stream of mailed message forms, each consisting of a single sheet of paper specifying a guess together with a suitable space for the teller's reply. On receiving such a message the teller writes high, low or got_it in the space and returns the sheet to the sender. To save effort, blank message forms might be pre-printed. The history of a typical message form might be:

| Guess: ___ | Guess: 125 | Guess: 125 |
| Reply: ___ | Reply: ___ | Reply: high |

| When blank | As sent by guesser | As completed by teller |

Admittedly this game would be awesomely dull but there is no denying its feasibility.

Let us consider a PARLOG model of this communication style. A totally blank message form could be represented by a term such as

   msg(Guess, Reply)

which is a structure having msg as functor. Of course, the choice of functor symbol is arbitrary. What is important is that the term contains two unbound variables corresponding to the two spaces on a blank message form: binding the variables will correspond to filling in the spaces. So the history of such a term is directly analagous to the history of a message form:

| msg(Guess, Reply) | msg(125, Reply) | msg(125, high) |

| When blank | As sent by guesser | As completed by teller |

The end product of the PARLOG interaction would be a list of completed messages that is something like

   [msg(500, high), msg(250, high), .., msg(107, got_it)]

where the value of the guess term in each message has been contributed by the guesser, and the value of the reply term has been contributed by the teller. As sent out by the guesser each term is an 'incomplete message' in that it contains a variable that has been deliberately left unbound in order to accomodate the reply.

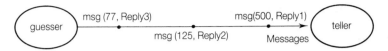

Figure 6.8   The guesser's messages contain unbound variables.

The interesting aspect of the PARLOG version is that having received a message and supplied the reply, the teller need not bother to do anything about mailing the return. This means that we shall only need one communication channel and hence, given suitable procedures, the interaction can be specified by the query

← guesser(Messages), teller(Messages).   **M5**

To understand this, consider the following. Assume that the guesser process produces for Messages a first binding of

Messages = [msg(500, Reply1)|Msgs]

representing a first guess of 500 and the supply of Reply1 as the unbound response variable. Then M5 becomes

← guesser([msg(500, Reply1)|Msgs]), teller([msg(500, Reply1)|Msgs]).

The Reply1 variable occurs in *both* calls. So when this variable becomes bound to high by the teller process, the guesser process will be able to read the value immediately. There is an *automatic* communication backwards from the teller to the guesser that removes any need for a separate feedback channel. (We shall overlook the fact that the analogy with conventional mail breaks down at this point!).

Let us modify the procedures of the previous section so as to implement the new scheme. The teller relation is the consumer of the message stream (although notice that it actually *produces* values for the unbound reply variables) and now needs only a single argument. Its mode declaration will be

mode teller(messages?).

The messages stream can be represented by [msg(Guess, Reply)|Messages] where the teller process will be supplied with an integer value for Guess and an unbound variable for Reply (see Figure 6.8). We must ensure that the three clauses for teller will result in Reply becoming bound to the appropriate feedback response for Guess.

If the value of Guess is the correct answer, the teller process should bind Reply to got_it. This can be represented by the clause

```
teller([msg(Guess, Reply)|Messages]) ←
    correct(Guess) :
    Reply = got_it.
```

The '=' in the body of the clause is PARLOG's **full unification** primitive. Logically it is read as equality: operationally a call to the primitive tries to find substitutions for variables that make the arguments identical. When the clause is the selected candidate the effect will be to bind the unbound call variable to the constant got_it that is to be communicated back to the guesser process.

The unification call here is essential. Perhaps it would be tempting to specify the clause in the form

```
teller([msg(Guess, got_it)|Messages]) ←
    correct(Guess) :
    true.
```

which is logically equivalent. But this version would not give correct behaviour. Because of the input mode, such a clause could only be a candidate for a call that *itself* supplied the constant got_it. No such call will ever be made: in our scheme, the call will always supply an unbound variable as the reply component of the message term. It is the role of the teller process to bind this variable to got_it when it finds the guess component of the message to be correct. This is the effect that the unification call is designed to achieve.

Similar modifications are needed to the other clauses. The procedure becomes:

```
mode teller(messages?).

teller([msg(Guess, Reply)|Messages]) ←
    correct(Guess) :
    Reply = got_it.
teller([msg(Guess, Reply)|Messages]) ←
    high(Guess) :
    Reply = high,
    teller(Messages).
teller([msg(Guess, Reply)|Messages]) ←
    low(Guess) :
    Reply = low,
    teller(Messages).
```

The guesser relation of the previous section must also be revised. The second argument is now redundant and the first argument should represent the new type of message list. A definition is:

```
mode guesser(guesses↑ ).

guesser([msg(500, Reply1)|Msgs]) ←
    synch_guess(interval(0, 500, 1000), Msgs, Reply1).
```

It is important that the Reply1 variable that will be sent unbound to the teller in the message containing the initial guess is also made available to the process evaluating the synch_guess call. This process should suspend until the teller has bound this variable to one of the terms high, low or got_it, at which point it should commit to a clause that determines the behaviour to follow. A suitable definition is:

```
mode synch_guess(lastinterval?, messages↑, lastresponse?).

synch_guess(interval(Min, G, Max), [], got_it).
synch_guess(interval(Min, G, Max), [msg(Guess, Reply)|MoreMsgs], high) ←
    NewMax is G − 1,
    midpoint(Min, NewMax, Guess),
    synch_guess(interval(Min, Guess, NewMax), MoreMsgs, Reply).
synch_guess(interval(Min, G, Max), [msg(Guess, Reply)|MoreMsgs], low) ←
    NewMin is G + 1,
    midpoint(NewMin, Max, Guess),
    synch_guess(interval(NewMin, Guess, Max), MoreMsgs, Reply).
```

Notice that there is no attempt in the body of the two recursive clauses to specify a value for Reply in the output message. The variable will be sent unbound by default.

Actually the messages sent by the guesser are momentarily even more 'incomplete' than intended. This is because the synch_guess process created by the guesser call will commit to a clause as soon as the teller process binds the Reply1 variable to high or low. At that point synch_guess will output the term msg(Guess, Reply) on to the Messages channel. The second variable in the term is intentionally unbound, but Guess too will be briefly unbound until the body calls of synch_guess have computed for it the appropriate value for the guess. The slight delay is just a consequence of PARLOG's test-commit-output-spawn evaluation strategy in which a process supplies output bindings before any spawned sub-processes have necessarily run to completion. Notice that no harm will result from it here because the teller procedure has the sufficient tests property – its guard evaluations will suspend until the call supplies bindings representing integer terms.

Generalization

An **incomplete message** is simply a term like any other that is communicated between two processes, except that it is a compound term (a list or structure) that initially contains at least one unbound variable. Sometimes such a term is described as 'part constructed'. The variable is deliberately left unbound by the producer process: it represents the 'space for reply' part of the message. By binding the variable the consumer process effects what is known as a **back communication** (it is 'back' in the sense that it is from the consumer to the producer, which is in the reverse direction to the main communication). The sharing of the reply variable is what effects the automatic transfer of feedback. This technique enables two-way communication between processes along a *single* communication channel.

The use of incomplete messages blurs the distinction between producers and consumers. In M5 the 'official' producer for the value of the shared variable Messages is the guesser process since the variable occurs in an output mode argument position for this relation. In practice the list that is the final value of Messages is co-operatively constructed by the two processes. The guesser process produces the binding

Messages = [msg(500, Reply1), msg(250, Reply2) .., msg(107, ReplyN)]

and the concurrent teller process contributes the bindings

Reply1 = high, Reply2 = high, ..., ReplyN = got_it

Because of the co-operative construction of the Messages variable, guesser is an example of an **incomplete producer** and teller exemplifies a **contributing consumer**. In general, a producer process for some variable is regarded as 'incomplete' if it intentionally does not bind the variable to a ground (variable-free) term. A consumer process is regarded as 'contributing' if it makes bindings to a call variable that has been accessed via an input mode argument. Notice that such bindings *must* be made by body calls – they cannot be made by guard calls or the procedure for the contributing consumer would not have the safe guards property.

Sometimes the term **weak** is used to describe a communication channel that carries incomplete messages. The communication is said to be 'weak-directional' because of the presence of back communication, and the input argument for the consumer is called a 'weak input' because the call supplies only part-constructed terms to which the consumer itself contributes bindings. All examples of process interaction studied up until now have specified only **strong** communication channels. Producers have always supplied consumers with (ultimately) complete terms. In dataflow diagrams weak channels can be indicated with a second, smaller arrow to represent the back communication from consumer to producer, as shown in Figure 6.9 for the example above.

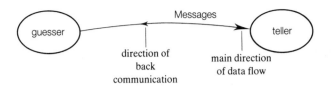

Figure 6.9 M5 implements a two-way communication channel.

The incomplete messages technique depends upon the so-called **logical variable** property which is a characteristic of logic programming languages. This is the property whereby a call can bind a variable to a term containing other variables that can themselves become bound by other calls. In PARLOG it provides the capability whereby a data structure can be cooperatively constructed by two or more concurrent processes, with the variable that represents the structure implementing a flexible communication channel between them; some of the possibilities that result are indicated in the following sections.

6.7   Solving the response-routing problem

Earlier we modelled a multiple-guesser version of the game. However, the approach used would not easily extend to allow incremental and individualized feedback from the teller to the different guesser processes. With the technique of incomplete messages it becomes straightforward to implement this kind of interaction. Each guesser process requires only a single communication channel and these need only be merged to create a single stream of incomplete messages connected to the teller process. This is illustrated by Figure 6.10 for two guesser processes. A PARLOG query to create such a network is

```
← guesser1(Msgs1),
   guesser2(Msgs2),
   merge(Msgs1, Msgs2, MergedMsgs),
   teller(MergedMsgs).                              M6
```

where the two guesser and the teller relations could be exactly as defined in the previous section (although it is better to make guesser1 and guesser2 cosmetic variations upon the previous guesser definition such that these processes generate different sequences of integers). The problem of how to re-route the teller's responses back to the appropriate guesser has vanished.

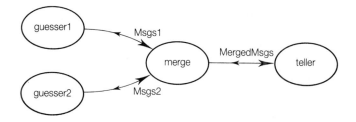

Figure 6.10   Multiple guessers with the 'incomplete messages' technique.

This is because in M6 each message term (a structure) contains an unbound variable shared by the guesser process from which the message has originated. As a component of the message term the variable simply passes through the merge process and hence reaches the teller. When the latter gives its reply by binding the variable, the appropriate guesser automatically obtains the feedback. These back communications of the reply values are represented by the smaller arrows in Figure 6.10.

Unfortunately if you implement and test this version you will discover that this solution has a slight flaw. As soon as the teller process in M6 receives a message containing the correct guess it will bind the corresponding response variable to got_it. At that point the teller process will terminate and so too (on reading the got_it response) will the successful guesser process. But the other guesser process will have no way of knowing what has happened. When subsequently this process generates a guess and awaits the reply, none will be forthcoming because the teller process no longer exists. The result will be a deadlock.

A remedy is not hard to find. The specification of the teller process must be changed so that this process does not immediately terminate after replying got_it to a correct guess. Instead it should spawn a sub-process that handles any subsequent messages from the remaining guesser process. A suitable replacement first clause for the previous version of teller is:

```
teller([msg(Guess, Reply)|Messages]) ←
    correct(Guess) :
    Reply = got_it,
    tell_quit(Messages).
```

The tell_quit procedure has mode

```
mode tell_quit(messages?).
```

The procedure can be defined in such a way that the behaviour is correct for any number of guesser processes. Where the input to tell_quit is the empty list it is certain that no active guessers remain and at that point the tell_quit process (and hence the teller process) can itself terminate. Otherwise any message that arrives should be given a feedback signal quit, say, to indicate to the sender that the game is over. A suitable definition is:

```
mode tell_quit(messages?).

tell_quit([]).
tell_quit([msg(Guess, Reply)|Msgs]) ←
    Reply = quit,
    tell_quit(Msgs).
```

Finally, we should also modify the synch_guess procedure so as to accommodate the new possible reply value. A single extra clause

```
synch_guess(interval(Min, G, Max), [], quit).
```

will effect the desired early-terminating behaviour on the part of the guesser processes.

Generalization

This example shows how the response-routing problem for the client-server interaction is solved by the incomplete messages technique. A client requiring feedback from the resource process sends a message containing an unbound variable for the reply. The need for a separate response channel is obviated by back communication and by implementing a suitable merge utility the resource process can service any number of clients without the need to change its procedure.

In Section 6.4 we demonstrated how two processes can synchronize tightly to one another by means of two single-way (strong) communication channels. M5 and M6 demonstrate that a single two-way (weak) communication channel can achieve the same effect. A guesser process is constrained by the supply of back-communicated responses (represented by the third argument of synch_guess) and a teller process is constrained by the supply of forward-communicated messages. Deadlock is still a hazard, as the above showed.

Another hazard relates to unsafe guards. Suppose for example that the second clause of the teller procedure is specified as

```
teller([msg(Guess, Reply)|Messages]) ←
    high(Guess),
    Reply = high :
    teller(Messages).
```

where the guard has been enlarged so as to encompass the unification call. Then the clause guard is no longer safe; it now contains a call that will attempt to bind an input mode call variable, namely whichever call variable is accessed via Reply. Recall from Section 4.7 that the safe guards property is a *mandatory* requirement in PARLOG. Of course there could be no justification for extending the guard in this way (and to do so would contradict the minimum guards principle also). But the requirement for guard safety should be especially borne in mind whenever the incomplete messages technique is exploited. A contributing consumer process will by necessity make bindings to an input mode call variable (this is how it 'contributes', after all) but to avoid unsafe guards you must ensure that these bindings are effected by calls in the *bodies* rather than in the guards of the procedures concerned.

6.8 Lazy producers

Our games until now have featured rather enthusiastic guessing players who have been eager to volunteer guesses. Their counterpart PARLOG processes have behaved with a similar keenness. So eager was the guesser in M1 that it was liable to run far ahead of the teller's capability to check the guesses produced. For M5 we had a guesser whose eagerness was constrained by the supply of feedback from the teller, so that the former process was able to generate only one guess ahead, but even so it was this guessing-ahead that effectively pushed the interaction forward. Let us imagine a guessing player who exhibits none of this eagerness – a 'lazy' player who participates in the game only with the greatest reluctance.

The truly lazy player is one who will volunteer nothing. Far from seeking to push the interaction forward, its natural state is one of non-communication; although, perhaps out of politeness, the lazy guesser will muster a guess when actively prompted for one by the teller. The interaction is therefore driven by the latter, who must make regular demands for guesses in order to achieve progress towards the end of the game. If the teller makes no demands then the lazy guesser produces no guesses: this is very different from the style of the eager guesser process with its tendency to race ahead.

This last thought provides a clue as to how lazy guessing behaviour may be modelled in PARLOG. The teller can be specified as the producer of a stream of messages representing demands rather than as the consumer of a stream of messages representing guesses (see Figure 6.11). Each demand message can contain an unbound variable that acts like a blank piece of paper. On receipt of such a message the guesser supplies a binding for the variable to specify the reluctant guess. The back communication of the guess value to the teller process will be automatic, just as was the back communication of the reply value in the incomplete message interactions of the previous sections.

Figure 6.11   Message flow for lazy guessing.

The teller process could provide a lazy guesser with any of the types of feedback discussed so far. For an interaction with feedback each demand message should be a structure having two components, one to specify the response to the previous guess and one an unbound variable to represent the next guess. However, in order to concentrate on the concept of laziness we shall implement a feedback-free interaction like that of M1. The advantage of this is that each demand message need be no more than an unbound variable. We will consider how the definitions of the guesser and teller procedures given in M1 should be transformed so as to implement a lazy guesser.

Figure 6.11 shows that the main direction of communication is reversed for the lazy interaction. The modes become

mode teller(demands↑), mode guesser(demands?).

and the interaction can be specified by

←teller(Demands), guesser(Demands).   **M7**

The solution to this query will be a list of integers

Demands = [0, 1, 2, 3, ...]

similar to the solution to M1. The difference lies in the *way* the list will be produced. In the lazy version, we intend that the teller process will produce a stream of unbound variables

Demands = [D1, D2, D3, ...]

representing demands, and the guesser process will contribute the bindings

D1 = 0, D2 = 1, D3 = 2, ...

representing guesses. As soon as each demand variable becomes bound to an integer the teller process will produce another, unless the integer specifies the correct answer. In contrast to all previous versions, the input constraint now works to hold back the progress of the guesser: this process will be forced to suspend until each demand variable representing a request for another guess is supplied by the teller process.

The definition given in M1 for the guesser relation can now become:

```
mode guesser(demands?).

guesser(Demands) ← lazy_integers(0, 1000, Demands).
```

Thus the stream of demand variables is passed through to lazy_integers for binding. This relation should have the same logical reading as the standard integers relation (Section 4.8.6) but its behaviour should be lazy rather than eager. That is, its modes are

```
mode lazy_integers(from?, to?, intlist?).
```

and its production of integers should be demand-driven. A call such as

```
← lazy_integers(0, 1000, [D1, D2, D3|Demands]).
```

in which the variables are unbound, should create a process that makes the bindings

```
D1 = 0, D2 = 1, D3 = 2
```

representing the lazy production of the first three integers. The process should then wait for more demands. If Demands subsequently becomes bound to [D4, D5|MoreDemands] then the call should respond by supplying the bindings D4 = 3, D5 = 4. When all integers in the range have been lazily produced the process should bind the demands tail-list variable to the empty list and terminate.

A suitable definition for lazy_integers can be adapted from the standard integers version. The essential change is that the third argument is now an input mode for which the call will supply a stream of unbound variables representing demands for integers. These variables should be given suitable values by body calls to the unification primitive. The definition is:

```
mode lazy_integers(from?, to?, demands?).

lazy_integers(N, N, [D|Rest]) ←
        D = N,
        Rest = [].
lazy_integers(N1, N2, [D|Rest]) ←
        N1 < N2 :
        D = N1,
        Next is N1 + 1,
        lazy_integers(Next, N2, Rest).
```

This definition should be tested independently. Try it with the query

```
← lazy_integers(5, 10, [D1, D2, D3|Demands]),
    swrite_list([D1, D2, D3|Demands]).
```

which supplies three demands for integers and check that the integers 5, 6, 7 (and no others) are produced.

It is tempting to think that the only significant change that is needed to the teller procedure of M1 affects the mode declaration. We might try to specify the procedure as:

```
mode teller(demands↑).

teller([Demand|Demands]) ←
    correct(Demand) :
    true.
teller([Demand|Demands]) ←
    not(correct(Demand)) :
    teller(Demands).
```

Logically this has the desired interpretation. Unfortunately in M7 the procedure would result in deadlock. The teller call would suspend immediately on testing these clauses for candidate status because the guard calls would be made with Demand an unbound variable. This is a classic deadlock scenario: it arises from the fact that commitment must always precede output in the (test-commit-output-spawn) behaviour of a PARLOG process. The guard calls cannot succeed, and hence the teller call cannot commit to a clause, until the demand variable becomes bound – but the demand variable cannot possibly become bound (by the concurrent guesser process) until it has been output by the teller, and output must wait for the teller call to commit!

To avoid the deadlock we should re-formulate the logic so that the process *first* outputs the demand variable and *then* spawns a separate sub-process (which cannot be a guard evaluation process) whose job it is to await the guesser's binding and to determine future behaviour accordingly. We can do this by introducing an auxiliary relation read_tell, say, so that the teller procedure reads:

```
mode teller(demands↑).

teller([Demand|Demands]) ←
    read_tell(Demand, Demands).
```

A teller process will now output one demand variable unconditionally. It will then spawn a read_tell sub-process which should check any received binding for the variable, which of course will represent a guess; when such a guess is detected the process should terminate if it is correct, and should generate further demands otherwise. The latter can be accomplished by recursively calling teller, as follows:

```
mode read_tell(guess?, demands↑ ).

read_tell(Guess, Demands) ←
    correct(Guess) :
    true.
read_tell(Guess, Demands) ←
    not(correct(Guess)) :
    teller(Demands).
```

Notice that this defines a teller process that is synchronized by the guesser's supply of a response. The guard evaluations will ensure that the generation of demands does not race ahead.

There remains a problem. If you test these definitions you will discover that a deadlock occurs after the production of the guess that represents the correct answer. Why does this happen in M7, when M1 was deadlock-free? The explanation is fairly straightforward. Both M7 and M1 specify a teller process that terminates when the guesser communicates a correct guess. When this happens in M1 the guesser just continues alone, eagerly producing the remainder of the integers as guesses before terminating. But the lazy guesser of M7 produces nothing except on demand, and since after the termination of the teller no further demands can appear this means that the guesser will laze forever. (The query above to the lazy_integers procedure also ends in a deadlock for a similar reason.)

Once we understand why the deadlock occurs it becomes easy to remedy. We must first arrange that before terminating, the teller process sends some kind of signal to indicate that there will be no further demands. An obvious way to do this is to re-write the first clause of read_tell as

```
read_tell(Guess, []) ←
    correct(Guess) :
    true.
```

where the signal is the explicit 'closing down' or 'sealing' of the demands stream. Of course, the guesser process must be able to detect this event and behave accordingly. Here we need only add a single clause to the lazy_integers procedure, as follows:

```
lazy_integers(N1, N2, []).
```

Notice however that this changes the logical reading of the lazy_integers relation. Instead of having the same meaning as the standard integers relation, lazy_integers(N1, N2, Ints) must now be read as: Ints is the list of integers from N1 to N2, *or* is some *initial sublist* of that list.

Generalization

Eager producer behaviour represents the norm in PARLOG. In programs that specify only 'strong' communication channels (and most of the programs in this book are in this category) all producers are eager and the input constraint can only affect consumer processes. However, the above shows how the input constraint can be turned against the producer. A producer can be 'lazified' by making it the consumer of a list of demand variables; on receipt of such a variable the producer makes an appropriate binding to it (that is, 'lazily produces' the required data). The consumer is made the producer of the demand variables, the bindings for which it duly consumes as soon as these are made available by the lazified producer. By this programming technique the interaction becomes **demand-driven** – it is led by the consumer's production of demands rather than by the producer's supply of data.

This ability to specify lazy interactions is not just a curiosity: sometimes lazy producer behaviour can be genuinely useful. An example is suggested by the query

    ← primes(P), investigate(P).

If the primes program has the usual eager behaviour then it could generate prime numbers uncontrollably ahead of the ability of the investigate process to consume them. At best it will probably do more work than is necessary and at worst, all available memory might become filled with terms representing uninvestigated primes. Furthermore, because the production of primes is (presumably) an infinite process the evaluation of the query will be non-terminating. A lazy variant of the interaction could solve all of these problems: the primes program would act as a lazy producer, completely controlled by the supply of demand variables from the investigate process.

One way to obtain a lazy version of any program is suggested by the above, in which we derived the demand-driven M7 interaction by transforming the supply-driven M1 version. A similar *transformational* approach can be applied to most interactions led by eager producers. In attempting such a conversion, care is essential to avoid the risk of deadlock.

Lazy producer behaviour can be seen as the extreme case of the incomplete messages technique described earlier. In a lazy interaction such as that specified by M7 the process that is the official producer (according to mode declarations) generates 'completely incomplete' messages, *viz.* unbound variables; these represent the limit case of 'weak inputs' to the official consumer. The shared term is cooperatively constructed but the 'contributing consumer' contributes almost everything and the 'incomplete producer' virtually nothing. The communication channel is weak-directional to the point where the back communication from consumer to producer implements the only flow of genuine data.

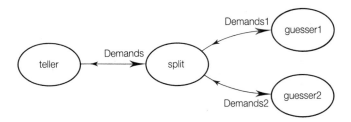

Figure 6.12 Two lazy guessers.

There is a compromise between 'totally lazy' and 'totally eager' producer behaviour. The compromise requires a **buffer** process that intermediates between the producer and its consumer: the producer is allowed to run ahead, but only by up to some fixed number of terms that represents the buffer size. Sizes of zero and infinity correspond to the two extremes of laziness and eagerness. The implementation of buffered interactions can be based on the techniques described above, but this represents an advanced topic that we shall not investigate here.

6.9   Lazy client-server interactions

We can extend the idea of lazy guessing behaviour to a game in which several guessers participate, all of whom are lazy. Admittedly such a game presents a dismal prospect. For left to themselves, the guessers remain sullen. To extract a guess from any one of them the teller must make an explicit demand upon that individual. For fairness all players should be kept involved in roughly equal fashion, which requires that the teller should distribute demands among them as equitably as possible. No feedback will be offered by the teller except to signal the end of the game when eventually a correct guess is extracted.

Modelling this version in PARLOG is fairly straightforward. For the guesser and teller procedures we can use the definitions of the previous section. But how should the communications be implemented? Recall that earlier models for multiple eager guessers used a merging process to combine the guess streams into a single stream for consumption by the teller process. In the demand-driven version it becomes more appropriate to use a splitting process to distribute the teller's demands among the lazy guesser processes. Figure 6.12 illustrates this for two lazy guesser processes, with arrows to indicate the two-way communication along each channel. Larger arrows indicate the flow of unbound variables representing demands and smaller arrows indicate the flow of bindings representing guesses. A query that can specify this interaction is

```
← teller(Demands),
    split(Demands, Demands1, Demands2),
    guesser1(Demands1),
    guesser2(Demands2).                                M8
```

For guesser1 and guesser2, you may like to implement minor variations upon the previous lazy guesser procedure so that these processes supply guesses over different integer intervals.

The split relation can be interpreted as a partition but without the usual test for ordering. Then the logical reading of split(X, L1, L2) is: L1 and L2 are lists containing terms that could be interleaved to give the list X. A possible definition is:

```
mode split(?, ↑, ↑ ).

split([], [], []).
split([X|Rest], [X|L1], L2) ← split(Rest, L1, L2).
split([X|Rest], L1, [X|L2]) ← split(Rest, L1, L2).
```

Operationally, the behaviour of the split process in M8 is to pass each demand variable onto one of the two guesser's input channels, the selection being made non-deterministically. The chosen guesser will bind the variable to the value of the guess and this binding will be automatically back-communicated to the teller. A bonus is that no special termination arrangements are needed: as soon as the teller process detects a correct answer it will close the demands stream, causing the split process to close the streams Demands1 and Demands2. At this point both guesser processes will terminate, including the process that did not generate the correct integer.

Generalization

This suggests that a client-server interaction might be specified with resource-controlled rather than client-controlled behaviour. The interaction becomes one in which the resource process circulates demands for its services among lazy clients, in contrast to the situation in M6 where eager clients are unconstrained and may make requests of the resource process at a rate that leads to a build-up of data on the latter's input channel.

6.10 Biased and fair behaviour

Do our models of the multiple-guesser games ensure *fair* treatment for all guessing players? Of course, 'fairness' is a difficult concept to define precisely. Intuitively an unfair behaviour is one that shows asymmetry or bias in the sense that similar processes receive dissimilar treatment. In the game for eager guessers (M6) it would be unfair for one player to have to wait longer than the others for the teller's responses to its guesses. In the game for lazy guessers (M8) it would be unfair for one player to have to wait longer for demands for guesses (we ignore the fact that the truly lazy player would probably regard this as favourable treatment!). Victims of such bias seem less likely to produce the winning guess. Extreme examples of unfair treatment are represented by the eager guesser who has to wait indefinitely for feedback and the lazy guesser who has to wait forever for a demand: these players are effectively excluded from the game.

Fair play in our models does not depend on the definitions of the guesser and teller relations. It depends upon the behaviour of the merge and split utility processes that implement the 'joins' between each guesser and the teller process. Let us consider first the split relation.

A fair split would be one that equitably distributed the teller's demands among both guesser processes. The non-deterministic version defined in the previous section is not guaranteed to do this. Whenever a demand is generated both recursive split clauses are candidates and if it should happen that the *same* clause is always selected then one guesser will receive all the demands and the other none. Such behaviour could arise from the presence of bias in the PARLOG run-time system, for example. Typically, the way to overcome it is to define procedures in such a manner that fair behaviour becomes the *only* evaluation option. A suitable definition for a fair version of the split relation is shown below.

```
mode fair_split(interms?, outterms1↑, outterms2↑).

fair_split([], [], []).
fair_split([X|Rest], [X|L1], L2) ← fair_split(Rest, L2, L1).
```

A fair_split process is deterministic. When used in place of split in M8, its behaviour is to pass the teller's first demand variable to guesser1 but the alternation of the argument terms in the recursive call means that the second demand will be passed to guesser2. The continuing alternation guarantees an equitable split of demand terms between the two processes. Logically, fair_split(X, L1, L2) means: the list X contains an alternating interleaving of the terms of the lists L1 and L2.

The standard merge is likewise capable of unfair behaviour. It is not impossible that an evaluation process for the call represented by

```
← merge(Guesses1, Guesses2, MergedGuesses).
```

could ignore the Guesses2 channel persistently, preferring to select terms from the Guesses1 stream whenever a choice is possible. In the extreme case a biased merge could degenerate to an append.

We cannot define a fair merge merely by use of the alternating arguments technique. For a strict alternation would hold back the data produced by the faster of the two guesser processes, and a property of merge that should be preserved is that it will not suspend providing data is available on at least one input channel.

What is needed is some way of detecting the situation in which a channel is empty. This offers another application for the var primitive: the test var(In) will succeed if In is an unbound variable, showing that it represents an input channel that presently contains no data. In the case where one channel is found to be empty and the other is non-empty, data should be taken from the non-empty channel. If both channels are non-empty then one term from the head of each channel can be passed onto the output stream. This suggests the following definition:

```
mode fair_merge(?, ?,  ↑ ).

fair_merge([T1|L1], [T2|L2], [T1, T2|L12]) ←
    fair_merge(L1, L2, L12).
fair_merge([T|L1], L2, [T|L12]) ←
    var(L2) :
    fair_merge(L1, L2, L12).
fair_merge(L1, [T|L2], [T|L12]) ←
    var(L1) :
    fair_merge(L1, L2, L12).
fair_merge([], L, L).
fair_merge(L, [], L).
```

The effect of the var tests is to impose fairness upon a merging process. They force an evaluation that gives highest priority to the first clause, for the second and third clauses can be selected only when one or other channel is empty. Thus whenever possible a reduction step will transfer one term from both lists onto the output stream.

For a known call, fair_merge is deterministic. If we know the bindings for L1 and L2 in the call fair_merge(L1, L2, L12) then we can identify a single candidate clause (if one exists) for the evaluation so that the output binding for L12 is predictable. This is in contrast to the non-determinism of the standard merge which we discussed in Section 5.3. But more typically, L1 and L2 are given bindings *incrementally* by other concurrent processes: the identity of the candidate clause is dependent upon the relative times at which the bindings become available. In this situation fair_merge shares with the standard version the non-deterministic behaviour that results from time-dependent computation.

Generalization

In a general client-server interaction the notion of **fairness** refers to the equality of access to (or treatment by) the resource for clients with similar status. An extreme case of unfairness in which a client process is effectively 'frozen out' of an interaction (like the eager guesser whose guesses are persistently ignored because of a biased merge) is known as a **starvation** or

lockout; this can be regarded as a local occurrence of deadlock. The above shows how ·fairness can be imposed by a suitable choice of procedure for merge or split.

The caution expressed previously concerning the use of the non-logical var primitive is worth re-stating. However, the fair_merge example is a (rare) legitimate use of the primitive. It implements an essential 'control' device for imposing fair priority upon the evaluation.

In a system of concurrent processes non-determinism often results from time-dependencies that simply do not arise in sequential evaluation. For example, in the query

```
← integers(1, 2, l1),
  integers(3, 5, l2),
  fair_merge(l1, l2, Digits).
```

the final binding of Digits could be *any* interleaving of the two lists of integers. In contrast, the sequential query

```
← integers(1, 2, l1) &
  integers(3, 5, l2) &
  fair_merge(l1, l2, Digits).
```

is *certain* to produce the binding Digits = [1, 3, 2, 4, 5]. In the concurrent query the non-determinism arises because the relative speeds of the different integers concurrent processes is not known in advance and so neither is the reduction behaviour of fair_merge. The solution is deterministic in the second query because the call to fair_merge can be guaranteed to be

```
←fair_merge([1, 2], [3, 4, 5], Digits).
```

and hence the resulting process is completely predictable.

SUMMARY

Of course, the game of 'guessers and tellers' is unimportant. What does matter is the set of concepts that underpin our various interaction scenarios; many of these are of general significance to concurrent logic programming. The main points are summarized below.

- A basic form of communication between two processes involves a producer sending a stream of completely constructed (that is, ground or variable-free) terms down a channel to a consumer. The channel is implemented by a shared variable that is incrementally bound by the producer. The consumer is held back by the input mode constraint but there is no constraint on the progress of the producer.

- Feedback from the consumer can be implemented by a second communication channel. If the channel carries a stream of reply terms to the producer then a tightly synchronized interaction can result.

- Feedback can also be implemented by the incomplete messages technique in which terms sent by the producer contain unbound variables. The consumer binds each variable to the value of the reply, effecting an automatic back communication to the producer. A channel that carries incomplete messages is called weak and it can take the place of two single-directional (strong) channels.

- Producer processes are normally eager. Lazy producer behaviour can be specified by transforming the producer into a consumer of a stream of unbound variables representing demands for terms.

- The client-server interaction presents the problem of how to manage the inputs and outputs of multiple clients. A solution is for each client to send a stream of incomplete messages to the serving or resource process. A utility merge process combines the streams into a single stream and feedback from the resource to the client is effected via back communication.

- Traps to avoid include deadlock, unsafe guards and unfairness. Deadlock is a non-termination behaviour that can arise in many ways. Unsafe guards are a particular risk in weak-directional programs since these make bindings to call variables that are accessed via input mode arguments. Unfair evaluation behaviour represents an operational bias that can be remedied by explicitly imposing the required priority on the evaluation.

EXERCISES

Select some simple examples of real-world process interaction and design, implement and test a range of corresponding PARLOG models. The following are two examples that you might care to try.

6.1 Model the interaction between a customer and a vending machine. Start with a very simple type of machine, (say) one that sells only a single type of item; its behaviour may be to output an item whenever a coin is supplied that exactly matches the item's price, and to do nothing otherwise. The mode declarations might be

```
mode vending_machine(coins?, goods↑ ),
mode customer(coins↑, goods?).
```

where the arguments are lists representing streams of coins and goods. Then progress to model machines with more realistic behaviour, such as a machine that can accept a sequence of coins to the correct total; a machine that can give change; a machine that offers several different types of item; a machine that contains finite stocks; a machine that tries to cheat customers; a machine that can serve several customers simultaneously; and so on.

6.2 Model the interaction between a bank account holder and the account manager. You should select the permissible range of communications but you should at least permit the account holder to deposit money, withdraw money up to some fixed overdraft limit, request a balance check, and so on. Then extend your model so that the account manager can handle multiple named customers.

7
Metalevel Programming

7.1 A database interface
7.2 Data representation and access
7.3 A lazy set constructor
7.4 Metacalls and shells
7.5 Multitask I/O

7.6 Fail-safe shells
7.7 Defining meta-predicates
7.8 Unification-related primitives
   Summary
   Exercises

PREVIEW   This chapter describes the set constructor and metacall primitives of PARLOG. These are often referred to as 'metalevel' primitives because calls to them contain terms that themselves represent relation calls. The set constructors are shown to provide an effective database interface and the worth of the two metacall primitives is demonstrated by the programming of some simple operating system shells. The chapter also reviews the unification-related primitives.

7.1   A database interface

Database applications have traditionally been a strong area for logic programming. A conventional relational database comprises a collection of tables specifying the relationships between the data: a typical example is the table of sales information shown below.

Item	Quantity	Date
bulbs	10	10th Jan
fuses	3	10th Jan
batteries	14	14th Jan
fuses	2	15th Jan
elements	1	28th Jan
bulbs	2	28th Jan
fuses	5	3rd Feb
solder	1	6th Feb

In logic, such a table can be represented by a relation defined by a set of assertions, one for each row. A 'logic database' version of the sales information is:

```
sales(bulbs, 10, date(10, jan)).
sales(fuses, 3,  date(10, jan)).
sales(batteries, 14, date(14, jan)).
sales(fuses, 2,   date(15, jan)).
sales(elements, 1, date(28, jan)).
sales(bulbs, 2, date(28, jan)).
sales(fuses, 5, date(3,  feb)).
sales(solder, 1, date(6,  feb)).            SALESDB
```

This definition could be made into a directly executable PARLOG program merely by adding a mode declaration. However, our experience with assertional programming in Chapter 3 suggests two reasons why this would not be satisfactory. Firstly, the chosen modes would constrain the allowable forms of query: some queries for which solutions logically do exist would produce deadlock. Secondly, PARLOG's committed-choice behaviour would prevent more than one answer from being returned to any query. A call can only commit to one clause, so that the query that asks (say) on which dates bulbs were sold could return at most one of the two possible answers, regardless of how the modes are specified. For a database application it is highly desirable both that every possible form of call to a defined relation should be supported and that the set of solutions returned should be complete.

There is a way. By using PARLOG's set primitive we can obtain the required behaviour without making any change to the SALESDB representation of information. The query

```
← set(Dates, D, sales(bulbs, Qnty, D)).
```

for example will return a solution of the form

```
Dates = [date(10, jan), date(28, jan)]
```

which is a list representing the required set of dates. The query should be read logically as

Find for Dates a list containing all values for D
satisfying the relation sales(bulbs, Qnty, D).

The set primitive has the special capability that it can interrogate a database like SALESDB directly in order to evaluate such a query. As another example, a query that asks what items were sold in the month of January is

```
← set(Items, I, sales(I, Qnty, date(Day, jan))).
```

The solution produced will be of the form

Items = [bulbs, fuses, batteries, fuses, elements, bulbs]

We say *of the form* because the ordering of the individual solutions could be different from this one. What is guaranteed is that the list will contain one term for each assertion in the database that satisfies the query relation; this could result in duplicates, as with bulbs in the example.

Thus the set primitive implements an interface between PARLOG and a database. For the present purpose, a **database** just means any collection of assertionally defined relations. Databases such as SALESDB are *not* PARLOG programs: they do not have mode declarations, for example. Rather a database is to be regarded as a passive store of information that is inaccessible to a PARLOG program except through calls to this special-purpose primitive. Implicitly set has the declared modes

mode set(solutionlist↑, term?, dbrelation?).

and the logical meaning of set(Solutions, Term, DBrel) is: Solutions is a list containing all values of Term for which DBrel can be unified with a database assertion. Operationally it is the use of full unification for *all* the arguments of DBrel plus the complete search of *all* the database assertions that ensures that every pattern of call is supported and that all solutions are returned for any query. But beyond the guarantee that set will produce a list of all solutions, PARLOG does not tightly define the behaviour of the primitive: access to the database assertions may or may not be sequential and the binding of the Solutions variable may or may not be incremental. Different implementations of PARLOG may differ in these respects.

7.2   Data representation and access

The contents of a database can be manipulated in a more general way by a query combining a call to set with other PARLOG calls. For example, a query that asks how many items overall were sold in January is

← set(Quantities, Qnty, sales(Item, Qnty, date(Day, jan))),
   total(Quantities, T).

where total can be as defined in Section 4.8. With the SALESDB database this query will return the solution

T = 10 + 3 + 14 + 2 + 1 + 2 = 32

The evaluation behaviour is to run the set process and the total process concurrently. If the PARLOG implementation is one in which solutions to set calls are constructed incrementally then the total process will accumulate the individual item quantities concurrently as these are produced by set; on other systems the total call will suspend until the set evaluation has completed.

Queries like the one above might be over-complex for database users. For convenience, it may be worthwhile to define some new database access predicates that 'wrap up' common combinations of call such as that of total with set. We might define for example a predicate dbtotal where dbtotal(T, N, DBcall) has the logical reading: T is the total of all values of N for which DBcall is satisfied in the database. Given such a predicate, the query above could be presented as

```
← dbtotal(T, Qnty, sales(Item, Qnty, date(Day, jan)).
```

and of course the solution for T should be as before. A suitable definition is:

```
mode dbtotal(total↑, numericterm?, dbrelation?).

dbtotal(T, N, DBrel) ←
    set(S, N, DBrel),
    total(S, T).
```

This program for dbtotal is effective for *any* database: it could contribute to a general-purpose query language for database users. Alternatively, if we know in advance the type of information that is to be interrogated then we could implement a completely 'customized' query language. For the SALESDB database we might define a relation salestotal, say, that would permit the previous query to be expressed more simply as

```
← salestotal(all, jan, T).
```

to obtain the solution. The constant all will be specially recognized by the program for salestotal. To discover the total sales of fuses in January the query would be

```
← salestotal(fuses, jan, T).
```

A suitable PARLOG procedure for salestotal is

```
mode salestotal(item?, period?, sales↑ ).

salestotal(all, Month, Total) ←
    set(Quantities, Q, sales(AnyItem, Q, date(Day, Month))),
    total(Quantities, Total).
salestotal(Item, Month, Total) ←
    not(Item == all) :
    set(Quantities, Q, sales(Item, Q, date(Day, Month))),
    total(Quantities, Total).
```

As another example, consider again the path-finding problem of Section 5.11. In that problem we represented the graph by a PARLOG procedure for neighbours, defined as follows:

```
mode neighbours(node?, nextnodes↑ ).

neighbours(a, [b, c]).
neighbours(b, [a, c, d]).
neighbours(c, [b, a, e]).
neighbours(d, [b]).
neighbours(e, [c]).                              PATHPROC
```

This representation has the property that a single call can produce the complete list of all nodes linked by an arc to a given node. This property is essential to an all-PARLOG program for path-finding because of the committed-choice operational semantics. However, the use of set now offers an alternative representation. We could specify the same graph by a database such as

```
arc(a, b).
arc(a, c).
arc(b, c).
arc(b, d).
arc(c, e).                                       PATHDB
```

Notice that there is no mode declaration – PATHDB is a *database* and not a PARLOG program. The only way in which a PARLOG program can access this representation is through set. We can arrange for this to happen by re-defining the neighbours procedure as follows:

```
mode neighbours(node?, nextnodes↑ ).

neighbours(Node, Nodes) ←
    set(Nodes1, N, arc(Node, N)),
    set(Nodes2, M, arc(M, Node)),
    append(Nodes1, Nodes2, Nodes).
```

You should satisfy yourself that the logical reading of this version is close enough to that of PATHPROC to make an acceptable logical substitute.

What are the merits of these alternatives? Certainly PATHDB avoids the redundancy of mentioning each arc twice and arguably it is easier to construct, verify and update than PATHPROC. On the other hand, the database version will be less efficient since much more work is now required to evaluate a neighbours call. But perhaps a more practically important factor is that in typical applications the representation decision may already have been made elsewhere. If a large version of PATHDB (or any other database) already exists and the task is to access it then the PARLOG programmer has no other choice than to use the set primitive (or subset, which we describe next) to implement the necessary interface.

7.3   A lazy set constructor

PARLOG has a second set constructor primitive. In addition to set there is also subset which is implicitly declared with modes

mode subset(solutiondemands?, term?, dbrel?).

The logical reading of subset is almost identical to that of set. Operationally, subset differs from set in having lazy behaviour in producing solution lists. The difference between lazy and eager evaluation behaviours was explained in the previous chapter: we can illustrate it here for the set constructors by means of an example using the earlier SALESDB database. Recall that a typical set call is

← set(S, Item, sales(Item, Qnty, date(D, jan))).

Once the evaluation process for this call has commenced nothing can hold it back. As fast as machine resources will allow, the process generates a complete solution list of items that have been sold in the month of January:

S = [bulbs, fuses, batteries, fuses, elements, bulbs]

As explained above, the list could specify any ordering and may include duplicates. But the point is that a set evaluation exhibits the standard 'eager' behaviour of a PARLOG producer process. In contrast, a subset evaluation process produces nothing except on demand. The first argument of subset is an *input* that accepts a stream of demand variables: bindings representing solution terms are made to these variables as they arrive. A typical call is

← subset([D1, D2], Item, sales(Item, Qnty, date(Day, jan))).

which supplies two demands for solution terms. The query should be read logically as

D1 and D2 the first two members of a list of solutions for Item to the database relation sales(Item, Qnty, date(Day, jan))

subset will respond by making the bindings

D1 = bulbs, D2 = fuses

at which point the evaluation process will terminate. We can be certain about the order of the terms in this list because unlike set, a subset call is guaranteed to be evaluated sequentially and the order of its solutions is determined by the textual order of clauses in the database. To obtain from subset the complete list of all six solutions it will be necessary to specify as many demand variables, as in the call:

```
← subset([D1, D2, D3, D4, D5, D6],
         Item,
         sales(Item, Qnty, date(Day, jan))).
```

which will produce the bindings

```
D1 = bulbs, D2 = fuses, D3 = batteries,
D4 = fuses, D5 = elements, D6 = bulbs
```

But these examples are untypical. A typical subset process is supplied *incrementally* with demand variables by some other concurrent process that (effectively) controls the database search. This demanding process receives the solution values by a back communication from subset; it can terminate the database search at any point by closing the demands stream. If the number of demand variables exceeds the availability of solutions then subset will respond by binding the excess variables to some system-dependent constant such as end. The lazy behaviour means that this primitive could be used to define a predicate that computes a fixed number of solutions to a database query, for example: this is left as an exercise to the reader.

Finally, we should reveal that set and subset are in two ways more powerful than the above examples have suggested. Firstly, their third arguments may specify a conjunction of database calls rather than only a single call. Secondly, the database to which these primitives provide an interface is permitted to be a *full* logic database: it may contain implications as well as assertions. The details are likely to vary between systems, but for some PARLOG systems a 'database' is likely to mean 'any PROLOG program' and the set and subset primitives will effectively implement a 'bridge' between the two languages.

7.4   Metacalls and shells

PARLOG has many attractions as a language for developing operating systems and for 'systems software' applications generally. This is a large and complex area but we can usefully introduce at this point the two forms of the call primitive which is essential to all kinds of systems programming in PARLOG. We shall show in particular how the primitive can be used to implement some simple shells.

The essential facility provided by call is the capability to execute other programs. The simpler form of the primitive has mode

```
mode call(?).
```

The single argument should be a term that itself represents a relation call. Then the behaviour of call(X) is simply to run the process corresponding to X, and the call evaluation succeeds or fails according to the outcome of this process. The fact that the argument term itself represents a call explains why this primitive is sometimes known as the **metacall** primitive.

Our first example is rather artificial. The query

$\leftarrow$ X = member(3, [1, 2, 3]), call(X).

creates two processes. While the variable X remains unbound the call process suspends, but as soon as the unification process has given X the value member(3, [1, 2, 3]) the call process becomes active. It creates and runs the specified member process and, since the member process terminates in success, so subsequently does the call. Of course, the call here is really redundant. The above is just a long-winded version of the query

$\leftarrow$ member(3, [1, 2, 3]).

which creates the member process directly.

A more typical application is one in which the value of the argument of call is not known until run time. Implementing a shell is an important example. A shell is basically a program that accepts commands from a terminal and executes them (or interprets them in some more general fashion). Generally a shell implements the topmost layer of an operating system – it represents the layer of software with which the user communicates directly. A simple sequential shell can be defined as follows:

```
mode singletask_shell(commands?).

singletask_shell([Command|Commands]) ←
    call(Command) &
    singletask_shell(Commands).
singletask_shell([]).
```

We can imagine a process created to evaluate the call

$\leftarrow$ singletask_shell(Cmds).

where the value of Cmds is some stream of commands such as

[printout(file23), wordstar('my.doc'), loadin(file17), mail, ...]

originating from the user's terminal. The identifiers printout, loadin, wordstar and mail are each intended to name programs (which could be the user's own programs, library programs, system utilities, or whatever) so that each command represents a request to execute some process or task. The shell is sequential or **single-tasking** because the conjunction operator in the recursive clause forces any task to run to completion before the next is begun.

A **multi-tasking** system requires a different kind of shell. In a multi-tasking system two or more tasks can run concurrently: it should not be necessary to wait for a printing task to finish before a text-editing task can begin, for example. We could convert the singletask_shell procedure into a shell for multi-tasking merely by replacing the ampersand by a comma in the recursive clause. But this would give an equal priority to all tasks, which is unrealistic. A more typical multi-tasking system expects the user to distinguish between two classes of task: 'foreground' tasks are those requiring interaction and 'background' tasks are those that can run (more or less) unattended. Printing would probably be specified as a background task whilst a task like text-editing would be a foreground task. We shall define a shell that allows no more than one foreground task, but any number of background tasks, to be active concurrently. To categorize each task the user is required to generate a stream of commands of the form

```
[bg(printout(file23)), fg(wordstar('my.doc')),
     bg(loadin(file17)), fg(mail), ...]
```

The multitask_shell defined below will obtain the desired behaviour.

```
mode multitask_shell(commands?).

multitask_shell([fg(Command)|Commands]) ←
     call(Command) &
     multitask_shell(Commands).
multitask_shell([bg(Command)|Commands]) ←
     call(Command),
     multitask_shell(Commands).
multitask_shell([]).
```

The parallel conjunction operator in the second clause will ensure that background tasks run concurrently with the shell's execution of further commands. Notice in contrast that once the foreground command has been executed, no more shell commands will be processed until the corresponding task has terminated.

7.5 Multitask I/O

Our definition for multitask_shell has ignored the problem of how to handle the inputs and outputs (I/O) of user processes. But when several concurrent processes exist, most of which will require access to a fixed set of peripheral devices such as the keyboard, display screen, disk system and printer, it would be disastrous to permit a free-for-all.

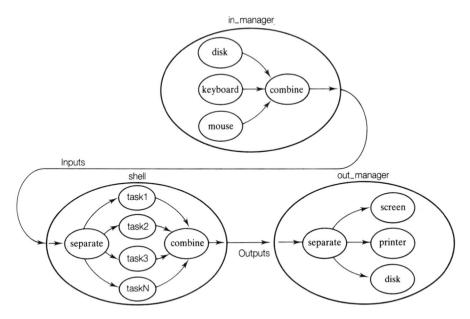

Figure 7.1 I/O management for a multi-tasking shell.

A coherent approach to I/O can be envisaged along the following general lines. It should be possible to represent the whole software system by a top-level query such as

← in_manager(Inputs), shell(Inputs, Outputs), out_manager(Outputs).

where the entire collection of inputs and outputs of the system are combined into two single streams Inputs and Outputs handled respectively by the special in_manager and out_manager processes. The latter are the managers or 'guardians' of I/O and each enforces a disciplined regime of access to the appropriate devices, typically on a basis of 'mutual exclusion'. A user process running under the shell must extract its own particular input terms from Inputs and similarly it must merge its own outputs on to Outputs (see Figure 7.1). It becomes the sole responsibility of the two managers to administer I/O resources: user processes need not and should not compete for them directly. This division of responsibilities provides the basis of a solution to the I/O problem for concurrent systems.

Unfortunately it also complicates the programming of the shell. It is no longer enough for the shell to create each user process – it must also arrange for the separation of inputs and the combination of outputs. Here we shall only show how the latter can be accomplished. Below is an extended version of the multitask_shell procedure that permits the user optionally to specify an output stream with each command: the shell then merges the different output streams into a single combined overall output stream ready for consumption by an appropriate out_manager process.

```
mode multitask_ioshell(commands?, output↑ ).

multitask_ioshell([fg(Command)|Commands], ShellOutput) ←
    call(Command) &
    multitask_ioshell(Commands, ShellOutput).
multitask_ioshell([bg(Command)|Commands], ShellOutput) ←
    call(Command),
    multitask_ioshell(Commands, ShellOutput).
multitask_ioshell([fg(Command, CommandOutput)|Commands], ShellOutput) ←
    call(Command),
    merge(CommandOutput, RestOuts, ShellOutput) &
    multitask_ioshell(Commands, RestOuts).
multitask_ioshell([bg(Command, CommandOutput)|Commands], ShellOutput) ←
    call(Command),
    merge(CommandOutput, RestOuts, ShellOutput),
    multitask_ioshell(Commands, RestOuts).
multitask_ioshell([], []).
```

This procedure for multitask_ioshell distinguishes between tasks that produce output and tasks that do not. For a task requiring no output one of the first two clauses is selected and the behaviour of the shell is exactly as before. For a task that will produce output the user is expected to specify a command of the form fg(Command, CommandOutput) or bg(Command, CommandOutput), where CommandOutput identifies the variable implementing the output channel of the process specified by Command. An example of such a term is

```
bg(integers(1, 100, Ints), Ints)
```

This command would request the shell to run a background integers process the output of which is represented by Ints. The shell's response is specified by the fourth clause. A metacall process is spawned that creates the integers process and a merge process is spawned to run concurrently with this process and with the rest of the shell. The merge serves to combine the output produced by the integers process with RestOuts, representing the combined outputs of future user processes, to obtain via ShellOutput a unified output stream for the whole shell. Assuming a fair definition for

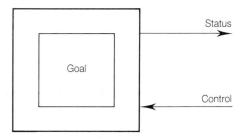

Figure 7.2   Control metacall evaluation of call(Goal, Status, Control).

merge, this stream should contain an equitable distribution of the output data that arises from each individual task.

Some elaboration is obviously necessary. User commands that produce output should also specify the required output device, for otherwise the out_manager could not discriminate between different terms arriving on the unified Outputs stream. This means that the shell should recognize commands of the form

```
bg(integers(1, 100, Ints), printer(Ints))

bg(integers(1, 100, Ints), screen(window3, Ints))
```

for example. The reader is invited to investigate the changes that must be made to multitask_ioshell in order to implement such commands.

7.6   Fail-safe shells

All the above shells suffer from a major flaw: if any user process should fail then so too will the shell (because call(X) fails if the call represented by X does). This is intolerable. An operating system that crashed whenever a user's program contained a bug would be hopeless!

Is there is a simple repair? Plausibly we might propose that within the shell procedures the calls call(Command) could be evaluated within guards. A 'fail-safe' clause could then be added to the end of the procedure to handle the failure cases. Unfortunately, this idea will not work for two reasons. Firstly, it would make concurrent user processes an impossibility (because the guard would have to terminate before the next user command could be executed by the recursive invocation of the shell). Secondly, it would rule out interactive user processes (output must always await commitment, so out_manager in Figure 7.1 for example would not 'see' the data produced by a user process running within the guard of multi-task_ioshell until the process had succeeded).

The real solution to the problem lies with a second, three-argument version of call that has the special property that it never fails. The fail-proof version, which is known as the **control metacall**, is declared implicitly with modes

mode call(goal?, status↑, control?).

Logically this metacall is read as true. Operationally its value lies in its capability to exercise tight supervision over a user process, which can be regarded as running within a 'black box' (see Figure 7.2). When the process represented by Goal terminates the Status variable becomes bound to one of the constants succeeded or failed depending on the termination state. If necessary the user process can be stopped at any time by binding the Control variable to stop, in which case Status is given the value stopped (these constants may vary between different PARLOG systems). To implement a minimum fail-safe behaviour in our earlier shells we need only replace each occurence of call(X) with one of call(X, S, C). With this change, the failure of any user process can have no effect upon a shell.

However, the control metacall is much more powerful than this simple application might suggest. As our final example, we use it to part-remedy another flaw in all the above shells: namely, that once a process has begun running under the shell there is no way in which it can be halted. Below we define multitask_abortshell, a modified version of multi-task_shell that has fail-safe behaviour and that additionally gives the capability to halt all current background processes whenever the shell registers a command bg_abort from the user.

```
mode multitask_abortshell(commands?).

multitask_abortshell(Commands) ←
    run_multitask_abortshell(Commands, Bg_control).

mode run_multitask_abortshell(commands?, backgroundcontrol?).

run_multitask_abortshell([fg(Command)|Commands], Bg_control) ←
    call(Command, S, C) &
    run_multitask_abortshell(Commands, Bg_control).
run_multitask_abortshell([bg(Command)|Commands], Bg_control) ←
    call(Command, S, Bg_control),
    run_multitask_abortshell(Commands, Bg_control).
run_multitask_abortshell([bg_abort|Commands], Bg_control) ←
    Bg_control = stop &
    run_multitask_abortshell(Commands, New_bg_control).
run_multitask_abortshell([], Bg_control).
```

A call

```
← multitask_abortshell(Cmds).
```

where Cmds represents a stream of user commands as before, initiates the shell with an unbound variable Bg_control as the second argument term. Notice that the second clause of run_multitask_abortshell creates each background process under the control metacall, with this *same* variable given as the common 'control line': this is the key to the shell's ability to abort background processes. For when a bg_abort command is received this variable is given the value stop by the third clause. At that point every background process is halted by its own supervising metacall. A new variable New_bg_control is created that will be the control line over any future background processes. For fail-safe behaviour, foreground processes are also run under the control metacall; but each of these is given its own independent control variable so that these processes are unaffected by aborts.

A limitation is that the shell cannot abort background processes whilst a foreground process is running. This could be remedied (basically) by re-specifying the first clause of run_multitask_abortshell so that a second process runs in parallel with the foreground process which searches ahead on the commands stream and which binds the background process control line to stop if an abort request is discovered.

7.7   Defining meta-predicates

Another application of the metacall primitives is in the definition of new **meta-predicates** – that is, predicates that take relation calls as arguments.

Our first example is not, the negation predicate. Of course, not is pre-defined by the PARLOG system but it is instructive to see how it could just as well have been defined by a PARLOG program. The program uses the one-argument metacall and the primitive fail which has the logical reading false and which behaves exactly according to its name. The definition is:

```
not(goal?).

not(Goal) ← call(Goal) : fail;
not(Goal).
```

The definition implements the operational semantics of **negation-by-failure**: to evaluate not(G), run G and invert the outcome. Does the procedure implement a logically sound interpretation of negation? Fundamentally its soundness depends on the **closed-world assumption** that the logical validity of G in the 'world' is equivalent to its validity in the program (informally, that the program contains all the 'relevant' information about G). Soundness requires also that if G is valid in the program then the evaluation of call(G) will not fail. For PARLOG this corresponds to the requirement that the program has the sufficient tests property which, of course, is an expected property of any well-constructed PARLOG program. Finally, it can be shown that the procedure is unsound in the case where the guard test call(G) succeeds by binding variables of G. Such bindings could only arise if the procedure for not has an unsafe guard, so this class of error *could* be flagged automatically (a sophisticated PARLOG compiler will detect unsafe guards).

A meta-predicate or for logical disjunction is easily defined. Logically, or(G1, G2) means: at least one of G1 or G2 is valid. We can define the relation as follows:

```
mode or(goal1?, goal2?).

or(G1, G2) ← call(G1) : true.
or(G1, G2) ← call(G2) : true.
```

An example usage is the query

```
← or(member(3, [1, 2, 3, 4]), member(3, [1, 3, 5, 7])).
```

Operationally, an or evaluation becomes a guards race. The first guard test to succeed makes the or call succeed, and the other guard test is halted at that point; if both tests eventually fail then so does the or. However, this program is limited to such uses as the example shown, in which the argument calls only *check* the value of given data. If the arguments contain variables that would become bound by an evaluation then the program for or would have unsafe guards.

In passing, you should check whether your PARLOG system supports a programmable operator grammar. This would make it possible for example to declare the or predicate as an infix rather than a prefix operator (the default case). The example query could then be re-specified in the syntax

```
← member(3, [1, 2, 3, 4]) or member(3, [1, 3, 5, 7]).
```

which is slightly more readable.

Interestingly, PARLOG's & sequential conjunction operator can also be substituted by a meta-predicate. We can define a predicate and such that the call

```
← G1 & G2.
```

could be rendered as a call

```
← and(G1, G2).
```

with equivalent behaviour. The definition is:

```
mode and(goal1?, goal2?).

and(G1, G2) ←
    call(G1, Status, Control),
    next_call(Status, G2).
```

This program uses the control metacall to bind Status to a system constant representing the outcome of the G1 evaluation. next_call should suspend until Status has a value and if the value is succeeded then it should proceed to evaluate G2. A suitable definition is:

```
mode next_call(outcome1?, goal2?).

next_call(succeeded, Goal) ← call(Goal).
```

It is the input mode of next_call that imposes the strict sequential behaviour with succeeded acting as a kind of 'token' marking the transfer of control. A similar **control token** approach could be applied to eliminate the sequential conjunction operator entirely, from *any* PARLOG program: the equivalent sequencing behaviour can always be obtained by a program that uses only the parallel conjunction operator with the control metacall (plus some additional constants that act as tokens). In fact, PARLOG compilers may effect such a transformation during program compilation.

As a final example, maplist is a well-known meta-predicate that relates two lists according to some specified relation. For example,

```
maplist(double, [1, 2, 3, 4], [2, 4, 6, 8])
```

is one instance of the relation and

```
maplist(translates, [chien, chat, cheval], [dog, cat, horse])
```

is another. The logical reading of maplist(Rel, L1, L2) is: each member of the list L2 lies in the relation Rel to the corresponding member of the list L1. A PARLOG program for maplist should obtain the value of L2 when values for Rel and L1 are given. A suitable definition is:

```
mode maplist(relation?, list1?, list2↑ ).

maplist(Rel, [], []).
maplist(Rel, [H|T], [H1|T1]) ←
    Goal =.. [Rel, H, H1],
    call(Goal),
    maplist(Rel, T, T1).
```

The =.. operator is the PARLOG system primitive that implements list-to-structure conversion – for example, the call G =.. [double, 1, X] produces the binding G = double(1, X). Notice that a maplist process is another example of 'peeling parallelism'. If the evaluation of each call(Goal) is a relatively long-lived process when compared to the time required to recurse down the list then many of these processes could exist concurrently.

7.8   Unification-related primitives

This is an appropriate point at which to gather together a vital class of PARLOG primitives: the so-called **unification-related primitives**. These are summarized in the table below. All but one of them have been discussed before but a brief reminder about the role of each may be helpful.

Primitive	Name	Mode	Logical reading	Operational reading
X = Y	Full unification	(?, ?)	X equals Y	X and Y are unified
X == Y	Test unification	(?, ?)	X equals Y	X and Y are syntactically identical
X <= Y	One-way unification	(?, ?)	X equals Y	X and Y are unified without binding Y
data(X)	data	(?)	true	X is bound to a non-variable term
var(X)	var	(?)	(has none)	X is an unbound variable

7.8.1   X = Y

A call to the full unification primitive never suspends: it can only either succeed or fail directly. A call succeeds whenever bindings can be made for variables in the argument terms in such a way that the terms become syntactically identical. The fact that bindings can result for both argument terms shows that these may represent 'weak' inputs. This primitive has an implicit usage in implementing 'output unification' in PARLOG (that is, unification between pairs of output mode arguments on commitment of a call to a clause). Where it appears explicitly within a program it is usually to effect a back communication from within the body of a clause: there were many examples of this is the previous chapter.

7.8.2   X == Y

The test unification or identity primitive cannot bind either argument term (that is, its arguments represent 'strong' inputs). A call to the primitive succeeds if the argument terms are syntactically identical (for example [1, 2] == [1, 2]). If the terms are unifiable but not syntactically identical, for example as with [1|X] == [1, 2|Y], the primitive suspends. A call fails if the terms are non-unifiable (for example [1, 3] == [1, 2]). PARLOG makes implicit use of this primitive whenever a clause head features a repeated occurence of the same variable in input argument positions. A call to == implements the test that the corresponding call argument terms are identical. A common explicit use is exemplified by the definition of member (see Section 4.8) in which the recursive clause contains a guard test of the form not(X == Y) to check that the variables represent distinct terms.

7.8.3   X ⇐ Y

We have not seen this primitive before but nevertheless its behaviour will be familiar. For this is the operation that implements 'input matching' between pairs of input mode argument terms when a clause is tested for candidate status to solve a call. The left and right arguments of ⇐ respectively represent 'weak' and 'strong' inputs, so that the left argument term (the clause head term in the input matching usage) can become bound whereas the right argument term cannot.

7.8.4   data(X)

data provides a test that X has a value – that is, has a binding to a term other than another unbound variable. The test can only suspend or succeed and this explains its constant logical reading as true. A typical usage is in the swrite_list program (see Section 5.1). This program reminds us that the success of an input matching test does not *necessarily* mean that the call has supplied genuine data to the clause – for example, if the clause head argument is a variable then input matching will always succeed, regardless of the call term. A call to data will implement the check where required.

7.8.5   var(X)

We discussed this logically troublesome primitive in the last chapter. Notice that var(X) does not have the same behaviour as not(data(X)) because when X is unbound a call to var(X) succeeds whereas a call to not(data(X)) suspends. An example of a justified usage is in the implementation of a fair merge program (see Section 6.10). Another use for var is to implement 'invertible' or 'multi-mode' procedures which can replace two or more ordinary (single-mode) procedures (for example, we could define a version of append that is able to split as well as join lists). Roughly, this is done by writing one or more clause for each desired form of call: each clause is guarded by suitably designed var tests in order to detect the call pattern for which the clause is an appropriate candidate. Output is implemented by 'weak' input mode arguments. But both efficiency and transparency suffer through such a treatment and it can only really be justified in exceptional circumstances.

SUMMARY

Metalevel programming means constructing programs and calls to manipulate terms that themselves represent programs and calls. Sometimes this is called 'second-order' programming. The main points of the chapter are summarized below.

- The set primitive can be used to implement a database interface. A call to set eagerly produces a list representing all the solutions to a specified database relation.

- subset is the lazy version of set. A subset evaluation will ultimately generate the same solutions as would be obtained by the equivalent call to set, but with subset each solution is produced lazily by making an appropriate binding to a demand variable.

- The metacall primitives execute PARLOG goals that are specified by argument terms. The one-argument version has the same logical and operational reading as the goal that it evaluates. The three-argument version has the constant logical reading true since it never fails: this version allows tight supervision over a goal evaluation. The metacalls can be used to implement shells and to define further meta-predicates.

- PARLOG's unification-related primitives are = for full unification, == for test unification, <= for one-way unification (as in input matching), data and var.

EXERCISES

7.1 The lists produced by both set and subset can contain duplicate terms. Use the primitives to define variations (predicates unique_set and unique_subset, say) that only ever return one occurrence of each solution to a database evaluation.

7.2 Among the minimum facilities required of a database system are programs to implement the following commands:

Query commands:	which(term, goals), is(goals)
Update commands:	add(reln), delete(reln)
Convenience:	list(reln)

Implement these commands, and any other commands that seem to be useful, as PARLOG programs using the set and subset primitives. For the update commands you will need to consult your system reference manual for predicates that can insert and remove database clauses (look for assert and retract).

7.3   If the requirement is to implement a database system from scratch (rather than interface to an existing database) then there is an alternative approach to the one using set and subset. This is to represent the database as a PARLOG term (probably a list) which is maintained by a long-lived (recursive) process. One way to define the top-level procedures is as follows:

```
mode dbase(commands?).

dbase(Commands) ← maintain_db([], Commands).

mode maintain_db(dbase?, commands?).

maintain_db(DB, [Command|Cmds]) ←
      transact(Command, DB, NewDB),
      maintain_db(NewDB, Cmds).
maintain_db(DB, []).
```

transact should be defined so as to enable user commands similar to those of Exercise 7.2. Then the query

```
← read_list(Commands), dbase(Commands).
```

should create a pair of processes that can respond to input of the form

```
Commands = [add(cost(bolts, 20)),
            add(supplier(bolts, 'Willis & Co')),
            is(cost(nuts, 10)),
            which(X, supplier(paint, X)),
            list(cost), ...]
```

Construct a definition for transact and implement this system. What alterations or extensions are needed in order to handle the replies of the dbase process to the user's commands?

7.4   Implement a variation of the multitask_abortshell procedure so that the shell provides greater control over background processes. In particular the shell should recognize two special commands: 'bg?' and halt(Proc), to produce the names of currently active background processes and to halt an individual named background process respectively.

8
Applications of PARLOG

8.1 A parallel system simulation   8.3 SLIM: a 'front-end' for PARLOG
8.2 A concurrent sentence parser

PREVIEW   This final chapter has three main aims. Firstly, it indicates a few of the likely PARLOG application areas and gives a flavour of the kind of programming that these applications can entail. The second aim is for coherence: we try to bring together in the context of an individual problem many of the concepts that have only been treated separately in earlier parts of the book. Thirdly, the chapter illustrates the process of PARLOG program development with more significant examples than those so far studied. The level and style of treatment continues to be introductory and informal: no significant prior knowledge of the chosen application areas is necessary.

8.1   A parallel system simulation

Simulations have long been an important application area for computers. By building a computer program (a 'working model') capturing the essential characteristics of a system we can hope to learn more about the system's operation. The system simulated could be a nuclear power station, the world economy, or a weekend supermarket; and the advantages of simulation over experimenting with the real thing can include safety, practicality, cheapness and flexibility. In particular, simulation experiments are typically high-speed and repeatable. Real time on the other hand has a habit of passing at its own rate and nobody has yet found a way to make it repeat.

   Many kinds of system that we might wish to model are inherently parallel. They consist of a collection of interacting processes that run together. Not surprisingly then, PARLOG as a concurrent language is a strong candidate for implementing models of such systems. On the other hand, simulation programs are primarily models of *behaviour* and as such they do not fully exploit PARLOG's logic programming capability. Most of the relations defined below are meaningful only in their procedural interpretation.

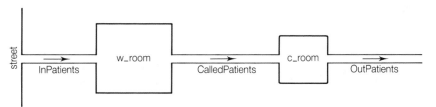

Figure 8.1 A doctor's surgery.

8.1.1 Modelling a doctor's surgery

A simple example is the doctor's surgery represented in Figure 8.1. Patients arrive from the street at intervals and queue up in the waiting room. When an individual's turn comes to respond to the doctor's call, he or she enters the consulting room, is examined and treated, and then departs. The parallelism within this 'system' is apparent: at any given time there is likely to be activity – in the form of patients arriving, waiting and being consulted – in all parts of the surgery.

If we can approximate to the rate at which patients arrive from the street and to the doctor's consultation times then we should be able to build a simulation model of the surgery. The aim would be to predict answers to such questions as:

- How full does the waiting room become at maximum?

- Given the times at which the street doors open and close for patient admission, and given that all admitted patients are eventually seen by the doctor, at what time does the doctor finish work?

- If two doctors were to work instead of one, how would this affect the flow of patients through the surgery?

An interesting fact about simulation diagrams like that of Figure 8.1 is that they are virtually PARLOG programs already. We can model the surgery by the query

```
← street(InPatients),
    w_room(InPatients, CalledPatients),
    c_room(CalledPatients, OutPatients).                    SIM
```

which is really just a representation for the same diagram in a different syntax. All that is necessary to complete the work is to specify definitions for street, w_room and c_room such that these processes accurately simulate the corresponding entities in the system. SIM will then create a network of concurrent PARLOG processes with an interflow of data that faithfully models the flow of patients through the rooms of the surgery.

The main difficulty is to simulate the passing of time. We must not merely leave the different processes to run as fast as machine resources will allow; for realism it is essential that the processes in the model should have the same *relative* speeds as the corresponding entities in the real system. In effect this requires that the simulation processes be explicitly regulated by a common clock. There are several ways to accomplish this: our program will adopt the simplest approach, which is to make use of a hardware (real-time) clock that is assumed to be accessible from PARLOG.

Representing the street

The street process created by SIM will act as the producer of InPatients. The final value of this variable will be a list of the form

```
[patient, patient, patient, patient, ..., patient]
```

Of course, real patients have individual characteristics – a name, a set of symptoms, a previous history, and so on. None of these are relevant from the point of view of this model. In the model each patient is just a 'blob' of data, a constant term patient generated by the street process. What is important to the model is the way in which these terms are generated.

Suppose that the surgery doors are open for ninety minutes during which people are admitted. In the model the opening of the doors can be represented by the starting of the clock. A suitable definition for the street procedure is:

```
mode street(arrivals↑ ).

street(People) ←
      set_clock(0) &
      pause(street, EndPauseTime) &
      admit_people(EndPauseTime, 90, People) .
```

The sequential operators are essential. The street process must *first* start the clock and *then* implement the pause and *then* spawn the admit_people process to produce the people until the ninety minutes are up. The pause is necessary because it happens that our definition for admit_people will produce the first patient immediately on call; in the real surgery there could be a delay between the time of opening and the time of the first arrival. The pause process will represent this delay by doing nothing until EndPauseTime. Details will be worked out later.

It is the job of the admit_people process to actually generate the value of InPatients in SIM. The generation must simulate the arrival of real people: the terms of the list should be produced incrementally, with a pause after the production of each term, until closing time is reached. The admit_people procedure can be defined by:

```
mode admit_people(timenow?, closingtime?, arrivals↑ ).

admit_people(TimeNow, ClosingTime, []) ←
    TimeNow >= ClosingTime :
    true;
admit_people(TimeNow, ClosingTime, [patient|Others]) ←
    pause(street, EndPauseTime) &
    admit_people(EndPauseTime, ClosingTime, Others).
```

With this definition, an admit_people process will initially test the guard in the first clause. This will ensure that no more patients are admitted after time is up. If the test fails, the second clause will be selected (the sequential clause search operator obviates the need for another guard test) and a new patient term will immediately be placed on the arrivals stream. A pause sub-process will then be spawned to simulate the gap that succeeds the new arrival, following which a recursive admit_people process is created to generate any future arrivals over the remaining time period. Notice that the sequential conjunction operator in the recursive clause is essential here too – there is no such thing as a concurrent delay!

Accessing the clock

The definitions above include calls to set_clock and pause, both of which will access the internal clock. set_clock is assumed to be predefined with the declaration

```
mode set_clock(starttime?)
```

A call to it should succeed with the side-effect of resetting the hardware clock to the specified time.

The pause relation is one for which we must supply our own procedure. The mode declaration should be

```
mode pause(location?, endtime↑ ).
```

Location is expected to be either street or c_room. These constants will identify distributions of time delay that correspond to street arrivals and consultation times respectively. A call pause(Location, EndTime) should do nothing from the time of the call until EndTime, the value of which will depend on Location. A suitable definition is:

```
mode pause(location?, endtime↑ ).

pause(Location, EndTime) ←
    required_delay(Location, Delay),
```

```
read_clock(TimeNow),
EndTime is TimeNow + Delay,
busy_wait(TimeNow, EndTime).
```

read_clock is expected like set_clock to be predefined. Its mode declaration is assumed to be

```
mode read_clock(time↑ ).
```

and the behaviour is the obvious one of binding the call variable to a term that represents the current clock time.

A busy_wait process does just what its name suggests: it keeps looking at the clock until the required end-time has been reached. A definition is:

```
mode busy_wait(timenow?, endtime?).

busy_wait(TimeNow, EndTime) ←
    TimeNow >= EndTime :
    true;
busy_wait(T, EndTime) ←
    read_clock(TimeNow) &
    busy_wait(TimeNow, EndTime).
```

The required_delay relation specifies the wait that is appropriate for each location. For a realistic simulation it would be crucial to specify these distributions accurately. However, for testing purposes a simple definition such as the following can suffice:

```
mode required_delay(location?, delay↑ ).

required_delay(street, Delay) ← Delay is random(0, 5).
required_delay(c_room, Delay) ← Delay is random(3, 10).
```

This specifies street arrivals and consultation times to occupy randomly selected amounts of time between zero and five units and between three and ten units respectively. (random is assumed to be predefined). The 'units' may each represent one minute of time in the real surgery but of course much finer units – each one-tenth of a second, say – can be used in the simulation. The finer the simulation units, the greater the speed-up on reality. The capabilities of set_clock and read_clock to measure advancing time will set an upper limit on the speed-up that can be achieved on a particular PARLOG system.

In practice there may be a more significant constraint on how fast the simulation should be allowed to run. Consider the street process in SIM: the validity of this process as a 'faithful' simulation depends upon the assumption that the time required to complete the process is negligibly different from the total time occupied by all the sequential pause sub-processes. Unfortunately, it is inevitable that the process will also spend some time on various 'overhead' operations such as input matching, executing calls to arithmetic primitives, and so on. None of these operations have counterparts in the real system and hence it is essential that this overhead time should be insignificant relative to the overall street process completion time. The same consideration applies to the other processes of SIM. What this means is that the delay periods should not be too short – or in other words, the simulation should not be allowed to run too quickly.

The waiting room

Patients arriving in a waiting room generally expect to have to queue. Periodically the doctor becomes free and calls through from the consulting room for the next in line: patients respond to these calls on a first-come-first-served basis. In terms of our simulation this means that the w_room process in SIM is a *lazy* producer of terms representing patients. It releases terms in response to demands from the c_room process rather than supplying these terms eagerly. An eager w_room process would correspond to a very disorderly surgery in which patients do not wait for a call but rush straight through into the consulting room regardless of whether the doctor is free.

The lazy programming techniques described in Chapter 6 will achieve the desired behaviour on the part of the w_room process. This process can be specified as a consumer of variables representing demands for patients. The c_room process will send a variable whenever it is ready to accept a new patient and the w_room process will respond by binding the variable to a term that represents the patient at the head of the queue. When the final patient has been dispatched the process can indicate the fact by supplying some special constant such as no_more_patients. The procedure below makes a suitable definition:

```
mode w_room(patientsin?, demands?).

w_room([patient|Pins], [Pcall|Pcalls]) ←
    Pcall = patient,
    w_room(Pins, Pcalls) .
w_room([], [Pcall|Pcalls]) ←
    Pcall = no_more_patients.
```

PARLOG's input mode constraint works very nicely for us here. It ensures the correct simulation behaviour in which suspension (waiting) occurs unless there is both a demand from the doctor and typically at least one patient who can respond to it. The 'first-in-first-out' scheduling of patients in response to calls is automatically simulated without requiring any special programming. Notice that body calls to the unification primitive are used to supply the demand variables with the appropriate bindings – this is typical of the lazy programming technique, as explained earlier.

There are a couple of possible objections. Firstly, with this definition the queue of waiting patients is represented in SIM by the variable InPatients. It is as if the queue forms not in the waiting room proper but in the corridor outside. Secondly, we have not simulated the fact that the real waiting room can become full. Both objections could be overcome by a more elaborate implementation of w_room as a 'bounded buffer' process, but we will not pursue this here.

The consulting room

The process that models the consulting room is quite simple. Its behaviour is to send out demand variables representing calls for patients. A patient who answers a call will occupy some process time (representing the consultation period): he or she will then be discharged, following which another demand variable will be sent out. As usual with lazy programming, we arrange that the c_room process first sends out a demand variable and then spawns another process the behaviour of which will depend on the reply.

```
mode c_room(patientcalls↑, patientdischarges↑).

c_room([Pcall|Pcalls], Discharges) ←
    read_respond(Pcall, Pcalls, Discharges).
```

The call for a patient is expected eventually to produce a response from the waiting room. Either the variable Pcall will become bound to patient, representing the entry into the consulting room of a new customer for treatment, or else the binding no_more_patients will indicate that the doctor can go home. In the first case the read_respond process should implement a delay and should then pass the term onto the discharges stream, creating a new c_room process to send out further calls for patients. In the second case the read_respond process should close the Pcalls and Discharges streams and terminate. This behaviour can be specified as follows:

```
mode read_respond(replytocall?, pcalls↑, pdischarges↑).

read_respond(patient, Pcalls, Pdischarges) ←
    pause(c_room, EndTime) &
    Pdischarges = [patient|Others],
    c_room(Pcalls, Others).
read_respond(no_more_patients, [], []).
```

Notice two features of this procedure. Firstly, the pause call that simulates the time spent by the doctor with the patient also makes available some information that is not used here, namely the clock time at which the consultation ends. However this information could contribute towards a general 'metering' of the simulation, as we shall see shortly. Secondly, the unification call in the recursive clause should be recognized as being essential. If we specified the clause as

```
read_respond(patient, Pcalls, [patient|Others]) ←
    pause(c_room, EndTime) &
    c_room(Pcalls, Others).
```

then there would be no delay on the output of the new patient term on to the discharges stream. Instead the behaviour would be that of a 'rogue' doctor who ushers each arrival directly to the surgery exit and then, after a pause, calls for another patient who will receive the same treatment – or rather, the same lack of treatment!

Gathering statistics

The basic simulation is now complete. With the addition of a concurrent call swrite_list(OutPatients) programmed into the SIM query we will be able to watch the generation of the list

```
[patient, patient, patient, .... ]
```

representing the stream of patients being discharged from the surgery. Unfortunately this will not help us to answer any of the questions that were originally posed, such as the one about the doctor's departure time. This is because our program gathers no statistics to record the progress of the patients through the various parts of the surgery system.

In the real surgery there is an easy way in which to gather such statistics. On entry each patient could be provided with a timesheet like the one shown in Figure 8.2. At each critical location the sheet would be stamped to record the time at which that location was reached, so that on discharge a patient's timesheet would contain all the important statistics. In PARLOG we can simulate such a timesheet-carrying patient by using a structured term such as

```
patient(in(T1), called(T2), out(T3))
```

in place of the simple constant patient used above. Initially the variables T1, T2, T3 in each term will be unbound but suitable 'time-stamp' bindings will be contributed by the street, w_room and c_room processes respectively as the term passes through. Thus the value produced for OutPatients will now become a list something like

```
[patient(in(4), called(4), out(10)),
 patient(in(6), called(10), out(19)),
 patient(in(9), called(19), out(24)), ... ]
```

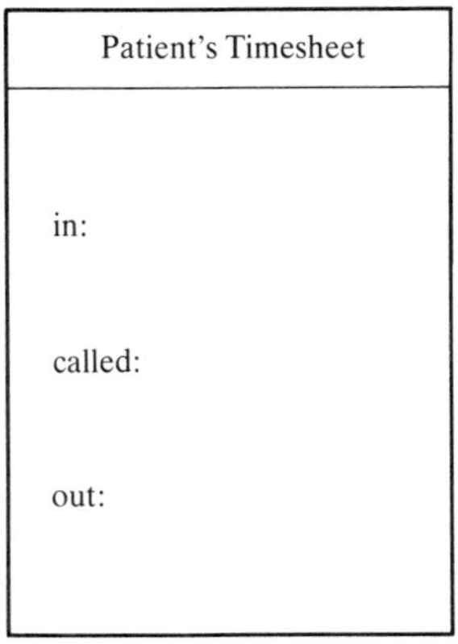

Figure 8.2   A timesheet.

that has been jointly constructed by all three processes. This is a nice application of the logical variable property discussed in Chapter 6. By reading the exit time recorded for the final patient we will be able to answer the question about the doctor's time of departure. More generally, the timing statistics can be analysed by a process that runs concurrently with SIM and that does the job of 'metering' the simulation.

It is a straightforward matter to adapt the program for this new representation of patients. We shall only show the changes needed for the street procedure: the implementation of the w_room and c_room time-stamps will be left to the reader. Actually street itself requires no modification but the definition of the subsidiary admit_people should be changed so that this process produces terms of the new type, as follows:

```
mode admit_people(timenow?, closetime?, people↑ ).

admit_people(Now, Close, []) ←
    Now >= Close :
    true;
admit_people(Now, Close, [patient(in(Now), called(T2), out(T3))|Othrs]) ←
    pause(street, EndPause) &
    admit_people(EndPause, Close, Othrs) .
```

Notice the duplicate occurrence of the variable Now in the head of the recursive clause. Operationally this will simulate the stamping of the time-of-entry statistic on the newly admitted patient's timesheet.

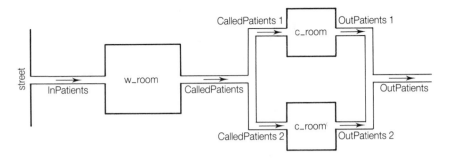

Figure 8.3   A two-doctor surgery.

Extending to a two-doctor surgery

A surgery with two doctors is shown in Figure 8.3. To simulate this system
we can specify the query

```
← street(InPatients),
   w_room(InPatients, CalledPatients),
   merge(CalledPatients1, CalledPatients2, CalledPatients),
   c_room(CalledPatients1, OutPatients1),
   c_room(CalledPatients2, OutPatients2),
   merge(OutPatients1, OutPatients2, OutPatients).                    SIM2
```

This creates a network of six processes in which the corridor junctions of the
diagram are represented by two merge processes. One of these combines the
two streams of outgoing patients. The other actually combines streams of
variables representing doctors' demands for patients – these demands flow
from the c_room processes to the w_room process, which is of course opposite
in direction to the flow of patients. (This should recall our discussion of
client-server interactions in Chapter 6, for the w_room process is essentially a
lazy server of data to the two c_room client processes.)

Only one change is necessary to the earlier definitions and this is to
secure the termination of the simulated system. Recall that the termination
of a c_room process depends upon its eventual receipt in response to a
demand for another patient of a message no_more_patients from the w_room
process. After sending such a message the w_room process as defined above
terminates. This is satisfactory behaviour for the one-doctor surgery, but for
the two-doctor version of the simulation it will leave one of the c_room
processes (whichever one was not the recipient of the message) in limbo.
This process will deadlock when it sends out a call for a patient after the
w_room process has terminated. It is as if one doctor waits forever not
realizing that the surgery has shut for the night.

The solution is to modify the w_room definition so that this process remains active for as long as necessary. A suitable revision is as follows:

```
mode w_room(patientsin?, demands?).

w_room([patient|Pins], [Pcall|Pcalls]) ←
    Pcall = patient,
    w_room(Pins, Pcalls).
w_room([], [Pcall|Pcalls]) ←
    Pcall = no_more_patients,
    w_room([], Pcalls).
w_room([], []).
```

Termination of the w_room process now requires the closure of the demands stream, which is taken as the signal that both c_room processes have terminated.

The version of the simulation that gathers statistics may require to distinguish between the two consulting rooms. If so then this is quite easily achieved. The representation of each patient can become a term of the form

```
patient(in(T1), called(time(T2), doctor(RoomNumber)), out(T3))
```

so that it will be possible to identify the doctor who treated the individual as well as the times of entry, call and exit. RoomNumber can be an integer 1 or 2 (or some other appropriate constant such as a doctor's name) and c_room can be re-defined with an extra argument in order to label each c_room process accordingly; the revised procedure could be given modes

```
mode c_room(roomnumber?, patientcalls↑, patientdischarges↑).
```

for example. Instead of being a stream of unbound variables as before, the demands stream CalledPatients in SIM2 can become a list of the form

```
[next(P1, 1), next(P2, 2), next(P3, 1), next(P4, 1), next(P5, 2), ...]
```

where each term next(Pi, N) represents a demand to the w_room process for a patient Pi to be sent to room N for consultation. The values of Pi and N are contributed respectively by the w_room process and by whichever c_room process has sent the demand. Making these changes is straightforward and the reader is invited to tackle them as exercises.

. 8.2   A concurrent sentence parser

The parsing problem is the problem of establishing the grammatical structure of a phrase or sentence. Logically we can distinguish two aspects of the problem: the first is to test that a sequence of words *does* have a valid structure, and the second is to discover what that structure (or **parse**) actually is. In practice the distinction becomes blurred because the usual approach to testing for validity involves trying to find a possible parse.

Parsing is a rich topic with many important applications. Two examples are real-time natural language processing systems, for which high performance parsing programs (or just **parsers**, for short) are a key requirement, and the compilation of computer programs, for which parsing represents an essential stage. Although the first example stands to gain more from a parallel execution behaviour than the second, it seems to be the case that opportunities for parallelism exist in all kinds of parsing. We shall develop a concurrent parser for a grammar which specifies some very simple English sentences, but which can be adapted for other languages too.

8.2.1 Specifying the language

A **grammar** is a set of rules that specify how the sentences of a language are put together. For a very small subset of the English language we might propose a (somewhat flawed) grammar as follows:

```
sentence           --> noun_phrase + verb.
sentence           --> noun_phrase + verb_phrase.
noun_phrase        --> determiner + noun_expression.
noun_expression    --> noun.
noun_expression    --> adjective + noun_expression.
verb_phrase        --> verb_expression + noun_phrase.
verb_expression    --> verb.
verb_expression    --> adverb + verb.
verb               --> likes|kicks|smiles|admires|eats.
determiner         --> the|a|an.
noun               --> boy|girl|table|tree|apple|ball.
adverb             --> quickly|easily.
adjective          --> big|small|lazy|eager|bad|good.
```

Of course, this is inadequate to express more than a miserable collection of uninteresting sentences, but it makes a place to start. The grammar has a straightforward interpretation. Each is a rule of the type

```
FORM --> EXPANSION
```

that defines an expansion or structure for some particular grammatical form. The first pair of rules specify the most important form, namely the sentence, which has two possible expansions – it can comprise a noun phrase followed by a verb, or alternatively it can be a noun phrase followed by a verb phrase. Other rules define these other forms: notice that the form of a noun (which is an example of a *terminal* form) is defined by a rule with a slightly different appearance which in effect says that a noun is one of boy, girl, table and so on.

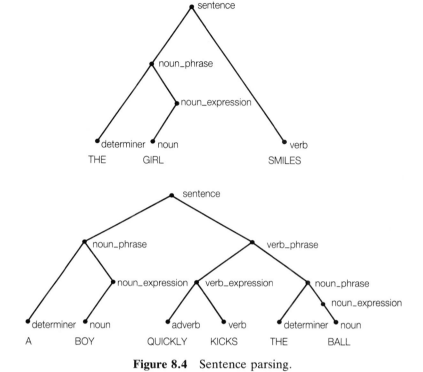

Figure 8.4   Sentence parsing.

With these rules we can validate such sentences as the girl smiles and a boy quickly kicks the ball. Figure 8.4 indicates how these sentences can be derived from the grammar. Diagrams such as these are known as **parse trees**: the generalized parsing problem can be regarded as the problem of building a parse tree from a given list of words. The reader may like to draw parse trees for some other lists that are valid sentences according to the grammar, such as the bad boy likes an apple and a table easily smiles an tree. The fact that this last example is non-English suggests that the grammar is less than perfect linguistically!

8.2.2   Representing the grammar

How can we represent the grammar in PARLOG? A fairly obvious scheme is to translate each rule into one assertion. For the first rule we might write

```
grammar(sentence, [noun_phrase, verb]).
```

to represent the fact that a sentence may expand into a noun phrase
followed by a verb. But this representation is not well suited to PARLOG's
'committed choice' clause search strategy: the grammar specifies *two*
possible expansions for sentences, and it would be better to have both
made accessible by the same single call. The representation

    grammar(sentence, [[noun_phrase, verb], [noun_phrase, verb_phrase]]).

meets this requirement and will be used instead. However, the rules for
terminal forms (such as nouns) deserve a scheme of their own: we shall
adopt for them the representation exemplified by

    dictionary(noun, [boy, girl, table, tree, apple, ball]).

to indicate that the noun is a terminal form composed of the specified
dictionary of words. Altogether then, the PARLOG version of the
grammar becomes two procedures:

    mode grammar(form?, expansions↑).

    grammar(sentence, [[noun_phrase, verb], [noun_phrase, verb_phrase]]).
    grammar(noun_phrase, [[determiner, noun_expression]]).
    grammar(noun_expression, [[noun], [adjective, noun_expression]]).
    grammar(verb_phrase, [[verb_expression, noun_phrase]]).
    grammar(verb_expression, [[verb], [adverb, verb]]).

    mode dictionary(form?, words↑).

    dictionary(verb, [likes, kicks, smiles, admires, eats]).
    dictionary(determiner, [the, a, an]).
    dictionary(noun, [boy, girl, table, tree, apple, ball]).
    dictionary(adverb, [quickly, easily]).
    dictionary(adjective, [big, small, lazy, eager, bad, good]).

There are of course many alternative representations. But this scheme
facilitates PARLOG-style committed-choice computation; it is reasonably
concise and transparent; and it is nicely self-contained, so that changes to
the grammar are potentially easy to implement.

8.2.3 Top-level predicates

We want to define a predicate parse say, where the logical reading of
parse(S, P) is: P is a term representing the parse of the sentence S.
Operationally, we want to find the parse so the modes will be

    mode parse(sentence?, parse↑).

A sentence can be represented by a list of words. With what kind of term
should we represent a parse? Since a parse is really a binary tree, the

obvious representation scheme is a compound term (structure) that has sentence as the principal functor. The term will look like one of

```
sentence(noun_phrase(....), verb_phrase(....))
```

or

```
sentence(noun_phrase(....), verb(....))
```

depending on the sentence. For the query

```
← parse([the, girl, smiles], P).
```

we would hope to obtain the solution

```
P = sentence(
        noun_phrase(determiner(the), noun_expression(noun(girl))),
        verb(smiles))
```

and so on. Thinking about this scheme should remind us that although parsing is usually equated to sentence parsing, parsing to other grammatical forms is important too: for example, the list

```
[the, girl]
```

parses as a noun phrase according to our grammar. So the top-level parse predicate is just a restricted case of another relation that specifies the parse of a list of words according to *any* specified grammatical form. This observation enables us to write a useful definition immediately:

```
mode parse(sentence?, parse↑ ).

parse(S, P) ← parse_form(S, sentence, P).
```

The parse_form relation is our real target. parse_form(Words, Form, Parse-Tree) has the logical reading: ParseTree is a term representing the parse of Words as a form Form of the grammar.

8.2.4 Scope for parallelism

Our parser will be 'top-down' in the sense that it would construct the trees in Figure 8.4 by starting from the root and working down towards the words in the input sentence. Of course parsing in the opposite, bottom-up direction is quite feasible too: parsing is a big subject and some very sophisticated approaches have been developed, often combining both top-down and bottom-up directions. Top-down parsers tend to be simpler, however, and for parsing artificial languages they can be perfectly adequate.

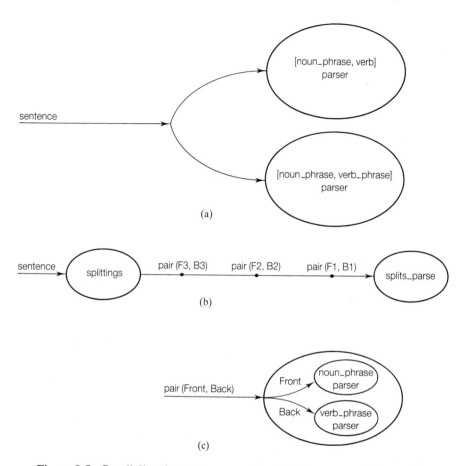

Figure 8.5 Parallelism in top-down parsing: (a) Try to parse alternative expansions in parallel; (b) Produce splittings concurrently with the process which tries to parse them; (c) Try to parse the two sublists in parallel.

Opportunities for parallelism in top-down parsing arise from at least four main sources. Firstly, observe that our grammar specifies two possible ways in which to parse a sentence – it might be done using the expansion [noun_phrase, verb] or using the expansion [noun_phrase, verb_phrase]. We could try both expansion possibilities in parallel (see Figure 8.5 (a)). Secondly, consider the task of trying to parse the sentence using the [noun_phrase, verb_phrase] expansion. The basic mechanism is to try to split the list of words into a pair of sublists in such a way that the front sublist will parse as a noun_phrase and the back sublist will parse as a verb_phrase. We could run a splittings process concurrently with a splits_ parse process that tries to parse the sublist pairs (Figure 8.5 (b)). Thirdly, there are usually many ways in which a sentence can be split into sublist pairs. The splits_parse process could create an individual concurrent parsing process for each pair. Fourthly, such a process that works on an individual pair could try to parse the two sublists in parallel, the front sublist as a noun_phrase and the back sublist as a verb_phrase (Figure 8.5 (c)).

Of course, similar opportunities for parallelism apply equally to parsing noun phrases, verb phrases and so on, as they do to sentences. The parser described below takes advantage of this and implements all the types of concurrency indicated here.

8.2.5 PARLOG definitions

A procedure for parse_form should handle two types of call. A call such as

    ← parse_form([smiles], verb, P).

merely requires that the word smiles be checked for membership of the verb clause of the dictionary procedure, following which the call should succeed with the output binding

    P = verb(smiles)

A more typical call requests a parse of a list according to a non-terminal form. An example is

    ← parse_form([the, girl, smiles], sentence, Parse).

To solve this call requires that the expansions for sentence should be determined from the grammar procedure, and the list of words parsed according to one or other of these expansions. This suggests the following definition:

```
mode parse_form(words?, form?, parsetree↑ ).

parse_form([Word], Form, Parse) ←
     dictionary(Form, Dict) :
     member(Word, Dict),
     Parse =.. [Form, Word].
parse_form(Words, Form, Parse) ←
     grammar(Form, Expansions) :
     expansions_parse(Words, Expansions, ParseList),
     Parse =.. [Form|ParseList].
```

Depending on whether the call specifies a terminal or non-terminal form, a parse_form process will commit to the first or second clause. The =..

primitive implements list-to-structure conversion (see Section 7.7) and is necessary to assemble the parse tree from its functor and components; this may not be very elegant, but for the second clause the alternative is to pass the functor Form into expansions_parse and this is baggage that we would rather not carry.

The logical reading of expansions_parse(Words, Expansions, ParseList) is: ParseList represents a parse of Words according to one expansion on Expansions. As an example, the second call to parse_form above would result in a call to expansions_parse of the form

```
← expansions_parse(
    [the, girl, smiles],
    [[noun_phrase, verb], [noun_phrase, verb_phrase]],
    Parse).
```

This specifies two alternative expansions that can be tried concurrently in order to parse the sentence. Other calls to expansions_parse (arising from noun_phrase parsing for example) will offer only a single expansion. A procedure that can handle both cases is:

```
mode expansions_parse(words?, expansions?, parselist↑ ).

expansions_parse(Words, [Expansion1, Expansion2], Parse) ←
    one_expansion_parse(Words, Expansion1, Parse) :
    true.
expansions_parse(Words, [Expansion1, Expansion2], Parse) ←
    one_expansion_parse(Words, Expansion2, Parse) :
    true.
expansions_parse(Words, [Expansion], Parse) ←
    one_expansion_parse(Words, Expansion, Parse).
```

With this procedure, a call that offers two expansions will result in a 'guards race' to establish one of the first two clauses as candidates. This will implement the first type of concurrency forecast above. Examples of calls to one_expansion_parse might be

```
← one_expansion_parse(
    [the, girl, smiles],
    [noun_phrase, verb],
    Parse).
```

and

```
← one_expansion_parse(
    [smiles],
    [verb],
    Parse).
```

The first example is more typical. It requires that the list of words should be 'split-parsed' into two sublists such that the front sublist parses as a noun_phrase and the back sublist parses as a verb. Calls like that of the second example will arise from grammar rules such as the rule for verb_expression that feature an 'expansion' specifying just one grammatical form, and these examples can always be re-specified as calls to parse_form. The procedure below provides two clauses accordingly.

```
mode one_expansion_parse(words?, expansion?, parselist↑ ).
```

```
one_expansion_parse(Words, [Form1, Form2], [Parse1, Parse2]) ←
    splittings(Words, Splits),
    splits_parse(Splits, Form1, Form2, Parse1, Parse2).
one_expansion_parse(Words, [Form], [Parse]) ←
    parse_form(Words, Form, Parse).
```

With the first clause we have specified the second type of forecast concurrency – the splittings process will generate incrementally a list Splits of all sublist pairs that can be concurrently tested by splits_parse. We will give the definition of splittings shortly. As an example, the value of Splits for an input sentence [the, girl, smiles] is

```
[pair([], [the, girl, smiles]),
    pair([the], [girl, smiles]),
        pair([the, girl], [smiles]),
            pair([the, girl, smiles], [])]
```

and a call

```
← splits_parse(Splits, noun_phrase, verb, Parse1, Parse2).
```

where Splits has this value, should be able (by using the third pair) to compute the bindings

```
Parse1 = noun_phrase(determiner(the), noun_expression(noun(girl)))
Parse2 = verb(smiles)
```

In general, the logical reading of splits_parse(Splits, Form1, Form2, Parse1, Parse2) should be: the list Splits contains a pair of word lists pair(Front, Back) such that the parse of Front as a grammar form Form1 is Parse1, and the parse of Back as a grammar form Form2 is Parse2. Operationally it is only necessary to recurse down the list, testing the two halves of each pair by calls to parse_form. The definition of splits_parse can be:

```
mode splits_parse(listofsplits?, form1?, form2?, parse1↑, parse2↑ ).
```

```
splits_parse([pair(Front, Back)|Splits], Form1, Form2, Parse1, Parse2) ←
    parse_form(Front, Form1, Parse1),
    parse_form(Back, Form2, Parse2) :
    true.
splits_parse([Split|Splits], Form1, Form2, Parse1, Parse2) ←
    splits_parse(Splits, Form1, Form2, Parse1, Parse2) :
    true.
```

This procedure delivers both the third and the fourth types of concurrency that were forecast earlier. The third type is implemented by a 'peeling' or-parallel behaviour, like that of the path-searching algorithm that we studied in Chapter 5 – here the effect will be to investigate concurrently the various sublist pairs representing different ways to split the list. The fourth type is specified by the and-parallel evaluation of the two parse_form guard calls in the first clause. Notice how and-parallelism realizes an 'efficient failure' behaviour here – if either sublist of any pair fails to parse then the attempt to parse the other half of the pair will be terminated at once. Or-parallelism on the other hand realizes an 'efficient success', in that a splits_parse process will terminate as soon as parsing succeeds for one sublist pair.

8.2.6   The splittings relation

The splittings relation is not specific to parsing. However, it is an example of a non-trivial list relation and to develop a PARLOG implementation of it makes an interesting exercise.

The logical reading of splittings(L, Splits) is: Splits is a list containing (in some order) all possible pairs pair(F, B) of front and back sublists of L. Operationally we want to compute such a list so that the required program will have modes

mode splittings(list?, listofsplits↑).

A few examples may help us to construct a logical formulation. Although we have been thinking about word lists until now, there seems to be no reason why the relation should not operate over all types of lists. Consider two short lists of integers:

T = [1, 2, 3]

and

[0|T] = [0, 1, 2, 3]

What are the 'splittings' of these lists, and how are they related? If we can identify the relationship between the splittings of T and those of [0|T] then we may be able to do the same for two general lists T and [H|T], and thus induce a recursive definition. For T the splittings can be represented as

```
[pair([], [1, 2, 3]),
      pair([1], [2, 3]),
           pair([1, 2], [3]),
                pair([1, 2, 3], [])]
```

and for [0|T] they are

```
[pair([], [0, 1, 2, 3]),
      pair([0], [1, 2, 3]),
           pair([0, 1], [2, 3]),
                pair([0, 1, 2], [3])
                     pair([0, 1, 2, 3], [])]
```

The relationship is not too hard to see: all but one of the pairs for [0|T] can be obtained from a pair in the splittings of T by inserting a 0 into the head of the front sublist. The one exceptional or 'new' pair is pair([], [0, 1, 2, 3]), which is pair([], [0|T]). By careful generalization, we can capture this idea in the following clause:

```
splittings([H|T], [pair([], [H|T])|Insertions]) ←
      splittings(T, Tsplits),
      front_insert(H, Tsplits, Insertions).
```

To complete the procedure we need a non-recursive clause. This is supplied by an obvious special case: the only way to split the empty list is as a pair of two empty sublists. The assertion

```
splittings([], [pair([], [])]).
```

can specify this case. Then the procedure becomes as follows:

```
mode splittings(list?, listofsplits↑ ).

splittings([], [pair([], [])]).
splittings([H|T], [pair([], [H|T])|Insertions]) ←
      splittings(T, Tsplits),
      front_insert(H, Tsplits, Insertions).
```

For the sake of completeness, here also is a definition of front_insert:

```
mode front_insert(term?, listofpairs?, insertedpairs↑ ).

front_insert(T, [], []).
front_insert(T, [pair(F, B)|Pairs], [pair([T|F], B)|InsertedPairs]) ←
      front_insert(T, Pairs, InsertedPairs).
```

Does our definition for splittings generate lists of pairs incrementally? It does, and you may like to analyse why this is so. Incrementalism is essential if our parser is to implement the second type of concurrency which we described earlier.

8.2.7 Strengths and limitations

Now that the program is complete, we should check that it works. We might also give some thought to its strengths and limitations.

A strength seems to be that we have implemented an (almost) total separation between the parser and the grammar, which should make the parser applicable to other languages. The *almost* is necessary because the definition which (for the sake of simplicity) we offered for the expansions_parse relation requires that each grammar assertion will specify no more than two alternative expansions. This would prevent (for example) an extension to the given grammar for the rule

    verb_expression --> verb + adverb.

because the extra rule would enlarge the corresponding grammar clause to contain three expansions. In fact, the restriction can easily be removed. If we re-specify the expansions_parse procedure as

    mode expansions_parse(words?, expansions?, parselist↑).

    expansions_parse(Words, [Expansion|OtherExpnsns], Parse) ←
        one_expansion_parse(Words, Expansion, Parse) :
        true.
    expansions_parse(Words, [Expansion|OtherExpnsns], Parse) ←
        expansions_parse(Words, OtherExpnsns, Parse) :
        true.

then the parser will be able to cope with rules that specify multiple expansions. Like the previous version, this revised definition implements a concurrent investigation of alternative expansions but it does so through a 'peeling' or-parallel behaviour.

A second restriction on the grammar is that at most two forms may appear in each expansion. This is because the parser is limited to two-way splittings of the list of input words. Fortunately, the restriction is not too severe because any grammar rule such as

    Form --> E1 + E2 + E3

that specifies a three-form expansion, can always be replaced by two rules

    Form --> E1 + X
    X --> E2 + E3

that introduce a new grammatical form X, for which some name can usually be invented. And since our program places no limit on the permissible number of grammar rules, the restriction is only a matter of inconvenience.

With these observations in mind, the reader is encouraged to experiment with a variety of substitute grammars. Try writing a grammar for arithmetic expressions or for regularly patterned strings of symbols, for example: the parser should be able to handle any grammar of the kind known as 'context-free' in formal language theory. However, natural languages (and some artificial ones too) have more elaborate grammars than these and efficient parsers for them require a more sophisticated approach than the pure top-down technique such as we have implemented here. The reader may like to investigate other types of parser and their implementation in PARLOG.

Our program specifies an impressive amount of concurrency. But this will not suit every computer system; if you run the parser on a small-memory sequential machine, the number of spawned processes may swamp the available storage (even for a fairly short input sentence!). One remedy for this is to reduce the amount of concurrency, for example by replacing the parallel search operator in the splits_parse procedure with a sequential operator. (Another remedy is to buy a more powerful machine!)

Obvious inefficiencies in the program should also be removed. Perhaps you have recognized already the fact that the one_expansions- _parse procedure contains a significant source of inefficiency. Recall that the first clause of the procedure is

```
one_expansion_parse(Words, [Form1, Form2], [Parse1, Parse2]) ←
    splittings(Words, Splits),
    splits_parse(Splits, Form1, Form2, Parse1, Parse2).
```

When this clause is selected to solve a call, the splittings process will always produce the *full* list of pairs representing sentence splits. It will insist on running to completion even if one of the first produced pairs causes the splits_parse process (which is the sole consumer of this list) to succeed, and of course when this happens the subsequent activity of splittings will be wasted work. We could eliminate the inefficiency by arranging for the splits_parse process to send splittings a feedback message to signal the event of a successful parse. This modification is left to the reader.

Our program produces at most one parse of a given sentence. This is no disadvantage with the grammar given above because for this grammar there never *is* more than one parse – the grammar is 'unambiguous'. But not all context-free grammars are unambiguous, and it would be fair to ask whether the program can be extended so as to return a list representing all possible ways in which to parse any sentence. To achieve this requires that each parsing procedure should be re-defined so that its output mode argument specifies a list of all parses rather than a single parse. If no parse exists then the corresponding call should return the empty list rather than fail. For example, the revised version of expansions_parse could be re-specified as follows:

```
mode expansions_parse(words?, expansions?, parselists↑ ).

expansions_parse(Words, [], []).
expansions_parse(Words, [Expansion|OtherExpnsns], AllParsings) ←
    one_expansion_parse(Words, Expansion, Parsings1),
    expansions_parse(Words, OtherExpnsns, Parsings2),
    merge(Parsings1, Parsings2, AllParsings).
```

Thus an expansions_parse process would output via merge the combined parses obtained from all possible expansions. For this to work, one_expansion_parse must be able to produce a list (maybe empty) of parses obtainable from one particular expansion, and this in turn will necessitate a re-definition for splits_parse. So the answer to the question is: yes, an all-solutions version of the parser is possible – but not without a considerable amount of extra work!

8.3   SLIM: a 'front-end' for PARLOG

An important role for PARLOG lies in the specification and development of software for computer operating systems. We use the term 'operating systems' broadly here, so as to cover all manner of software intended to make hardware usable by programmers: examples include text editors, language compilers, programming tools and system utilities, as well as the machine's basic resource management software. This 'systems software' application area for PARLOG is not really too surprising since, after all, the study of concurrent programming in computing was originally motivated by the need to develop operating systems that could manage multiple processes. Perhaps the surprise is how far the pioneers in this area were able to progress using only imperative and sequential languages as their main development tools.

Of course, systems programming is another big subject. We can only illustrate it here by describing one modest project: a 'front-end' or shell system for PARLOG. But many of the ideas are quite generalizable and it is hoped that what follows will spur the reader into further investigations in this area.

8.3.1   An informal specification

We shall begin with a brief overview of the system that we propose to implement. This can double as a kind of informal specification of the system's requirements.

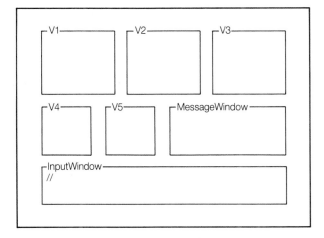

Figure 8.6   SLIM screen display.

First things first, however. Everyone knows that a new system only begins to exist when it has been given a name: let us christen this one SLIM, for Shell with Learners In Mind. The name fits quite well because the expected users of SLIM are novice PARLOG programmers. The raison d'être of the system is to help these people test programs (or better, to 'explore' programs – 'testing' sounds more single-minded than the activity that we envisage), in particular by making input and output easy to manage. Ideally SLIM should implement an ultra-convenient environment for studying PARLOG processes.

Users will interact with SLIM via the screen display depicted in Figure 8.6. Commands – which will usually represent relation calls to the procedures under test – are typed into the Input Window: we shall use the system prompt // to indicate such commands in the foregoing. SLIM executes each command, typically by creating a new process to evaluate the user's relation call, and prints helpful messages such as OK – process is now running in the Message Window. The remaining windows (with names V1, V2, etc.) are all Process Windows. Each Process Window represents a special kind of variable known in SLIM as a 'window variable'. A window variable is like any other PARLOG variable save in two respects: it has a 'global' scope, and any bindings made to it by a user process are automatically displayed in the corresponding screen window. Conceptually the logic variable is 'hard-wired' to the physical Process Window.

This hard-wiring of variables to windows is the most significant feature of SLIM. It means that to test a program for the integers relation for example it will only be necessary for the user to enter the command

    // integers(1, 100, V1).

The occurrence of a window variable in the output argument position will cause the required list of integers to be automatically displayed in the Process Window V1. It will not be necessary for the user to supply an explicit call to swrite_list, for example, in order to observe the data generated by the process.

A second feature of the system is that commands are incremental. Suppose for instance that having entered the integers command the user then decides to experiment with programs for randoms and merge, where merge is the usual relation and where the modes of randoms are

    mode randoms(quantity?, randomintegers↑).

Then the pair of commands

    // randoms(50, V2).
    // merge(V1, V2, V3).

will result in the concurrent display of the randoms output data in the V2 Process Window and the merge output data in V3, in addition to the integers data which has been generated (or which may still be being generated) for V1. This explains the significance of the 'global scope' property of window variables: for the merge call to access the variables V1 and V2 in this way would have been impossible if the above had been three ordinary separate PARLOG queries. In SLIM, a 'query' really corresponds to an entire sequence of commands entered up to an explicit reset command that will restore the system to 'scratch' state. Thus a network of processes can be created in convenient, piecemeal fashion. However, we should permit a user process to fail gracefully. Strictly speaking, since a session of SLIM commands corresponds to a conjunctive query, one failed process should logically terminate the session. It will be more helpful for SLIM simply to ignore the failure.

As a convenience we shall permit the input of explicit conjunctions of commands. For example

    // randoms(50, V2), merge(V1, V2, V3).

is an alternative to entering the previous two commands separately. Of course, the provision of incremental queries makes this capability strictly unnecessary.

Window variables will obviously contribute to output management. But they can help with input too. In SLIM we will implement an input command whereby a named window variable can become bound incrementally to terms entered at the keyboard. This will mean that a program for a relation spell_check (for example) having modes

      mode spell_check(words?, replies↑).

could be tested by the command

      // spell_check(V4, V5).

which names window variables for both input and output. Subsequently the user's commands

      // input(V4, coelostat).
      // input(V4, coeaesthesis).
      // input(V4, coetaneous).

will cause three terms representing words for checking to be sent as messages to the spell_check process. Automatically the corresponding outputs will be displayed in the V5 Process Window. In this way SLIM will support the testing of interactive programs.

    The only other command to be recognized by SLIM will be quit. The table below provides a summary of what should be possible with the system – all we have to do now is build it!

Command	*Effect*
<user_relation_call>	Create new process to evaluate a call to a user-defined relation
reset	Restore system to scratch state
<Cmd>, <Cmds>	Run a conjunction of commands concurrently
input(<Var>, <Term>)	Bind <Var> according to <Term>
quit	Exit system

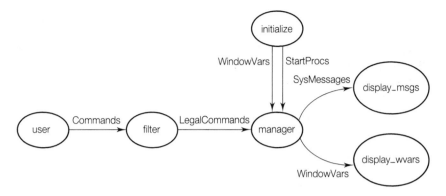

Figure 8.7   Data flow diagram for SLIM.

8.3.2   Top-level design

Figure 8.7 is a data flow diagram that shows how SLIM can be modelled by
a system of six communicating concurrent processes. A user process directs
the stream of commands gathered from the Input Window to a filter process
that traps invalid command terms and converts valid terms into some
standardized form. The initialize process specifies suitable terms to represent the window variables, and performs other such initialization: this
process will quickly terminate, unlike the others which will remain active at
least until a reset command ends the current session. The manager process
is the heart of the system: it supervises the execution of the user's
commands and sends a stream of response messages to a display_msgs
process that controls the Message Window. The manager process also links
the user's commands to the window variables. A display_wvars process is
responsible for displaying bindings made to the latter in the Process
Windows.

To implement this design requires that each process should be
defined by an appropriate procedure. From the data flow diagram the
necessary modes appear to be:

```
mode user(commands↑ ).
mode filter(cmds?, legalcmds↑ ).
mode initialize(winvars↑, startprocs↑ ).
mode manager(legalcmds?, winvars?, startprocs?, smsgs↑ ).
mode display_msgs(smsgs?).
mode display_wvars(winvars?).
```

(Notice that the diagram shows WindowVars as implementing both an input
and an output channel for manager – the second argument of this relation

will specify a 'weak' input.) Given suitable procedures for these relations, we will be able to run the system by entering the query

```
← user(Commands),
    filter(Commands, LegalCommands),
    initialize(WindowVars, StartProcs),
    manager(LegalCommands, WindowVars, StartProcs, SysMessages),
    display_msgs(SysMessages),
    display_wvars(WindowVars).                              SYS
```

which represents the system of processes as a conjunction of relation calls (that is, it is just the diagram in a different syntax). Of course, a query as lengthy as this one is much too tedious to type. If we declare a predicate

```
mode slim.
```

which is defined by a single clause with the calls of SYS in the body, then the system can be set running by the command

```
← slim.
```

which is more convenient.

8.3.3   Terms and relations

Which types of data will the variables of SYS represent? And what is the logical meaning of the relations between them? Let us first consider the matter of data representation.

Commands is an easy one. Its value can be a list containing terms each representing a user command. A typical value might be

```
[randoms(50, 'V2'),
    input('V1', 1),
        intgers(1, 20, 'V4'), ...]
```

which specifies the beginnings of a command 'history' for some particular session. The reason for the quotes around the window variables will become clear shortly.

LegalCommands is just a validated version of Commands. For the above value of Commands, our definition of filter would give to LegalCommands the value

```
[run(randoms(50, 'V2')),
    input('V1', 1),
        unrecognized(intgers(1, 20, 'V4')), ...]
```

SysMessages can be a list of terms each representing a SLIM message produced by the manager process and intended for display in the Message Window. In our system a typical value will be

```
[running(randoms(50, 'V2')),
     input('V1', 1, done),
          unrecognized(intgers(1, 20, 'V4')), ...]
```

WindowVars should implement a kind of look-up table that associates window variable identifiers with their current values. It will be a term of the form wvars(WControl, Windows), where the purpose of WControl will be explained later. The look-up table proper is represented by Windows and this term can be a list of pairs such as

```
[window('V1', ...), window('V2', ...), window('V3', ...), .... ]
```

where the second component of each pair will specify the current value of the window variable named by the first component. The use of quoted constants is essential to provide the necessary look-up capability; if 'window variables' were stored as PARLOG variables then the significance of their names would be lost.

StartProcs specifies an empty set of initial user processes. We shall represent this by the term procs(PControl, []), where the role of PControl will be explained later. A more general, non-empty set of user processes can be represented by a term procs(PControl, Procs) where Procs is a list exemplified by

```
[randoms(50, 'V2'), integers(1, 10, 'V1'), merge('V1', 'V2', 'V3')]
```

Each term of the list will represent one user process created by the manager process.

What about the logical interpretation of the relations of SYS? There is no useful logical reading for the user, display_wvars and display_msgs predicates. These predicates exist solely for their input/output operational side-effects.

The logical meaning of filter(Commands, LegalCommands) is: Legal-Commands is a list obtained by applying the validating function map__command to each term of Commands. The definition of map_command will be given shortly.

initialize(WinVars, StartProcs) means: WinVars is a term representing a set of unbound window variables and StartProcs is a term representing an empty set of user processes.

manager(LegalCommands, WinVars, StartProcs, SysMessages) means: SysMessages is a list representing a history of system messages that arises from the history of commands LegalCommands when the starting state of the system is given by WinVars and StartProcs.

8.3.4   Channels and processes

By describing terms and relations we have considered SLIM from the logical viewpoint. We should now address the complimentary, operational interpretation in which the variables of SYS become communication channels and the conjoined relation calls become concurrent processes. Both perspectives are important to our understanding of the system and each provides a cross-check on the other.

All variables of SYS implement single-directional communication channels. 'Strong' stream communication is implemented by Commands, LegalCommands, and SysMessages (recall that a 'strong' channel is one in which the producer process completely constructs the value of the data). The producer processes for these variables are user, filter and manager respectively. The main constraint on these processes is the supply of user commands.

StartProcs implements the communication of a single constant. Its value is produced in a single reduction step by initialize. The latter is also the 'official' producer for WindowVars, but for this variable the value given by initialize is incomplete – the second component of each pair window(Name, Value) will be left as an unbound variable. Incrementally these variables will become bound by user processes created under the manager, and the display_wvars process which also shares WindowVars will display these bindings concurrently as they are made. Thus for WindowVars, initialize acts as an incomplete producer; manager is a contributing consumer; and display_wvars is a non-contributing consumer. This use of the 'logical variable' property will prove to be a very convenient means of handling user process output.

What about the termination of processes? The initialize process is ephemeral. The filter and manager processes should terminate in response to the closure of the commands stream by the user process, and of course user itself should terminate at that point. However, the manager's life must not end before it has sent a termination signal to display_msgs, display-_wvars, and to any user-created processes that may still be active. With display_msgs this can be done by closing the SysMessages message stream. The termination signals to display_wvars and to the user processes will comprise the binding to stop of the WControl and PControl variables mentioned earlier.

8.3.5   Predicate definitions

We are now ready to give PARLOG definitions for the main relations. Some of these – particularly those concerning input and output where machine dependencies are almost unavoidable – may require adaptation by the reader in order to suit the implementation of SLIM to his or her own system.

Defining user

A simple-minded first effort at defining the user predicate is:

```
mode user(commands↑ ).

user([Cmd|Commands]) ←
    write('Input Window', '//') &
    read(Cmd) &
    user(Commands).
```

Unfortunately this definition is unsuitable for several reasons. Firstly, the read primitive may have the property that a call to it will suspend all other concurrent processes (in sequential machine implementations of PAR-LOG this behaviour is to be expected). Hence this procedure threatens to lock out all the other processes of SLIM. Secondly, read is likely to substitute internally devised names for any variable names appearing in user commands: it may convert merge(V1, V2, V2) into merge(_109, _110, _111), for example. In view of the special significance of the window variable names, such behaviour would be disastrous. Thirdly, the definition allows neither for conjunctive commands nor for termination.

We can surmount the first problem by preceding the read call by a call to a keyboard 'polling' primitive. All PARLOG systems will have such a primitive, which we assume to be named key: its behaviour is to succeed if some key has been pressed since the last call to read, and to suspend (but without disrupting other processes) otherwise. By using this primitive we can limit calls to read to those occasions when there actually *is* something to be read. To solve the problem of preserving variable names we shall replace read with gread (for 'ground-term read'), which is assumed to behave exactly like read except that it preserves any variable names that may occur in input terms. It does this by 'freezing' the names into quoted constants – merge(V1, V2, V2) is converted into merge('V1', 'V2', 'V3'), for example (notice that this is consistent with our earlier remarks about the representation of SLIM's window variables). You should find that gread, or a pseudonym, is available on your system as a primitive or 'library' predicate. Finally, conjunctive commands and termination can be provided for by introducing a sub-procedure user_check, say, that inspects the input term and selects appropriate behaviour accordingly. The following pair of procedures is satisfactory:

```
mode user(commands↑ ).

user(Commands) ←
    key &
    write('Input Window', '//') &
    gread(Cmd) &
    user_check(Cmd, Commands).
```

```
mode user_check(cmd?, cmds↑ ).

user_check(quit, []);
user_check((Cmd, Cmds), [Cmd|Others]) ←
    user_check(Cmds, Others).
user_check(Cmd, [Cmd|Cmds]) ←
    user(Cmds).
```

Consider the process that evaluates the call user(Commands). As long as key suspends, the process suspends and other parts of the system are not affected. As soon as a keypress is detected key succeeds. The SLIM prompt is then displayed in the Input Window (notice the assumption that the write primitive accepts a window name for its first argument) and a term is read by the call to gread. This call may suspend all other activity, but only temporarily: when the gread is completed and user_check has acted upon the entered term, the suspended processes will resume and they will run uninterrupted until a further keypress causes key to succeed. user_check closes the commands stream if the entered term is quit. Otherwise the new command or commands are passed on to the commands stream and a further user process is spawned in the anticipation of further commands.

Defining filter

The role of filter is to impose some control over the form of inputs entering the manager. It is straightforward to implement the logical reading given above as a pair of PARLOG procedures:

```
mode filter(cmds?, legalcommands↑ ).

filter([], []).
filter([Cmd|Cmds], [Lcmd|Lcmds]) ←
    map_command(Cmd, Lcmd),
    filter(Cmds, Lcmds).

mode map_command(cmd?, mappedcommand↑ ).

map_command(reset, reset).
map_command(input(Var, Term), input(Var, Term)).
map_command(Call, run(Call)) ←
    defined(Call) :
    true;
map_command(Cmd, unrecognized(Cmd)).
```

map_command serves to scrutinize and (possibly) transform each user command. Although this procedure performs only an elementary level of validation, it is enough to guarantee that only four types of term (reset, input(Var, Term), run(Call) and unrecognized(Cmd)) can reach the manager. A command Call is permitted to pass through the filter as run(Call) only if defined(Call) is true, where the intended logical reading of defined(X) is: X represents a call to a currently defined PARLOG relation. defined (or a pseudonym) is likely to be a PARLOG system primitive. Notice how the sequential search operator is used in the map_command procedure effectively to implement an 'otherwise' case; there is no need for a complex guard test in the final clause because the non-candidacy of the clauses in the parallel group is established before this clause is tried.

Defining initialize

This relation specifies the starting parameters of SLIM. For a system that has just two window variables named 'V1' and 'V2' say, a suitable definition is

```
mode initialize(winvars↑, startprocs↑ ).
```

```
initialize(WindowVars, StartProcs) ←
    WindowVars = wvars(WControl, [window('V1', Value1), window('V2', Value2)]),
    StartProcs = procs(PControl, []),
    create_screen.
```

The body calls to the full unification primitive are not essential; we could just insert the appropriate terms directly into the head of the clause. Perhaps the version above is tidier, although this is a matter of taste.

The task of create_screen is to create the necessary screen windows. Since this procedure is machine-dependent its definition is left to the reader.

Defining manager

The manager process does the real work. We can define a suitable procedure in five clauses, one for each type of message that can be sent by filter and one for termination, as follows:

```
mode manager(filteredcmds?, winvars?, startprocs?, sysmsgs↑ ).
```

```
manager([run(Call)|Cmds], Wvars, Procs, [running(Call)|Msgs]) ←
    install_call(Call, Procs, ProcsPlusCall, Wvars),
    manager(Cmds, Wvars, ProcsPlusCall, Msgs).
manager([input(Wvar, Term)|Cmds], Wvars, Procs, [Inputreply|Msgs]) ←
    input_term(Wvar, Term, Wvars, Inputreply),
    manager(Cmds, Wvars, Procs, Msgs).
manager([reset|Cmds], Wvars, Procs, ['System reset ok!'|Msgs]) ←
    reinitialize(Wvars, Procs, InitWvars, InitProcs),
    manager(Cmds, InitWvars, InitProcs, Msgs).
manager([unrecognized(Cmd)|Cmds], Wvars, Procs, [unrecognized(Cmd)|Msgs]) ←
    manager(Cmds, Wvars, Procs, Msgs).
manager([], Wvars, Procs, []) ←
    terminate(Wvars, Procs).
```

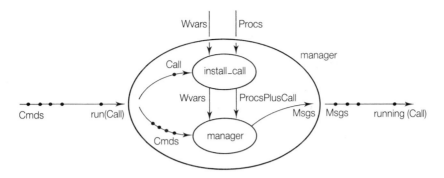

Figure 8.8   A procedural view.

You should satisfy yourself that this definition is consistent with the logical reading of manager given earlier. Each clause can be read as a logical specification of the history of system messages that is valid for a particular history of commands when the system starts in some 'logical state' represented by the two middle argument terms. For example, the logical interpretation of the first clause is: for a starting state represented by Wvars and Procs, a history of messages starting running(Call) is valid for a history of commands starting run(Call) if in the new state that arises from installing Call, the remainder of the history of messages is valid for the remainder of the history of commands.

The procedural interpretation of manager gives an alternative perspective. A call to manager creates a process that accepts a stream of command terms and produces a stream of system messages. In response to each command term the process commits to an appropriate clause, outputs a system message and (typically) spawns two concurrent sub-processes: one sub-process executes the command and the other (a recursive manager process) responds to the subsequent command terms. Figure 8.8 illustrates this when a run command term commits the process to the first clause. In passing, readers acquainted with 'object-oriented' programming terminology may prefer to think of the manager process as an **object** that responds to a run **message** by selecting the install_call **method**, and so on: this kind of PARLOG program seems to lend itself well to an object-oriented interpretation.

Defining install_call

The logical reading of install_call(Call, Procs, Procs2, Wvars) is: Procs2 is the list of user processes obtained by adding Call into Procs, and Wvars is consistent with every relation on Procs2. The mode declaration should be

```
mode install_call(call?, procs?, procs2↑, wvars?).
```

Operationally install_call does not merely perform a list insertion. It must also create the new process specified by Call. If the arguments of the latter mention any window variables then these should be substituted for by their current values, which can be obtained from the Wvars look-up table. A suitable definition is:

```
mode install_call(call?, procs?, procs2↑, wvars?).

install_call(Call, procs(Ctrl, Procs), procs(Ctrl, [Call|Procs]), Wvars) ←
    map_arguments(Call, Wvars, MappedCall),
    call(MappedCall, Status, Ctrl).
```

The map_arguments call performs the replacement of window variables. As soon as MappedCall has become bound to a term that represents an atom the required user process is created by the control metacall. Because this metacall never fails, SLIM is automatically protected from the possible failure of a user process. Notice that the manager copies the *same* control variable (it is the one that appears as PControl in the initialize procedure) to all user processes: this implements a common 'control line' whereby the manager process can terminate all user processes in response to a reset command. Hence SLIM exploits the control metacall in a similar way to the multitask_abortshell program of the previous chapter.

The definition of map_arguments is left to the reader. As an example of its behaviour, suppose that the call is

```
← map_arguments(Call, Wvars, MappedCall).
```

where the first two argument have values

```
Call = merge([1, 2, 3], 'V1', 'V2')
Wvars = wvars(Ctrl, [window('V1', [4, 5, 6|X1]), window('V2', X2)])
```

Then map_arguments should compute for MappedCall the result

```
MappedCall = merge([1, 2, 3], [4, 5, 6|X1], X2)
```

Notice that the user's merge process in this example will make bindings to X2, showing that the fourth argument of install_call represents a 'weak' input.

In fact it is not necessary for install_call to insert the new call into the list of current user processes. The manager process as described above makes no use of this information. However, future elaborations of SLIM (some suggestions for which are given later) are likely to find it useful.

Defining input_term

The role of input_term is to permit incremental binding of the window variables to terms supplied by the user. For example, if Wvars has the current value

```
Wvars = wvars(WCtrl, [window('V1', X1), window('V2', [2, 4|X2])])
```

then the call

← input_term('V2', 6, Wvars, InputReply).

should 'add' 6 to the value of the window variable 'V2'. It can do this by extracting from Wvars the appropriate 'tail' variable X2 which should then be given the binding X2 = [6|Y]. The result for Wvars will be

Wvars = wvars(WCtrl, [window('V1', X1), window('V2', [2, 4, 6|Y])])

(The binding of Wvars by the call shows that this argument represents a 'weak' input to input_term.) InputReply should be given a value that will convey the system's response to the user's attempt to perform such an input operation. In the example the binding InputReply = input('V2', 6, ok) will indicate the successful outcome, but of course the operation might not have been possible: the essential condition is that in the Wvars look-up table, 'V2' names an unbound variable or a list with an unbound tail. Had 'V2' named the empty list for example then InputReply could return the value input('V2', 6, not_ok). A suitable definition is:

```
mode input_term(winvar?, interm?, wvars?, inputreply↑ ).

input_term(W, InTerm, Wvars, input(W, InTerm, ok)) ←
    vartail(W, Wvars, Tail) :
    Tail = [InTerm|Y];
input_term(W, InTerm, Wvars, input(W, InTerm, not_ok)).
```

The vartail call should extract from Wvars the appropriate variable Tail for binding, and if the 'unbound variable or list with unbound tail' requirement is unsatisfied then the call should fail. The definition of vartail is left to the reader.

Defining reinitialize

reinitialize(Wvars, Procs, InitWvars, InitProcs) has the logical reading: Wvars is unifiable with wvars(stop, W), Procs is unifiable with procs(stop, P), and InitWvars and InitProcs are terms that satisfy the initialize relation. Operationally the unifications will bind the control variables in Wvars and Procs to stop and hence will terminate the display_wvars process and all user processes. The call to initialize will restore the system to scratch state, with fresh window variables and an empty user process list. However, we must not forget to create another display_wvars process to replace the one that has been killed off. The definition is:

```
mode reinitialize(wvars?, procs?, initwvars↑, initprocs↑ ).

reinitialize(Wvars, Procs, InitWvars, InitProcs) ←
    Wvars = wvars(stop, W),
    Procs = procs(stop, P),
    initialize(InitWvars, InitProcs),
    display_wvars(InitWvars).
```

The terminate procedure is even simpler than this (it does nothing more
than make the bindings to stop) and its definition is left to the reader.

Defining display_wvars

The display_wvars procedure should spawn one sub-process to manage the
output to each Process Window. It can be defined as follows:

```
mode display_wvars(winvars?).

display_wvars(wvars(Control, [])).
display_wvars(wvars(Control, [window(Wname, Term)|Others])) ←
    control_write(Control, Wname, Term),
    display_wvars(wvars(Control, Others)).
```

control_write should specify the process for a single window display. This
predicate is assumed to have modes

```
mode control_write(control?, window?, term?).
```

and it is a distant cousin of the swrite_list relation described in Chapter 5. Its
behaviour is to write the value of the named term into the specified
window, with writing proceeding incrementally as data is generated for the
term by a user process. If the control variable becomes bound to stop then
the window should be cleared and the control_write process should terminate. The definition is left to the reader.

Defining display_msgs

This procedure has the simple job of writing into the Message Window the
system messages produced by the manager process. It can be defined as:

```
mode display_msgs(messages?).

display_messages([]).
display_messages([Msg|Messages]) ←
    swrite('Message Window', Msg) &
    display_messages(Messages).
```

This assumes the availability of a two-argument version of the swrite predicate defined in Chapter 5. The first argument specifies the screen window into which the writing is to take place.

8.3.6 Extending and adapting SLIM

SLIM is now complete, at least according to our original specification. But there is still enormous scope for enhancement. Some suggestions for extensions are:

- A status command that would give current system information, such as the state of user processes (active, succeeded or failed) and of window variables (bound or free).

- A capability to accept commands that are calls to PARLOG's unification-related primitives.

- A vars command that would enable users to declare new identifiers as variables, or some other means to extend the set of variables beyond the existing provision for window variables.

- A kill command that can be used to terminate a named user process.

- An elaboration of the input command so that the second argument can be a list of terms rather than an atom or number. Further, some means should be provided to complete the list value of the window variable that is the recipient of the input.

- A set of program development commands, such as edit, compile, listing, and the usual file commands, that will begin to make the system into something closer to a support environment for programming.

Some of these changes will require a revision of earlier decisions. For example a selective kill needs a representation for user processes that implements a unique control variable for each process. Other extensions, such as the provision of program development commands, may involve little revision to the existing procedures but they could require a significant amount of new work. Building and adapting a system of this kind can be very worthwhile. However, if you make too many changes and extensions then one further facility that may become necessary is

- A help command that displays in the Message Window a reminder of all the other commands.

But perhaps by that time you should have re-named the system to STOUT!

Appendix A
GHC and Concurrent PROLOG

PARLOG has two sister languages with the names **Guarded Horn Clauses** (GHC) and **Concurrent PROLOG** (CP). This appendix describes the main differences between the three languages. It should provide enough information to suggest what is required to convert a PARLOG program into GHC or CP.

A.1 Horn clause syntax

Syntactically, the three languages are virtually identical. All construct procedures from modified Horn Clauses of the form

$$A \leftarrow G1, .., Gj : B1, .. Bk.$$

where the head A, the guard G1, .., Gj and the body B1, .., Bk are all atoms. The guard and body are both optional. There are some trivial differences: in GHC and CP the implication operator is ':-' and the guard operator is '|'. More significantly, programs in PARLOG are uniquely characterized by the presence of mode declarations. CP programs are distinguished by the use of question-mark labels to annotate selected clause variables as 'read-only' variables, as explained below. GHC syntax is the closest to that of pure unadorned Horn clause form.

A.2 Operational semantics

Operationally the three languages share the same basic evaluation strategy that has been described in this book for PARLOG. That is, to evaluate the conjunction of relation calls (say)

$$\leftarrow call1, call2, ..., callj.$$

a network of concurrent processes is created with shared variables acting as communication channels. The evaluation process for a call tests the clauses in the appropriate procedure as far as the clause guard. Ultimately the process commits to one clause and spawns (reduces to) sub-processes as specified by the clause body. A process terminates when it reduces ultimately to an empty set of sub-processes.

From this common evaluation strategy follows a strong set of family resemblances. PARLOG, GHC and CP all share the characteristics of stream and-parallelism, with recursively-defined relations giving rise to the incremental binding of variables; restricted or-parallelism, in which the individual clauses of a procedure are investigated concurrently, but only up to the moment of commitment; the possibility of genuine non-determinism arising when there is more than one candidate clause for a particular call; and the limitation which results from the 'committed-choice' strategy that a call evaluation can result in at most one solution.

The committed-choice strategy imposes upon each language the same crucial 'safety' requirement. This is the requirement that a call variable must not be allowed to become bound until a clause has been selected for commitment. It is an essential requirement because the clause that would give such a premature (pre-commitment) binding may turn out not to be the eventually selected candidate clause, and bindings once made are never retracted. In particular, for a guarded clause the test for candidate status includes the evaluation of the guard: a call variable must not become bound by a guard evaluation. Guards must be 'safe' in this respect. This is not the same as saying that a guard may not bind *any* variable – a variable that occurs only 'locally' in the guard (for example) can become bound without breaching the safety requirement.

The differences between the languages stem from their contrasting approaches to implementing the safety requirement. Related to this is the mechanism that is used to determine when a call (process) should suspend. We now describe in turn the approach that characterizes the three languages.

A.2.1 PARLOG: inputs and outputs distinguished by modes

The situation for PARLOG can be briefly re-stated. Every PARLOG procedure has a mode declaration that designates each relation argument as an input or an output. Testing a clause for candidate status means input matching between corresponding pairs of input argument terms, plus guard evaluation. Input matching is a constrained (one-way) unification: if it could only proceed by binding a call variable, input matching – and hence possibly the call – suspends. The use of input matching has two effects: it enables the compiler to generate efficient code, and it ensures that unification cannot bind input mode call variables. The responsibility of ensuring that guard evaluations do not bind input mode call variables is left to the programmer (possibly aided by a compiler check – no run-time safety check is applied). Taken together this strategy ensures the safety of input mode call variables. Output mode call variables are automatically made safe by a compilation that arranges to hold back the unifications between pairs of output mode arguments until the point of commitment.

A.2.2 GHC: safety and suspension through sus-unification

For GHC there is no explicit distinction between the input and output arguments of a relation. In testing a clause for candidate status a special form of unification (let us call it **sus-unification**) is used that suspends if an attempt is made to bind a call variable to a non-variable term. A sus-unification test is applied between the call and the clause head for *all* pairs of arguments: this requires that output be implemented by variables (not structured terms) in the clause head which receive their values by means of suitable calls to an assignment primitive in the clause body. Guard evaluations also use sus-unification, which means that a guard suspends if it attempts to bind a call variable (notice that in PARLOG, this would represent an illegal event in the case where the call variable occurs in an input mode argument position). Thus sus-unification becomes the means both of implementing the safety requirement and also of determining when a process should suspend.

In practice this scheme has proved very difficult to implement efficiently. In the absence of any distinction between input and output terms being available at compile time, sus-unification seems to require an expensive run-time check on variable bindings. So far implementation effort has focussed on a restricted version of the language known as 'flat' GHC (FGHC) in which guards are limited to test-only calls to primitive relations (henceforth referred to as **flat guards**). Sus-unification is thus only required for testing the call with the clause head, and this is equivalent to performing PARLOG-style input matching over all pairs of arguments.

Some of the programs in this book, such as the concurrent sentence parser described in Chapter 8, feature 'non-flat' or 'deep' guards (that is, guards that contain calls to programmer-defined relations). For translation to FGHC these programs must be transformed into a form in which all guards are flat. This is always possible (in fact, PARLOG programs can be *compiled* into flat guard form) perhaps at some cost in terms of effort and a loss of transparency. But for PARLOG programs with only flat guards the translation should be simple. The main need for change arises where PARLOG programs specify non-variable terms (for example list patterns) in output mode argument positions of clause heads. These terms must be replaced by variables in the FGHC versions, with suitable calls to the assignment primitive added to the body of the clause to implement the required output. This is because a non-variable clause head term that is intended for output would probably cause the indefinite suspension of the call in the FGHC version.

A.2.3   CP: read-only variables and multiple environments

CP distinguishes itself from both PARLOG and GHC in two main ways. Firstly, the input/output designation of the arguments of a relation is specified by each call rather than being fixed by the defining procedure (in PARLOG it is explicitly fixed by modes, in GHC it is implicitly fixed by assignment calls). This is achieved by the programmer's annotation of call variables that are to be used for input with special read-only ('?'-character) labels. CP implements a modified form of unification that suspends when an attempt is made to bind a read-only variable to a non-variable term and this in fact represents CP's sole process suspension mechanism. Secondly, CP implements the safety requirement in a radically different way. During the search for a candidate clause, each clause is given only a *copy* of the call argument terms. The copy is stored in a 'local environment' that is identified with the clause; a typical call will therefore create multiple local environments, one for each clause in the relevant procedure. Any bindings that might be made in testing the call with a clause head and in evaluating the guard affect only the local environment for that clause. Only on making a commitment to a clause are the bindings from the corresponding environment transferred to the variables of the call. This mechanism automatically makes call variables safe.

Here is a CP version of the pqsort relation defined for PARLOG in Section 5.5:

```
pqsort([N|Rest], Sorted) :-
    partition(N, Rest?, LessN, MoreN),
    pqsort(LessN?, SortedLess),
    pqsort(MoreN?, SortedMore),
    append(SortedLess?, [N|SortedMore?], Sorted).
pqsort([], []).
```

Note that in general, variables that are not annotated with read-only labels can be used either for input or output. With this CP program, a call that specifies a non-empty list for sorting will create four concurrent sub-processes as given by the body of the recursive clause. Because of the read-only status of the variables LessN and MoreN in the pqsort body calls, these sub-processes will suspend until the partition process has supplied the variables with bindings. Overall the evaluation behaviour will be the same as that of the PARLOG version of the program.

Because CP specifies the communication constraint by annotations on calls rather than on procedures, the possibility exists that the same CP procedure may support two or more distinct patterns of call. However it seems likely that only very simple CP procedures will be able to exploit this possibility. This is because clause bodies themselves usually specify communication constraints via read-only variables. The read-only annotations in the procedure above would make it impossible for this program to be 'run in reverse' so as to produce a permutation of a given sorted list, for example.

As with GHC, there have been major difficulties in implementing CP's approach in its full generality. The multiple environment mechanism seems to be complex and potentially inefficient, and the semantics of the 'read-only' variable has turned out to be troublesome. To date the CP implementation effort has centred on a simplified flat guard subset of the language, FCP, which (analogously to FGHC) prohibits calls to non-primitive relations in guards.

In converting the PARLOG programs in this book into FCP the remarks made above concerning the restriction to flat guards apply equally to FCP. But for FCP there is the additional requirement of translating from PARLOG's representation of communication constraints by mode declarations into the FCP form of annotating call variables with read-only labels. Basically, call variables that occur in input mode argument positions in the PARLOG program should become read-only variables in the FCP version.

SUMMARY

PARLOG, GHC and Concurrent PROLOG form the 'committed-choice' family of concurrent logic programming languages. They have a great deal in common. They differ firstly in their approach to meeting the safety requirement that is mandatory for the family, and secondly in the mechanism that is applied to determine process suspension.

So far only PARLOG has been successfully implemented with full guards. Implementations of GHC and CP have been mainly restricted to the 'flat' versions FGHC and FCP, in which guards are limited to calls to primitive relations. These flat languages suffer from a reduced expressiveness and PARLOG programs that exploit 'deep' guards will require to have these 'flattened' to enable a translation. However, many PARLOG programs themselves use only flat guards and to translate these programs into FGHC or FCP should be fairly straightforward.

Appendix B
PARLOG syntax and primitives

B.1 Syntax

These syntax diagrams represent PARLOG syntax pictorially. Language symbols are enclosed in circles and language constructs defined by other syntax diagrams are enclosed in rectangles.

B.1.1 Procedure

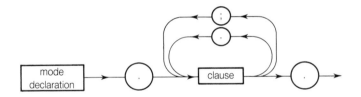

The semi-colon appears above the period for a reason – it represents the fact that the sequential operator has a higher precedence than the parallel operator (that is, in a mixed group of clauses the parallel operator binds more tightly).

B.1.2   Mode declaration

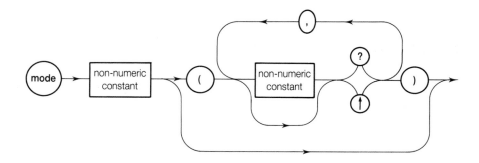

B.1.3   Clause

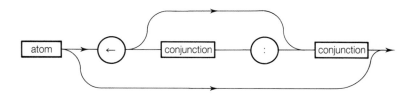

B.1.4   Conjunction

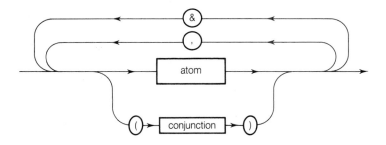

As with B.1.1 the sequential operator has the higher precedence. But in a conjunction, brackets can be used to override the default precedences.

B.1.5   Atom

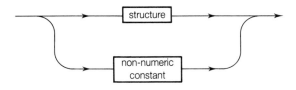

B.1.6   Term

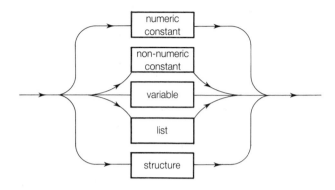

In these diagrams numeric constant, non-numeric constant, and variable are undefined. Numeric constants are just numbers. Variables are distinguished from non-numeric constants by beginning with an upper-case letter. For examples, see Section 1.10.

B.1.7   List

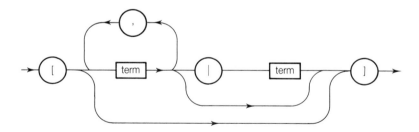

B.1.8   Structure

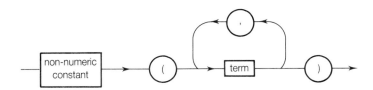

This diagram represents prefix-syntax structures only.

B.2   Primitives

The table below lists the PARLOG primitives which are used in the text.

Name	Modes	Purpose	See Section
==	(?, ?)	test unification	3.13.1, 7.8.2
=	(?, ?)	full unification	6.6, 7.8.1
<=	(?, ?)	one-way unification	7.8.3
<, >, =<, >=	(?, ?)	tests for inequality	3.13.2
=..	(?, ?)	list-to-structure conversion	7.7
call	(?)	simple metacall	7.4
call	(?, ↑, ?)	control metacall	7.6
data	(?)	test for binding to non-variable	5.1, 7.8.4
is	(↑, ?)	arithmetic evaluation	3.13.3
not	(?)	negation	3.13.5, 7.7
read	(↑)	input	3.13.4, 5.1
set	(↑, ?, ?)	database interface (eager)	7.1
subset	(?, ?, ?)	database interface (lazy)	7.3
var	(?)	test for unbound variable	6.2, 7.8.5
write	(?)	output	3.8, 3.13.4

Bibliography

Books on committed-choice logic languages

As yet there are only two such books (other than this one):

Gregory, S. (1987). *Parallel Logic Programming in PARLOG: The Language and its Implementation*. Wokingham: Addison-Wesley.

Shapiro, E. (Ed.) (1988). *Concurrent PROLOG: Collected Papers*. Cambridge, Mass: MIT Press.

The first is a comprehensive study of the design, application and implementation of PARLOG. Based on Steve Gregory's PhD thesis, this text will be especially useful to researchers in language design and to those who intend to build PARLOG implementations on sequential or parallel hardware. It includes an extensive collection of references. The second book is an edited collection of research papers from a number of authors on various aspects of Concurrent PROLOG.

PARLOG research papers

The PARLOG Group at Imperial College maintains a library of the group's research papers. A current bibliography can be obtained from:

The Secretary to the PARLOG Group,
Department of Computing,
Imperial College of Science and Technology,
University of London,
180 Queen's Gate, London SW7 2BZ.

At the time of writing the bibliography lists approximately 50 papers on a wide range of topics. Included are PARLOG applications to expert systems, simulations, and systems programming; environments and tools for PARLOG programming; relationship of PARLOG to other languages such as CCS, LOTOS, object-oriented languages, PROLOG, GHC and Concurrent PROLOG; implementation of PARLOG; and many others.

General logic programming

The foundations of logic programming are described in a classic book:

Kowalski, R. (1979). *Logic for Problem Solving*. North Holland.

A large and expanding literature is devoted to PROLOG. Two books that can be especially recommended are:

Bratko, I. (1987). *PROLOG Programming for Artificial Intelligence*. Wokingham: Addison-Wesley.

Sterling, L. and Shapiro, E. (1986). *The Art of PROLOG*. Cambridge, Mass: MIT Press.

Index

and-parallelism   64, 97, 131, 248
arity   17
assertion   58
atom   13
atomic formula   13
atomic propositions   2

back communication   191, 194
backtracking   94
backwards chaining   123
backwards reasoning   30
bindings   33
broadcasting   180, 186
buffer process   201, 235

candidate clause   71, 97
candidate status   95
child process   90
clause choice strategies   81
clauses   16, 97, 269
client-server interaction   179, 185, 194, 202, 238
committed choice strategy   72, 131, 242, 270
commitment   69, 72, 95, 124
communication,   75, 77, 174, 177, 182, 191, 200
completeness   39, 49, 82
components   43
compound terms   43
concurrency   63, 65, 66
Concurrent PROLOG   269, 272–3, 280
connectives   2
constant   17

contributing consumer   191, 195, 200, 259
control metacall   224, 264
control tokens   224
correctness   49

database   211
dataflow diagrams   75
dataflow synchronization   75
deadlock   59, 73, 88, 99, 182, 198, 200, 205, 238
debugging   127
declarative semantics   23, 81
deep guards   147
demand-driven interaction   200
difference lists   161

eager producer   200
efficiency   39, 124
execution stage   43

fairness   202, 204
false commitment   94
feedback   177, 182
flat guards   271–3
forwards reasoning   31
functional relation   134
functor   43

generate-and-test   132
GHC   269, 271
goal clause   24
goal selection strategies   81
graphs   161
ground formulae   23

guard 95,
    guards race 131, 147, 165, 246
    properties associated with 100
    safety of 102, 195, 223, 270

I/O 218
implication clause 86
implications 16
incomplete messages 102, 191, 193–6, 200
incomplete producer 191, 200
incompleteness 72
incremental production 114, 117, 153
incrementalism 115
input 58, 127
input constraint 59
input matching 59, 94
input substitution 34, 47, 59
instantiations 14, 33
interleaving 65
invertible procedures 70, 226

lazy behaviour 214
lazy interaction 200
lazy producer 200, 234
lists 44
lockout 205
logic
    Horn clause form of 2, 15
    logic database 44, 210
    logic interpreter 8
    logic program 7
    predicate form of 2, 12
    propositional form of 2
    syllogistic form of 2
logical variable 192, 237, 259

merge 133, 205
message tagging 186
metacall 216, 221
meta-predicates 222
minimum guards principle 101, 195
mode declarations 57, 67, 69, 269
multiple environments 272
multiple solutions 124
multi-tasking 217
mutual exclusion 179, 218
mutual recursion 164

negation-by-failure 80, 222
network of processes 118

non-determinism 71, 124, 135–7, 153, 156, 205

object-oriented programming 263
operational semantics 39, 40, 81, 269
operator grammar 223
operators in Parlog
    commit 97
    parallel clause search 63
    parallel conjunction 64
    sequential clause search 63, 110, 133
    sequential conjunction 66
or-parallelism 61, 96, 131, 248
output 58, 67, 69, 127
output substitution 35, 47, 59
output unification 67, 69

parallel conjunction 64
parallel evaluation 66
parallel search 60
parent process 90
parsing 239
partial completeness 101
predicate 13
primitives 19
primitives in PARLOG 77, 279
    < 78
    <= 226
    = 189, 225
    =.. 225
    =< 78
    == 77, 158, 226
    > 78
    >= 78
    call 215, 221
    data 128, 178, 226
    is 79
    key 260
    not 80
    read 79, 127
    set 210
    subset 214
    var 176, 178, 226
    write 68, 79, 128
procedure 20, 58
procedure call 35
procedure definitions in PARLOG
    absval 94, 95
    add_few 91

add_four 88
admit_people 237
and 224
append 113
bonus 99, 101
busy_wait 233
c_room 235
characteristic 71
characteristics 72
clerical 100
common_term 132, 133
correct 173
current_version 67
dbase 228
dbtotal 212
dictionary 242
display_msgs 266
display_wvars 266
expansions_parse 246, 250, 252
fair_merge 204
fair_split 203
filter 261
front_insert 249
grammar 242
guesser 172, 175, 181, 184, 190, 197
high 184
initialize 262
input_term 265
insert 151
install_call 264
integers 116
larger 125
lazy_integers 197
maintain_db 228
make_ord_tree 156
make_tree 155
manager 262
map_command 261
maplist 224
maxfiles 74
member 108, 110
merge 134
multitask_abortshell 221
multitask_ioshell 219
multitask_shell 217
natural_sum 126
neg_filter 125
neighbours 162, 213
next_call 224

not 222
official_user 59, 60, 63,
on_both 130
on_either 131
on_ord_tree 149
on_tree 146
one_expansion_parse 247
one_way 164
or 223
ord_insert 154
owner 68
parse 243
parse_form 245
partition 138
path 163
posints 105, 120
positive 86
pqsort 143
profile 160
programmer 99
qsort 143
read_respond 235
read_tell 199
reinitialize 265
required_delay 233
run_multitask_abortshell 221
salary 100
salestotal 212
same_profile 158
singletask_shell 216
slim 257
small_plus 69
split 202
splits_parse 247
splittings 249
status 74
street 231
swrite 129
swrite_list 129
synch_guess 182, 185, 190
technician 99
tell_quit 194
teller 173, 175, 181, 184, 189, 198
total 110
user 260
user_check 261
w_room 234, 239
while_guess 177
zeroes 103
process 77, 122

process behaviour   123
PROLOG   40, 57, 80, 282

query formula   8

read-only variables   269, 272
recursive relations   102
reduction   87
relation call   35
relational database   209
resolution   32

safe guards property   102, 195
safety requirement   270
semantic rules   4
semantics   42
sharing   37
shell   216–22
simulations   229
sorting   141
soundness   49
spawn stage   86
specification stage   43
starvation   204
stream communication   121
stream feedback   186
strong communication   191, 194, 200,
    259

structured terms   43
structures   17, 43
sufficient tests property   100, 110, 124
suspension   59
sus-unification   271
synchronization   75, 143, 177, 182
syntax of PARLOG   275–9

termination,   87, 131, 199
testing   127
time-dependent computation   136,
    205
timesharing   65
top-down inference   30
top-down resolution   32
trees   144–61
truth-table strategy   10

unification   32, 46, 81
unification-related primitives   226
uniprocessor   62
universal quantifier   14

variable   14, 17, 59, 72

weak communication   191, 194
weak input   191, 200, 227, 265